To You, for being curious and brave enough to pick up this book and believe that More is possible for you. I'm honoured you've chosen me to be on this journey with you. From the bottom of my heart, thank you...

be
ANXIETY
FREE
FOREVER

Reawaken the Brilliance of Your **Subconscious** in 7 Easy Steps and Find the **Lasting Freedom** that's **Meant for You**

EMMA UPTON

For more information, email morethanthisbyEmmaUpton@gmail.com

ISBN: 979-8-88759-657-0 (paperback)
ISBN: 979-8-88759-659-4 (hardcover)
ISBN: 979-8-88759-658-7 (ebook)

GET YOUR FREE GIFT!

Hello, friend. Welcome to the work. Click the image below to hear Emma's overview of the brilliance you're going to find within these pages.

To help you overcome anxiety faster – and forever! – download The Anxiety-Free Workbooks **HERE** and make them a part of your path.

To take the first step toward your freedom and implement The 7 Steps faster, join Emma Upton's free live workshop by CLICKING HERE!

Join the community by visiting: www.thereismorethanthis.com
Or join us on Instagram @morethanthisbyEmmaUpton

DEDICATION

To the broken version of me who somehow found the strength to believe (with absolutely no proof) that something More lay outside of my *right now*, back then. This belief gifted me these 7 Steps which changed my entire world.

To my three darling boys, my mum, my dad and my sister, who have been and continue to be everything I need.

My Grandpop, my shining light, thank you for showing me that magic exists in the most ordinary places. Knowing this enabled You to see the true magic of this world – only now am I able to see.

TABLE OF CONTENTS

LETTER TO THE READER

There is no such thing as a coincidence. You are here because you're meant to be. And I'm flippin'-well THRILLED that you are!

You're here reading this to overcome anxiety as seamlessly as possible, yes? You're chomping, "Let's just jump into the *how* now, Emma Upton. I am SO over feeling this way!" Right?!

First, real quick, I want to ask: how's it going right now?

Let's do a mini check-in before we begin.

I see you striving for *better* or *bigger* – or just "not **this AGAIN!"** Working and hoping for something different, which you go all-in on – again, but you keep drawing blanks.

Maybe you've gotten dead good at being able to say, blow by blow, what's "wrong" and "why".

You're missing that final piece of the puzzle – **the** means to know what the funk to **actually** do about it. You're spinning in circles. Whatever *it* is, it feels like something's missing, right?

You blame yourself. It feels like your heart is on the outside of your body, and no matter how hard you try, your happiness is determined by the things and people around you – what they think, do and say. No matter what accolades you get, how much you gain or lose, how much you give – you're numb. You're trapped in your default survival mode setting, like Dory...

"Just keep swimming...just keep swimming...just keep swimming, swimming, swimming..."

Functioning. Holding on. Hoping for *"More"* and that one day, it'll just get different.

You've built a space around you for protection, but it's gotten so thick that it's suffocating. You've nailed the door shut – tight! And inside, there isn't any space, not even for joy.

It's just you and your thoughts. And they're confusing AF! You don't dare open that door for anything new, even if it promises glory. Because why the hell would you risk opening yourself up? Doing that might let in everything else – the very things you built the original wall to keep out. That would be stupid...duh!!

You're going through the motions of living, spinning never-ending plates, and you feel like You've gotten lost within it all.

In your hunt for *More* (stillness, peace, love, joy, gratitude, inner kindness, endless energy, happiness, abundance, just feeling less shitty or whatever the funk it is you want to feel whilst you're still a living, breathing human), you give more of yourself away.

You strive to achieve, and maybe even get some pretty gnarly results, but the world demands more from you each and every time. And out there, they don't play fair. Another chunk of You is lost in the ether, with little hope of it being returned to sender.

What's the point? What's my purpose? Why am I here? And why does it feel so bloody hard to exist the majority of the time?!

These questions plague you because you believe that what you see reflecting back at you in the "mirror of your life" is You. I am here to

SHOW you that it's not You and that There Is More Than This. You are not the human limits impressed upon you by your busy brain. You are SO much more...

If I just described you, this is **the book** that will allow you to make it all different.

The truth is that overcoming anxiety is easier than your anxious, busy brain would have you believe.

> *Life isn't about waiting for the storms to pass.*
> *It's about learning how to dance in the rain.*
>
> —*Vivian Greene*

This human experience will NEVER be simple. Please stop waiting for it to be simple for you to start living and enjoying your life. With these 7 Steps, you will learn how to beat anxiety at its own game with a complexity you actually enjoy. As you journey with me, you will create an **ease** in your existence that you didn't believe could be available to you. With each Step, you will quieten your busy brain more and more. With a less busy brain, you will have the clarity to see how to choose ease in some of the least simple situations available to a human being.

I know this feels like a lie right now, but I promise you're going to see it all differently. You possess the power of choice.

There is no "try"; there is only *do* or *not do*. Both are okay, but you need to commit to which you are choosing.

You are ultimately in charge of your thoughts. The ideas and beliefs that create your life are run by you every day. You choose whether to allow them in. I know this might feel like a lot, and you might want to take a running swing at me for suggesting this, but I promise you're going to see this too. I will teach you how to be aware and involved in what you let into your mind, and thus, your life.

Your brain is in charge of **EVERYTHING.** Without the quiet persuasion of virtuous cycles, your mind will continue to peddle the self-perpetuating shit cycle you're currently in. If you're dealing with anxiety, it feels like there is no room in your mind for change – so I get that it might feel like a lot right out of the gate! We've just gotta keep going and pretty soon the evidence that change can exist for you too will start to stack up...

Our purpose in being here together is to become SUPER interested in what the brain – our computer program – is getting up to. The Dark Web of our minds has a way of seeping into our **everythings** – in spaces that, unless we are aware of our Unconscious programming, we can't actively control.

You *can* interrupt anxious thoughts before they happen (I'm gonna teach you how). But first, you have to know what's going on underneath.

In 7 Steps, you'll learn how to bring your busy brain and closed-up heart into alignment so that you Find who You truly are. When you deeply know who You are, your quest for a life filled with *More* feels like...

- A deep love for life you thought only existed in films.
- Gratitude for all the stuff you KNOW you "should" feel grateful for.
- Working with the world instead of against it. You stop letting it all hurt you so hard. You instead start leaning into learning and genuinely enjoying your day-to-day world.
- Realising that the bitch in your brain – who currently dominates one **heck** of a lot of your existence right now – isn't actually You. Seeing this means you get to see Actual You in a **whole** new light!
- A deep mind-body connection that fills you up with an endless energy – from your smallest little piggy toe to the tip of that crown resting on that Goddess head of yours.

- A warm bubble bath you can actually enjoy without a racing mind telling you **everything** that "should" be happening instead.
- Not giving a hoot about the stuff you wish you didn't care so blooming much about. Letting go of the *shoulds* and truly just doing what feels magical for You – and only You!

This process will allow you to come back to the Youest version of You.

Picking up this book in itself, however, won't cause this to happen. It's not like you'll hear trumpets and see the heavens opening up with God shining his spotlight upon you in one big epic moment and it all makes sense and you're FINALLY fixed! *Phew!* This is what the busy brain will have you believe, but true, lasting change doesn't work this way.

Your whole life can truly change, in all the places you want it to, but this change most often happens through a series of moments. The most powerfully enlightening moments of acute awareness come in little droplets.

The most profound ones, the ones that create lasting change, are often the retrospective ones in which we look back and say, "Holy smokes! Being relentless in choosing something different for myself over and over again was how it got to be different for me..." Luckily, making this **easy** to do is what this work is based upon entirely!

You create More for yourself when you **do the work**. Read this book to the very end. And when you look back after doing life a little differently each day, you'll realise that it all <u>had</u> to be...

Are you excited and nervous all at the same time?

ME TOO! Let's dive in, shall we? Change can be scary, but don't worry. I'll be with you every step of the way.

All my love,

Emma xo

INTRODUCTION

Neuroplasticity is the brain's ability to rewire itself in order to make new connections, mature from the state of infancy to adulthood and heal itself from injuries.

This phenomenon proves that you are not destined to be one way your entire life. Just because you held a certain belief or had certain struggles in your life doesn't mean it has to repeat. Your role in constructing this change, however, is imperative and is more in your hands than you probably think.

THE 6 WRONG RULES

For 30 years, I gave my brain the wrong message. I gave it the message that life was meant to feel difficult and uncomfortable and that I was meant to feel lost in the constant, painful pendulum swing of my emotions.

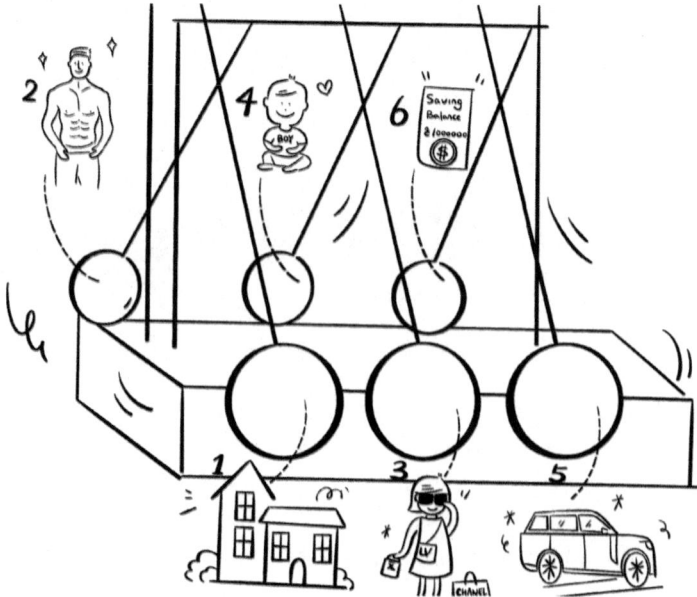

Ding: *moments of heightened elation* (holidays, spa days, new designer handbag days, first day on the job days)

Dong: *deep, dark lows* (most days – even my Ding days would Dong if they didn't go the way I wanted them to!)

I was wrong! So. Blooming. WRONG! For 30 years!

My life felt like an endurance test because I was dedicated to playing it by The 6 Wrong Rules. You know, those Rules which no one actively sits you down for and outrightly tells you but you just "know". Those Rules which promise you'll finally catch up with that elusive state of happiness and fulfilment that we're all desperately searching for. I've narrowed them down to the following 6.

We're told that to live a happy and fulfilled life, we must follow these 6 Wrong Rules:

1. You must secure the career with the well-known, well-respected title that pays MEGA bucks!

2. You must acquire the handsome husband, wife or significant other!
3. You must buy the big, beautiful house!
4. You need to get the fancy car!
5. You need to have a rockin' body to hang the latest designer handbag off of!
6. You need to have kids!

If you're old enough to have these things, and you're missing one of them, you think that ticking it off your Wrong Rules List is your answer, right?

And, if you aren't old enough, you've got your eyes on the 6-Tick prize. You think life will get better once you have them all, yes?

MY MISSING TICK

I wanted a baby so badly. I had 5 out of 6 of the things I needed "to be happy" except that one.

Without a babe, I had a gaping hole in my heart. I spent weeks in Ibiza off my rocker and thought having a child was **the missing piece in my life**.

A baby was that next mission for me to accomplish and tick off my list. I was desperate. Friends I loved deeply would tell me their news – "It's a boy!" – and I wanted to scream in their faces, "Screw you and your perfectly working uterus!" But instead, I smiled and fake-squealed in "delight".

"Congratulations!"

I'd escape at the first opportunity, go home, curl into a ball feeling like the worst human in existence (jealousy towards your best friend is pure evil!) and want to die.

I was 30 years old when they arrived. FINALLY! The answer I'd been looking for. My happiness. The final tick on the list. And I got two of them. Twins. TWO! The Universe made doubly sure that I'd never feel that gaping hole within my heart **ever** again.

I had hit the jackpot, and they turned out to be the best boys, too. They had been delivered from the heavens, so how could I expect any less?

But one day, as I sat on the scatter back, cream, plush sofa of our lavish home surrounded by my Selby Mama changing bag and my **super-cute** babes, I looked at my boys and felt numb. It was in this moment, looking at their perfect little pudding faces, that I had a realisation: I'd never been happy.

A PICTURE-PERFECT HAPPYLESS LIFE

"Never happy!? As in EVER?" I pondered in disbelief.

Frantically, I tried to recollect every landmark event that'd ever happened in my life. This was quite the challenge for me since anxiety had wiped 99% of my memories. (Living in survival mode will do this to your brain.) There were SO many lovely things to recall, but I couldn't remember a moment of life in which I didn't feel worried.

I had always worried. Worry and numbness were my default setting, and living this way didn't leave me much space for anything else. And what made me feel **worse** was that there were no murders or (too extreme) life-shattering moments to report that justified this level of unhappiness.

Loving parents, loving partner, loving family, loving friends, pretty stable everything else. White privilege to the MAX! How embarrassing! How pathetic! What the hell is my problem?! I need to get a grip!

I was horrified! With a guilt-ridden shove (something I was **very** familiar with executing!), I pushed this feeling back into the belly of where it came from, hoping it would never return, and continued to function through life.

I continued in my quest to get everything perfect. This hopeful need to control led to an eating disorder, insomnia, alcohol dependence and an addiction to anything which provided me some light relief from the grips of anxiety.

Life continued. And any time anything encouraged me to ponder my happyless existence, it was met with more embarrassment, shame and guilt (which I shoved deeper into the abyss of my being). So, I created more distractions in my life:

- I could French plait my hair like a pro.
- I learned to plaster and became a DIY master.
- I was the queen of fancy days out and became an activity-planning extraordinaire (24-hour binge at Ibiza again, anyone!?).

Externally, to the world, I had it all. And "having it all" added more pressure to just keep going...

So, of course, my body started to revolt.

THE BODY'S REVOLT

As I continued to ignore the signs screaming inside my head, I started to get physically sick. I had fatigue, to start. I'd wake from 12 hours of sleep and my immediate first thought would be, "What time can I go back to bed?!"

Then, my physical appearance started to change. I had sunken eyes with dry, dark rings around them. People would see me without makeup and cry, "Jesus, are you sick or something!?!"

Mortified, I'd fib, "Oh, I've just got a bit of a headache," when in actuality, I didn't know what the heck was happening to me!

My body began to ache as if my bones were in a vice and someone kept turning the key.

When I looked in the mirror, I could see my fringe thinning and bald spots creeping in where curls once bounced.

I fancied sex as often as I fancied cleaning out the plughole[1] with my tongue.

Catching a glimpse of my naked body in the mirror was enough to make me wanna puke! No amount of protruding collarbone could make me believe I was thin enough.

"I can sort this out!!" I'd scream internally, "I've just gotta keep going..."

Meat was out. Raw vegan was in. If it was good enough for Gwyneth P, it was good enough for me.

I googled, Instagrammed, and *MedDoc*ed every last nutrient I suspected I might be deficient in and intravenously dripped it into my system.

I contorted myself into downward dogs morning, noon and night. Forrest Gump had nothing on the miles I trudged to try and outrun the silently deadly mayhem of my existence.

As I did all the stuff on the outside, I continued to squish my thoughts about my life a little bit deeper into myself. Then one day, whilst standing at the sink preparing dough balls to make pizza after a day of distractions at the pub then the park and now home for movie night, my toes went numb.

"That's weird", I thought, as I continued to stand and "do".

"Just another minute or two. I'll finish this off, and then I'll go sit down".

---

[1]   The hole in the sink or bath where the water runs.

The numbness began to travel up into my feet.

I stopped what I was doing. This was demanding my attention *now*.

It tracked up both legs – to my knees.

Still, I said nothing. I stood in disbelief at what was unfolding. This paralysis went up to my bum and into my hips. Motionless, I whispered, "I can't move my legs".

My younger sister was with me. She panicked – I am the one who "knows". I am the one who is strong, in charge and tells everyone what needs to happen, no matter how challenged I am by what's unfolding...

"It's fine!" I lied, "I just need help getting to the sofa".

Following this, I spent days in bed, and we all thought something was chronically wrong. I never stopped. Ever! I always did the "stuff" and the stuff got done because I did it.

Three weeks of lying in bed. Three weeks of uncertainty. Three weeks of tests and scans, of being helped to the toilet and of being bathed by my husband.

My internal mess felt so familiar to me that I thought it was normal. But paralysis was forcing me to see something new.

"What wrong, Ma-mam?"

"Nothing, my sweetheart. Ma-mam be better soon," I sobbed as my little babes closed the door and left me in my darkness.

I lay in bed – done! I was done with a marriage that felt like a chore with obligatory sex once a month (if it was a "good" patch). Done with a teaching career which felt like I was on a never-ending countdown to the next half-term/full-term/6-week holiday.

I was done with painful gripes and digs from friends and family which were enough to leave me feeling like I'd been beaten with a bat. I sold parts of my soul to "keep the peace" and make their lives easier.

I was done with my shitty relationship with food where I controlled every last calorie in the hope of looking thinner and "hotter".

I was done with alcohol and how it gave everything a hazy tinge, making the moment a little more bearable – until waking in the morning with a freight train running over my brain.

In bed that day, I had no fight.

I was done.

Then, I heard words. Words which came into my mind so quietly I should've missed them; I would've if I was still within the noise of my life. But they were so impactful, they reverberated in my mind:

There is more than this...

There must be more than this.
There's got to be!
This can't be it!
It CAN'T!

I think medically, this moment would be defined as a nervous breakdown, but my nervous system and adrenal glands were so shot, I don't think I could've had a nervous breakdown, even if I'd wanted to. I'd taught myself to be so high functioning that I couldn't even "let go" enough to have a genuine nervous breakdown. I didn't have an edge, but if I did, this was it.

It was *do something different or die.*

I didn't want to die. I also didn't want it all to continue to feel like this.

It was time to do things differently.

But HOW?!?!

IT'S MY BONES AND BODY – NOT MY BONCE[2]!

I took action the only way I knew how: in "doing".

I went to see the best doctors. I was prodded and poked, scanned and X-rayed. Tested. Retested. All inconclusive.

We were drawing blanks wherever we went.

Then, I met him: the final doctor who saw me in my quest to "get better and just get back to my blooming life, thank you very much!"

He was different. He took his time examining me. He stepped back, looked me over and said:

"It is not inside your body that your problems lie. It is inside here".
And he tapped his head.

Dumbfounded, I distinctly remember looking past him, to a symbol positioned on his windowsill. I've since learned that it was Shiva looking back at me. It drew my awareness for a second; a moment I discounted before it began.

"Stuff and nonsense," I interrupted. I stormed from the hospital, FUMING! "How dare he!? How very DARE he!? 'All in my head'!!! He isn't a shrink. He's a bone doctor. It's my bones and my body that's the problem, not my bonce! Keep outta my lane, Buddy!"

With no physical answers, nothing was making any sense.

I had to get curious. I had to do something different because, at that moment, it was just getting worse...

---

[2]   An alternate word for *head*.

So, I started to get curious about what options were available to me to sort out this inconvenience. I had a life to live! I needed to get back to doing what I'd always done so life could just continue as it was.

It felt like anyone I spoke to kept talking about the brain and depression and antidepressants.

"Freaking FINE!" I was desperate...

Spending money wasn't an option. I hardly made any. Our outgoings matched our incomings almost to the **letter**. And I never spent huge chunks on anything. That £50 an hour for counselling or therapy with nothing physical to "show" for it could kiss my incredibly hairy behind! I'd rather have bought a handbag or a holiday!

Then I remembered that my husband's work had a health insurance policy, which meant that I had access to a professional for free. Free was good, and I was desperate, so I gave it a try...

My first appointment with a counsellor was nothing short of horrific. It went from 0 to 1,000 in 0.3 seconds.

"Hi. How are you? What's the most traumatic thing that's holding you back?"

(Okay, it wasn't quite like this, but it was pretty close!)

WTFunk!?!? I was not ready for this. Yet, I gave it to her – both barrels. Things I'd spent the best part of 20 years actively repressing. Wasn't it what I was "supposed" to do??

Mid-sentence, my hour was up.

"If we can hold it there for today, Emma, that'd be great."

"I'm sorry, WHAT?!" I thought. But the polite and amenable me smiled, wiped away my tears and replied, "Of course, yes. Sorry for taking up so much of your time".

I remember being turfed out[3]. The blinding brightness of the outside light. The noise of the main-road traffic hurtling by.

Trembling and squinting through the tears, I looked around at this unfamiliar place. I couldn't focus. I scrambled to try.

I had an hour's drive ahead, and it was the lads' poker night at our house. *Lads, lads, lads.* Everyone would be there soon. And I'd promised to have the twinnies for the night so the boys weren't interrupted.

I remembered scolding myself for thinking that addressing what was happening inside my head was the "right" thing for me to do. "Stupid girl, I don't have time for this! I need to get back to my life!" I steadied myself, walked to the car, and felt more numb than I had before. The drive was out of body. Like I wasn't actually there.

I walked into the house. "SHOW TIME!" All smiles. "How are you?" "What can I get for you?"

"If you'll excuse me..." I took the boys to bed. We milked, we sang, we storied. And as I lay in between their cots[4], watching my beautiful babes drift to sleep, with a house full of people, I'd never felt more alone or more sad to be alive.

But not a tear in sight. Just nothing.

---

[3] To be thrown out.
[4] Another word for *cribs*.

It was horrible, but I wasn't a quitter. So, I kept trying with therapy. Still reluctant to pay, I was "matched" with their "best fits". Some were good, some were pretty great, some were bloody awful, but I was always left wide open, thinking:

"Okay, great! Now I can articulate precisely why I'm feeling so fluffed up – to the letter! So, what the HECK am I supposed to do about it?!"

Traditional talk therapy left me feeling like I had more questions than answers. All we ever did was talk. We'd talk it out, think and "understand".

But "understanding", thinking and talking didn't "work" for me.

It was annoying because I was trying SO bloody hard! *And <u>still</u>, I just wanted this case CLOSED!"*

Then, as I sat in the therapist's living room, indulging in the stories, again, even boring myself to tears, I remembered that day in the Bone Doctor's office. And behind the very offensive and RUDE (still hadn't forgiven him!!) doctor, that little golden Shiva sparkling…

Maybe that little guy had More for me?

Please. I'm desperate…

I went to a Christian school, so I just kinda had it thrust upon me that God was legit ever since I was small. This belief was just underlying for me. I only became sceptical when the big guy let me down **big time** when my friend died of a horrific brain tumour at the age of 12.

If there *was* a God, what in the world was he playing at?! Screw that! In that moment, I moved away from the idea of something bigger than myself. I became a "realist, thank you very much". I wanted to become more "sensible". I became driven by the facts and "seeing is believing".

But being this realist wasn't all it cracked up to be. Science and tests and logic and research wasn't helping. And it was getting bad!

With my sciency, logical, realist brain still fully leading the charge (but this time with that little Shiva still winking at me), I decided to explore The Breath. This was the furthest I'd "allow" myself to explore outside the realms of my known.

In my breathly pursuits, I found a dude called Satya Narayana Goenka. He taught Vipassanā Meditation and spoke of its profound healing benefits.

Profound healing...just by breathing!?!

I was **in.** I was literally game for anything at this point (not an ideal spot to be in – thank goodness I found Goenka and not Pablo Escobar)!

Goenka had online recordings of his renowned 10-Day Silent Retreat all over YouTube. So, I decided to do my own 10-day breathwork retreat of sorts. Outside of the time I spent with my babes, I remained in the silent pursuit of my breath.

The power of breathwork hit me like a freight train! It was almighty.

In these 10 days I had some profound moments – and I became obsessed.

My Western, logical, talk-therapy-conditioned brain, however, was still getting in the way. I wasn't "better". I **still** didn't know how to get "better". All of this sitting and waiting with no singular objective. I didn't know why **"it"** (whatever **"it"** was!?) wasn't just happening already when:

- I'd chosen not to die
- I'd chosen to search for more
- I'd done the talk therapy

- I'd had enlightening moments where I'd found a weirdly wonderful power within myself
- AND I kept bloody breathing, just like Goenka was telling me to...

There are only so many times you can sit down, meditate, get frustrated, journal your heart onto the page or chant in ancient Pali before getting discouraged as FUNK!

I was still searching for answers and guidance on how to process what I was experiencing. Saying I was confused and frustrated would have been an understatement!

It was time to look for **that** definitive answer, **again**...

THE POWER OF PURPOSE

He who has a why to live for can bear almost any how.

—*Friedrich Nietzsche*

Everyone and their wife always talks about how you'll never feel complete until you fully apply yourself to service and purpose.

So, whilst still attempting to rebuild my own world, it became my mission to help others in the hope that I could at least prevent at least one person from getting so alarmingly close to the edge that I'd reached.

I'd had a couple of powerful realisations, lessons I wish I'd known whilst sitting alone in those dark spaces, that I hoped to share with someone at that too familiar lowest ebb. This idea drove me forward. This would give me a feeling of purpose, a reason for everything I had endured.

Giving to others – that was the next fix I was looking for.

MONEY AND IMPACT

Back then, I had no money.

Mum pottered[5] in part-time jobs. Dad was a factory worker turned window cleaner. As a kid, we didn't have much. And, of course, that followed me into adulthood. Despite the nice house and holidays, we lived tightly from paycheque to paycheque. Every penny was accounted for.

So, I took the plunge. I went in HARD, as usual!

If you want money and impact, you've gotta invest money in learning how someone else made their impact. Them's the rules. So, I invested in my first business coach for £10,000 (I almost threw up and shit myself simultaneously when she gave me her fee!! It cost more than my car!!!)

I was hooked.

"This IS my answer!" I proclaimed as I stopped sleeping, eating and prioritising anything or anyone outside of my business's growth. It was like the devil had gotten a hold of me and refused to let go.

It all felt murky and messy.

Everything I did was always a way to scale, to get immediate short-term results, to create more...and more...and more. I had more "Get-Rich-Quick Tips" than my nervous system knew how to handle.

I was frazzled! I was chasing – permanently chasing – with no "That's enough!" in sight!

Business coaching was the third and final space in the triangle of feeling like I'd found my answer **but** then realising that I was even more lost than before.

---

5   To spend time in a relaxed way doing small jobs and other things.

THE LESSONS OF THERAPY, SPIRITUALITY AND BUSINESS

Exploring these three spaces taught me powerful lessons – mainly, how **not** to do things.

The Lost Triangle of Therapy, Spirituality and Business promised answers but just left me with more questions:

1. Talk Therapy taught me how helpful it can be to see *when* the shit hit the fan/my traumas.

It also taught me that being able to put your finger on the "problem," seeing that it's there and "understanding" why (from your past experiences) **isn't** enough to heal and move forward. It left me feeling empty...

2. Spirituality taught me that, on some level, you must believe in the power of something greater than yourself that holds answers the human brain cannot comprehend.

It also left me frustrated by the idea that I should simply just "have patience" and be able to be grateful for my shit-show existence because, "Everything happens for a reason", "It'll all work out" and "Time is a healer". BLEUGH!!! It left me feeling like there was a secret code that everyone else knew but me...

3. Business taught me the "Power of Push" and how there is always something bigger, better and more profound to embody, and that service and purpose are imperative to life (alongside an abundance of money!).

It also taught me that 99% of "successful" businesses run on stress and an endless chase of *not good enough*-ness – "Must do more to feel more worthy!". I was left feeling burnt the funk OUT...

I'd learned **a lot**. But I was left with more questions than answers, and back then, not having answers was the WORST!

Why wasn't it freaking working!?!?

MASLOW'S HIERARCHY

It didn't "work" because, it turns out, I never felt safe. No matter what I did, I was scared almost all of the time. My life was a soundtrack of sharp inhales and gasps every time **anything** happened:

- Unknown number calls on my phone: *panic* *gasp*
- Someone (**especially** if it was a work someone) asks to talk with me: *panic* *gasp*
- Stranger approaches me in the street: *panic* *gasp*
- Someone I *know* approaches me in the street: *panic* *gasp*
- ANYTHING happens in my life: *panic* *gasp*

There was nothing physically in front of me to be scared of. And yet, I always felt overwhelming fret, fear and anxiety tinged with a hint of shame and guilt underneath almost **everything** that happened in my life. And here's why:

MASLOW'S HIERARCHY GAME OF LIFE

Life is made up of bases. Each completed base unlocks a level in the human experience. Up-levelling from base to base is how you get to unlock You and your greatest life potential that's filled with all that juicy Moreness we all want.

I want to introduce you to The **ONLY** Rule when playing Maslow's Hierarchy Game of Life (which, if you're alive and a human, you are playing – whether you know it or not!).

The Rule: You must collect and complete all things in each base before you unlock the higher level.

Take a look at Base 1, and answer this: Are your physiological needs being met?

Quick. Answer before reading on. Are you rested, fed and hydrated?? Yes or no?

We're all normally super quick to say that all of our physiological needs are being met 100% (unless you have newborn twins!!). If you have a nice warm bed and an abundance of food and water, you might fancy yourself set to cross this base off the list.

But what about rest? I'm not talking 12 hours' sleep in your Egyptian cottons. I'm talking actual rest – deep and penetrating rest where you wake up and the core of your existence feels still.

Have you EVER experienced this?

I hadn't either!

Pretending to be okay and continuing to function whilst battling crippling thoughts, fears and anxieties puts the brain on hyper-alert **all** of the time. It's exhausting, no matter how much sleep you get! So, even after what "should" be considered "restful periods" (sleep, spa days [lol to having time for spa days] beach days, garden days), you're still knackered[6]. When you can't switch off the worry and mental unrest, you lack the ability to rest, and therefore, you're confined to Base 1.

Unrested, it's impossible to move to Base 2 – to feel safe emotionally or physically. This is why you're so anxious, no matter how many safety precautions you've invested in and how apparently "safe" you've constructed your immediate situation to be.

Without Base 2's emotional stillness, it won't matter if Zac Efron comes nakedly into your world and declares his undying love for you; you'll never be able to make a home at Base 3: love and emotional belonging and security. This is why your relationships keep failing.

If you're unable to experience true, unconditional love, it's impossible to build self-esteem. No matter how many people tell you how gorgeous you are or how much of a fabulous job you've done, it'll never feel enough. That's why billionaires and celebrities, who seemingly "have it all", kill themselves.

If you make it through all the bases, you make it to the climax of this triangle: self-actualisation. A space where Actual You lives, and not the Anxious Imposter who's living your life and pretending to be you. The You who was intentionally put on this spinning sphere for a purpose. The You who's meant to spend 99% of her life rested, safe, in love and knowing she's better than sliced freaking bread.

It's only when you've made it from Base 1 to the tip of the triangle that you'll feel fizzy with joy for life and see who You actually are. And you can **only** get here by building upon a secure base and going up.

This book screams the vibes of Meghan Trainor – it's **ALL** About that Base! (*No treble!*)

The problem is: we don't want the base. We've been taught that the base is boring and mundane and how much better than this we are!!

---

6   Incredibly tired.

So, we're all hunting to "win" at Maslow's Game of Life (as in, "Just let my life feel freaking GLORIOUS!!!"), but we're all trying different tricks and tips to hack our way to the very top of the triangle, leaving us feeling limp and a little bit pathetic...

Talking to cheap-ass (or really bloody expensive ones who're just a bit shit!) therapists, sitting in 10-day retreats breathing, investing life savings (and money you absolutely **don't** have!!) into the next "quick fix to get rich" – all done in an attempt to skip over the base; to indulge in the treble-climax at the top of Maslow's Game, to FINALLY feel bloody brilliant about who You are.

To get anywhere close to this climax, you must be willing to get real comfortable with Base 1 *first* – especially the elusive *rest* bit.

You want to rest, desperately, but a brain which has been busy with anxiety for **so** long has forgotten how to.

Looking at the tip of this triangle from the trenches of Base 1, it might very well feel like you winning Maslow's Game of Life is impossible!

The reason?

Instead of rest, your brain has become trained to revert back to something else...

THE EMOTIONAL "SAFEHOUSE" QUEST FOR REST

Experiencing anxiety is like running from an invisible bear 24/7 with your hands and legs tied together. It's like having one foot on the accelerator and the other hard on the brake.

Chemicals are coursing through your body - fight, take flight or freeze.

When you have anxiety, there are a LOT of spaces in your body that go into this sympathetic nervous response. You interrupt your body's regular program of nourishing, nurturing, resting and taking care of you in favour of survival.

In this panic, when you're feeling this way, I want you to tell me: where do you most wish to be?

At home, right?

Or, if your home doesn't feel like that much of a safe space, you wanna be somewhere familiar where you **know** you can "switch off" and "relax". You also know that, realistically, you can't actually relax (no matter where you are), but the *idea* of it is so temptingly nice and appealing, so you keep trying.

Let's explore this a little...

PART 1

YOU ARE NOT THE PROBLEM: LEARNING YOUR LANDSCAPE

Why do anxious thoughts persist no matter how hard you hope, wish and try to understand and be rid of them?

The answer to this question lies deep within Yourself. And to access this answer you must change Your Landscape.

Your Landscape is made up of the places in your mind that you frequent as you go about your day:

1. The most familiar place is what I call The Emotional "Safehouse". It's somewhere you revert back to whenever and wherever things get intense. It houses all sorts of inherited entities (all of whom you're going to meet soon). It resides inside the Unconscious Mind.

And then you have...

2. A pathway that naturally runs from that You part of you which exists in the Subconscious, through The Emotional "Safehouse" space in the Unconscious, and into the Conscious Mind where you think and "know". I call this path The Rainbow Road – a multicoloured medley of all things You. It's innate in **every** human being. Anxiety and overthinking block The Rainbow Road by constructing an Emotional "Safehouse" smack-bang right in the centre of it, which is how You got so lost.

The Subconscious, Unconscious, and Conscious Minds need to reconnect in order to create **lasting** change.

To stop scratching the surface of why life feels out of control, to get to the bottom of it and to *truly* live free from anxiety forever, the key is to go with your nature, not against it, and begin being curious around the unknown...

WELCOME TO THE UNKNOWN

This world is filled with an abundance of unknowns, and your brain spends a big-ass chunk of its time trying to make sense of it. It dedicates endless hours to thinking, scheming and manipulating in the hope of generating an outcome which will finally feel good for you.

Only…it's not really working. And that's because this isn't the way life was meant to be lived.

Your brain is a piece of technology far superior to any that can be crafted. Why? Because it harbours the gift of imagination. Imagination led the Wright brothers to imagine metal could fly; Guglielmo Marconi to imagine that invisible radio waves could be heard; Thomas Edison to imagine the electric light; Marie Curie to imagine that splitting an atom could provide life-saving radioactivity. Each physical, tangible outcome was first a conceptual spark inside the mind. What they each proposed was perceived as madness to the world (until it was done!)

Your imagination is a portal to You! It's something you KNOW how to "do". Your job is to remind yourself that accessing this portal gets to be really flippin' fun and easy!

That's why this book was created. It's been crafted to take inconceivable concepts and make them really real – like flying planes, electric lights, radio songs and living a life totally and utterly FREE from anxiety – using techniques and principles which might feel a little too far for a mind which is too used to thinking, scheming, rationalising, and manipulating.

I invite you to remember how much more fun the world felt when you lived through your imagination – when you got lit up by a small spark of an idea which you allowed to grow instead of pissing on your own bonfire with "realist" thinking every time you felt that fire begin. Every character, phrase, setting and situation in this book was created to be the spark of imaginative colour that lights Your Rainbow Road journey. Because a spark is all that's needed to make Your magic.

If you want it all to "make sense", stop reading right now – this is not your book! If you're DONE trying to "make sense" of this world, and being crushed by it over and over again, get ready to use your imagination. A sound wave will ring in your ear, a light will go on, a fire will start within the belly of your existence, and it'll all make sense in ways that no one else will ever be able to explain. At this point, You won't need to "make sense" of it – You'll **know**. And that is when you will start to truly live...

Imagine that...

THE EMOTIONAL "SAFEHOUSE"

How often do you fantasise about getting home, getting to the end of your jobs and sitting down in a nice, clean space – feeling still and relaxed?

If you're anything like me, this was THE "Ultimate Dream Goal". And when anxiety ruled my existence, that moment NEVER came – no matter how tidy the house was, how "done" my to-do list was, or how frothy I made my coffee.

That **didn't** stop my brain from searching for it, though!

Why stop, right?

The brain's a huge piece of software that uses around 20% of your body's energy when it's in a resting state (and remember, we ain't resting, so our number's got to be a whole heap bigger – that's a LOT of energy!). So, it's always looking for a break, a respite, the hope of making it off Base 1 (please!). Always hunting for the "easiest", more familiar option which'll allow it to conserve the most energy. Home.

"What in the world does this mean for me?!" I hear you...

Now, your brain doesn't just wanna take you back to your physical home; it's also anchored itself within an imaginary Emotional "Safehouse" that it's made up and housed inside your mind too. And, much like what it does with your physical space, it's always trying to get back there in its "Quest for Rest". It takes its "Energy Conservation Project" (lol!) so super seriously that it'll attempt to drag you back to familiarity in ANY way it can.

Unfortunately, the brain is wired to seek out danger so you can stay alive. So, "familiar" is often the things that you don't want more of in your world. This is why "Safehouse" has inverted commas[7] – they're intentional. It's because, despite the tantalising notion of the safety it promises, you **still** don't feel safe in this mental space of familiar thoughts and feelings.

If being worried, being angry, feeling guilty or being depressed has been the way your brain has worked for some time now, this is your familiar; this is your "Safehouse".

This is weird. I know. I don't make up the rules for how this works. I am just the messenger.

Because the feelings around this Emotional "Safehouse" are so familiar, you instinctively prime your brain to look for evidence to divert you back to this known Emotional "Safehouse" Space.

At the height of my anxiety, I had a permanently dull ache in the pit of my stomach. If I ever got a reprieve from this sensation, I would actively go in search of it. A feeling of, "It feels weird not feeling this way". I'd find a memory that was worry-filled enough to make me anxious again, taking me back to my Emotional "Safehouse", and I'd be on my complete-opposite-of-merry way, again.

The Emotional "Safehouse" feels so inviting, despite it feeling really shitty, because it holds a feeling of:

"Well, at least there are no bears, and I'm much less likely to die here".

---

[7]   Another word for *quotations*.

"Not dead" and "as close to rested as possible" is where your primitive brain thinks it can "rest" the easiest to allow it to come back to only using that 20%. So, you sit tight, peering from behind your net curtains, trapped DEEP in the familiarity of your Emotional "Safehouse" pains.

Even though what you've just read might suggest otherwise, all of you **really** wants to win Maslow's game. Somehow, though, the game and the rules got a little scrambled at Base 1.

"Logically", obtaining your Base 1 needs *should* feel like the cosiness of your tidy home, with a perfect brew the colour of He-Man's face (my fave) and a biscuit (Oreo for me, please!) – aka The Ultimate Level of Loveliness. Only...it doesn't feel that way!

Emotional "Safehouses" that we endure look like:

- Beatings from a partner. We go to this because pain and unworthiness is familiar, which is why domestic abuse victims keep going back.
- Poor diet leading to diabetes. Feeling out of control and hungry for affection is familiar to people with obesity. Often, they've only known **moments** of light relief when eating the foods they love; thus, gorging on food is familiar. This is why people keep gaining weight and choose to have limbs amputated over changing their diet and exercise habits.
- Obscene spending habits. This stems from the feeling of being out of control but loving that excited hit of something new, which is familiar. This is why people go further into debt over things they don't need.

You stay in your Emotional "Safehouse" because of the facade: the promise of "not-deadness". You stay. You hope. And nothing changes. There's a reason for this.

There are two *you*s at play in this scenario.

THE TWO YOUS

Your obsession with your Emotional "Safehouse" will reduce effort-lessly and naturally as you learn The 7 Steps housed in this book. There is NO shoehorning (we're **done** with that!). These steps will take you closer to who You are.

What do I mean here?

Well, pretty soon you're going to learn there are two yous (more mad-ness, yes, but stay with me...).

There's The Actual You (with a Capital Y)

This is the You you once knew, way back when, before you joined your parents in *their* Emotional "Safehouse" (more on that shortly). Back then, you were The You who:

- Knew what she wanted
- Didn't give a hoot what anyone else had to say about her
- Wore her roller skates, whilst only wearing pants, with the glitter-iest headband on
- Loved wildly, without limits, and without judgement
- Got whatever she wished for
- Shared instinctively
- Was excited to be alive

Then there's *Imposter you*: your "Ideal Self" Avatar

This is the "you" who is thoroughly convinced that The Emotional "Safehouse" is a helpful place to be; this is the you who's royally fuck-ing up your life.

Right now, you really think she's you, but she is not!

She is an imposter. She is not You. And she's obsessed with making up stories and finding "evidence" for why you're such a mess or why you don't deserve anything lovely in your life (LIES!! But you still believe them...and back to "Safehouse" you go...).

Imposter you is made up of three elements I call The Trio of Terror (you're gonna learn about this cast of characters in Part 2).

Right now, this trio has dedicated their existence to making up stories for why:

- You aren't enough
- You're too much
- Everyone else is doing it right
- You're the only one who's doing it wrong

In short, they're telling you that You as You are is an embarrassment and should be hidden from the world...back to...(you get the picture).

This allows them to continue to lead the charge of <u>your</u> existence! This makes you more fearful and pushes you deeper into the "Safehouse" Abyss with not so much as a tightrope to scramble your way back.

GET CURIOUS

Think for a moment...Before life got to the space you're in right now, do you remember being unafraid to express your Actual You? This freedom you once felt might've been lost in one of two ways:

1. An almighty moment of travesty
2. It's been blocked up for a while as you gradually, one brick at a time, forgot who you were

The loss of yourself usually comes slowly and covertly. My work is dedicated to teaching you HOW to come back to the Youest version of You – with a Capital Y!

To get a small glimpse of You, I want us to do a super-quick exercise together.

Although Little You has grown, the energy she carries is still alive within. This exercise is the first step to unlocking the door she hides behind.

LITTLE YOU VISUALISATION

1. Close your eyes and become aware of your breath.

2. Breathe in through your nose (or mouth! If this is tricky, no worries! Just do what you can.) for as long as feels comfortable, then out of your mouth until there is no breath left. Continue to fill yourself up, and empty yourself out.

3. As you do this, Imagine Little You, the one who doesn't give a hoot. Imagine her in your favourite place in the world, living her best life. Running, jumping, clothes off, roller skates on – having **the** best time. If you didn't make it to an age you can remember feeling like this (I can't! Anxiety hit me hard since before I left the womb, I think!!), then create it. Imagine what Little You could've created if she hadn't been so worried about everything all of the time.

4. Smile as you create. Hold the mental image of what could've been for as long as you wish.

CLICK HERE FOR THE AUDIO LINK TO THIS!

If this feels challenging right now, that's okay. It's unfamiliar and your brain might resist the heck out of it.

Keep coming back to Little You. Over and over again. She will become clearer and louder as your Conscious Brain becomes quieter, and your resistance to seeing her will become less determined as you learn The 7 Steps.

LET'S GO...

It's time to see where this Little You got lost along the way. In being lost, you left breadcrumbs leading you straight to that "Safehouse" in the centre of it all so you could find your way back to it each time you felt threatened. This house draws you in with the smell of freshly baked cookies and a seemingly cozy feel but is actually freaking FATAL if you stay there too long!!

We're going to go one better than the tightrope too. You're gonna learn how to make yourself a road filled with all the colours of the rainbow (much like Dorothy's yellow brick one!). And brick by brick, colour by colour, you're going to build your Rainbow Road. You'll enjoy a completely new Landscape. You will feel inspired to come out of that "Safehouse" space to explore Your new world as you wish to perceive it. Your perception of your life is imperative in this process. It's what we're going to explore next...

THE RAINBOW ROAD

THIS WORLD MAKES NO SENSE

The odds of you being alive is 1 in 400 trillion. For context, a trillion is a million million. And the probability of your even being alive is one in four of these. FOUR!

You grew from one single cell which somehow knew how to call towards it all of the things it needed to evolve into you. One cell turned fully formed human.

Look at you, sitting there all person-like and stuff. It all started with a single cell!

We're all here, floating around on a sphere which is suspended in an ever-expanding, endless Universe travelling at 1,000 miles an hour, which feels like complete stillness. We're being held down by a force we cannot see with no true understanding of how we got here or how and when it's all going to end.

It makes no sense!

If we were to spend our time trying to compute all of this from dusk till dawn, it would drive us into an early grave. You might be breaking a cold sweat as you read this. Truly contemplating this often is a feat too far for our humanness, so we end up bouncing to the other extreme and pretending it all makes sense.

Our sensory experience and how we perceive reality play a BIG part in how we do this.

UMWELT

Around the time I began to acknowledge that I even had anxiety, life wasn't making quite as much sense as I wanted it to. Upon spending some time getting curious about the bizarreness of our existence, I stumbled across a chap called Jakob von Uexküll and his term *umwelt*.

Umwelt comes from the German word for "environment". Uexküll uses the term *umwelt* to describe the animal kingdom, and it doesn't simply describe each animal's environmental surroundings; it's used to describe the animal's *perception* of the surroundings it senses and experiences. *Umwelt* is used to describe each animal's entirely unique perceptual world.

Getting curious around this is how I've been able to wave bye-bye to anxiety.

Although the human's existence is a sensory one where we perceive the world through our 5 fundamental sensory receptors, it **is** limited. LOTS is happening outside of our field of awareness. Just because you're not perceiving it doesn't mean it's not there. It's very *umwelt*-like to believe such.

Our eyes cannot see the ultraviolet hues of light like bumblebees can. Bumblebees only experience communication as ritualistic figure-of-eight dances.

Our ears cannot hear the infrasonic calls of the elephant – who only sees the world in shades of blue and yellow.

Our sense of touch cannot measure distance like the mouse, who perceives his environment through his map-making whiskers. His short-sightedness forces the belief that the visual world ends just beyond the tip of his nose.

As I dive deeper into this work, I'm learning that our levels of perception are limitless, but they do adhere to the part of the brain whose job it is to order the sensory experience we have each and every day for it to "make sense" to us. Remember, our brain is always on the lookout for how it can revert back to what is *known* and *familiar* so we can all go about our daily existence (brew and biscuit) with as little resistance as possible. Existing within this default setting means we're missing out on ALL kinds of *umwelt*!

To sense the world, we detect stimuli in the form of light, sound and chemicals. We then convert these stimuli into electrical signals which travel along neural pathways to the brain. Cells, which are responsible for detecting stimuli, are called receptors.

There are 3 types of receptors:

- Mechanoreceptors detect pressure or movement.
- Photoreceptors detect light.
- Chemoreceptors detect molecules.

These sense receptors are mostly in the eyes, nose, ears, mouth and skin.

This is how your brain receives and interprets your world:

1. Light, sound and/or chemical stimulation occurs
2. The body registers the stimuli through the ear, nose, mouth, eye or skin
3. Your sensory receptors convert stimuli into electrical signals
4. Electrical signals travel through the nervous system to the brain
5. The brain "makes sense" of it

It is this chain of events that then creates an awareness of **our** experience. Our *umwelt*.

Consider what you've read for just a moment....

- Light is just electromagnetic radiation.
- Smells are just molecules.
- Sounds are just waves of pressure.

But your body is created so that it perceives these things in precisely the way you want to perceive them in order to make sense of them. That's why coriander can taste like soap to some and a delicacy to others.

*How the heck have we been constructed so that we can detect any of these things...**then** convert them into electrical signals – and **THEN** smell freshly ground coffee, see the stars in the sky and hear the voices of our most beloved beings!? Mind-freaking-BLOWING!*

It's all done through the clever automated computer system that is the brain. Therefore, if you change the way your brain computes, you change your umwelt and the way you perceive it ALL!

There are so many sights, tastes, smells, sounds and things to touch that if you experienced everything at once, you would implode. This is why your brain listens to what you unconsciously tell it to focus on – Emotional "Safehouse" FM.

Choosing your *umwelt* is like tuning a radio to a specific frequency/station. Your inner "radio" has the capacity to receive infinite numbers of frequencies, but it will only pick up what you direct it to. Therefore, we experience exactly that: **our** experience. There is so much that we aren't perceiving whilst in our survivalist "Safehouse" existence. I'm not saying you're gonna grow whiskers to mind map your world or start seeing in infrared. This work is about discovering what you're truly capable of actualising.

> ***The world exists as you perceive it. It is not what you see, it is how you see it. It is not what you hear, but how you hear it. It is not what you feel, but how you feel it.***
>
> *—Rumi*

NO TWO UMWELTS ARE THE SAME

We're all living within our own *umwelts*. We inhabit the same spaces yet experience life very differently from one another.

Take two children with the same alcoholic parents:

- Child 1 becomes an alcoholic because of their traumatic childhood.
- Child 2 creates the 12-step program that helps those who want to recover from alcoholism.

When you look at your life, if you had to generalise completely, which child are you?

I was 100% Child 1 before The 7 Steps.

Why do we so willingly become the victim of our own circumstances?

We fear the unknown (the potential bears waiting in caves to spring out and eat you), so we go about trying to "make sense" of this bizarre worldly adventure we're on. Even though we think we'd ideally like to eternally spend our lives in trackie[8] bottoms in our boarded-up "Safehouse", we can't. We've got to work and live. Outside of our "Safehouse", we feel exposed. The only "bonus" is that "out there" in that big wild world, the more people we have who back up our perception of **our** *umwelt*, the more "real" and "secure" our existence on this spinning sphere feels. And remember: our brain LOVES "secure"!!

This is why so many people are out there *fighting* for what they believe is just and true and important. They bunker down in response to their perceived *umwelts*, and they rally as many people as possible to back up this notion. These beings with firm notions of what is "right" and what is "wrong" hold TIGHT to their version of *umwelt* and refuse to

---

[8]   Another word for *tracksuit*.

waver – for doing so might be taken as a sign of weakness/them not definitely "knowing" what is going on.

A perfect example of this is veganism (chill if you're a vegan – maybe I'm not talking about you...maybe...)

How many chilled-out vegans do you know that just quietly go about their plant-based diet?

I know I freaking didn't when I was vegan!

I was appalled by the conditions the animals lived in. How they were slaughtered. The loss of land due to mass farming for animal feed. The impact that animal protein has on the body. And the freaking milk industry...yuck!!

I'd tell anyone within a five-mile radius about it in the hope that what I was screaming at them (not screaming, but pretty close!) would make them "see the light", "get healthier" and "stop abusing helpless animals".

Back then (I'm no longer vegan – I practise balance to process all areas of my world now [I'm not "right" here – just a person making a choice]), I truly believed I was spreading the good message for all of humanity.

On reflection, I wanted to be "right". I wanted to feel "safer/less likely to die". I just wanted a feeling of being more in control of my life.

Internally, it was my cry for, "Please come bunker up in my Emotional "Safehouse" with me. It doesn't feel as safe as I want it to there, alone. More people there will make me feel better. Please come". Externally, I looked psychotic, screaming, "You're all fucked if you don't do it the way I do it, you morans!" I was a HOOT to have at BBQs as you can imagine!! (lolz)

To "successfully" maintain the "safety" of your *umwelt*, you're always on the lookout for the streets that look most familiar to you. You keep leaping into the same circles of friends with the same circus and shit shows unfolding and into the same toxic relationships. You keep entering the same suffocating, micro-managed work environments. You're buying the same cheap-ass cars, or perhaps even therapy, hoping that you'll be able to shortcut your way to happiness this time (which you can't!).

To change your Child 1 *umwelt*, you've gotta get curious about the landscape of the brain.

YOUR LANDSCAPE: THE BRAIN'S THREE FUNDAMENTAL LEVELS

Humans work on three fundamental levels:

The Conscious → this is what you "know". It's what you can put your finger on precisely and say "this". When you understand things with your Conscious thoughts, you say, "Ah...that makes sense". As humans, we LOVE being able to do this!

When working with this part of the mind, you do so without too much effort. It feels automatic, like "it's obvious" and doesn't require thought. This part of the mind massively feels like you.

This is where The Trio of Terror (whom I'm going to introduce you to soon) live.

The Unconscious → an unknown, endless chasm filled with feelings, thoughts, memories and urges, stored up over time, which you have no considered control over.

This part of the mind is like a guarded vault filled with all of the experiences/stories/emotions that've been important enough to you to shape you into who you believe you are today. Accessing it requires time and space. Mainstream mindset work tends to be more concerned with taking a pneumatic drill into this space with the mentality that "If you just keep going hard enough, long enough, you'll crack through".

This is where your Emotional "Safehouse" is.

The Subconscious Mind → the all-knowing, omnipresent part of you which makes decisions based within your highest and greatest good; no words or active thinking/choosing exist here.

The Subconscious Mind cannot be accessed through any means of "thought". It's a Universal Energy Space which holds light, oneness and freedom. Every answer you might ever look for is stored within this Universal Energy Space. Access is granted here through imaginative curiosity, which also makes space in The Unconscious.

This is where You (with a Capital Y) lives.

That Subconscious is filled with the juicy good stuff you want more of. Access to The Subconscious makes life feel easy freaking BREEZY!

Our mission, should you choose to accept it and read this book entirely, is to match up all three elements the way they were intended to be...

The ideal way to align all three levels of the mind is to create a "Rainbow Road". This Rainbow Road is made up of the 7 elements that, when combined, allow you to overcome overthinking and be free from anxiety. They work so well together because each one plays a huge part in aligning the different parts of your landscape: The Subconscious, Unconscious and Conscious Minds.

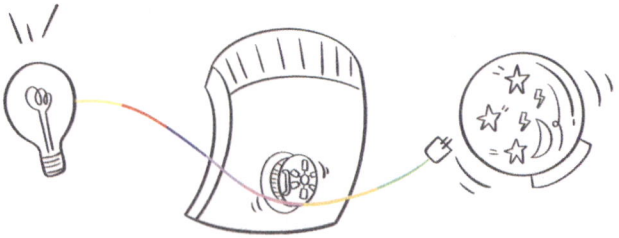

RAINBOW ROAD RESISTANCE

As you realise you know less than you thought you knew, you're going to see things (your *umwelt*) differently, with a different awareness.

Your Conscious Brain is gonna be screaming, *"What the funk are you doing!?!?!"*

This is because your Conscious Brain is still listening to the outdated message/established brain neurology of *Return to "Safehouse"*, which has been programmed into The Unconscious Mind for the number of years you've been alive...How many years is that?! A few, right?! So, give yourself a break here! With kindness and consistency (both of which I am going to teach you through this work), this pattern **will** change (there's gonna be a LOT that comes up which'll try to con-vince you otherwise, but I have a Formula for it all – just you wait...). **Harnessing awareness through a willingness to be curious is key. Why?**

The Conscious Mind will resist things which go against its "logic". Curiosity releases the resistance that arises when the traditional measure of "success" is challenged, which is what we're going to do with this work.

The truth is: you're gonna "fail". You're gonna get frustrated. It's part of the course! It's essential, actually. There will be days when you feel done and going one more round with your brain feels like a feat you just can't face. You might have fallen on your face one too many times and all you wanna do is sit and Netflix and chill over and over and over again...

Knowing this, accepting this, taking a day, having a massive nap and THEN coming back with a deeper level of curiosity **is** the work. The journey of alignment with Actual You is the reparation of your colourful Rainbow Road.

Every time you spot this resistance, remind yourself that failure and frustration actually means you are bridging the gaps among The Conscious, Unconscious and Subconscious from the bottom up through this new passageway you're building.

This resistance is actually a blooming great thing. It's a marker of things shifting and changing. A new brick being added to your new Road.

Curiosity combined with fun reduces resistance so moving into a new awareness actually gets to feel easy. You've gotta make it your mission to keep building your Rainbow Road in a light and fun way – **especially** when The Conscious Brain is screaming, "I couldn't possibly!!". Shifting your focus from overthinking to enjoying this process of reconstructing your Rainbow Road **is** what will allow you to navigate yourself through all of this into that freedom I promise exists for you (too!).

This might be the first time you're actively remembering how to do this again, as an adult.

Welcome. We're gonna have a **ball** together!!!

You are part of a tribe now! If you have access to any of my online materials, to me, my coaching and my team, it's in these moments of frustration that you reach out, lean in and say, "Flipping heck!!! I'm SO up for changing, but **this** thing keeps getting in my way. What the funk is it all about!?!?"

Follow us on Instagram: @morethanthisbyEmmaUpton

Or email us at: morethanthisbyEmmaUpton@gmail.com

We hold space for you to Find your answers as you move through and let that scramble for "Safe" familiarity go.

Let's just make one thing real clear right now. "Failure" is imperative.

"But I can't fail, Emma. I dunno how to!"

It's time to learn.

Make peace with it. Right now.

If you don't fail, you're not challenging yourself into unknown spaces and places.

Failure is a sign that you're making space for something new. So, embrace it. Learn the lessons and let's all freaking move ON – we've got a Subconscious Mind to unleash!

But doing this can sometimes feel like cracking a secret code which is being guarded by a fire-breathing dragon! The resistance is REAL!

Your Conscious Gatekeeping Mind is much like a dragon. Its life goal is to keep you locked inside your Emotional "Safehouse"! This is why you need a process that lasts.

Now, this *could* be just another one of those Conscious Mind/push-as-hard-as-you-can kinda books where you cross your fingers and hope and pray it has at least *some* kind of impact.

But this is NOT that book!

What if you didn't have to go rooting through your dirty knicker drawer and air your laundry for everyone to see? What if you didn't need to get to the "root" of past traumas and rip yourself in two to "heal"? What if you don't need fucking healing at all?! What if there's no need to dredge up and dance around in the shadows of all of the horrible things that have happened to you? What if you didn't need to know your rising moon star or the phase of the earth's orbit? What if your

Enneagram number or the human design you fell into didn't mean diddly squat?

What if the only thing you need ever do is to learn to live? To be totally and utterly alive to whatever is being presented to you right now – in **the** only moment which exists. And what if you already have **all** of the tools readily available, but you just forgot how to access them?

If all of this is true (which it is!!), and you decide to actively lower your resistance to it being so, it will allow you to actively change your *umwelt*.

With this book, you will learn how to use your senses in a different way. The scented sensory stimulants that these 7 steps will teach you to use makes it fun and easy to establish the path from The Conscious Mind, through the trenches of The Unconscious, on your way to The Subconscious – and back. This is a process I have trademarked as The Piggyback Sensory Hack System™.

The Piggyback Sensory Hack System™ will allow you to create space in The Unconscious (letting go of those painful feelings, emotions and stories you've made up to make "sense" of it all) for the big-ass Rainbow Road you're going to be laying down, bit by bit, colour by colour, scent by scent, taste by taste. This will change your entire perception of reality.

Allow me to explain.

THE PIGGYBACK SENSORY HACK™

If you're reading this part of the book in isolation, you might want to burn it, scream, "Madness!" at me, and do that weird little quick walk you do to escape when you don't wanna make too much of a scene.

Rainbow roads?! Made up of colours and scents!? Piggyback Hacking to a Subconscious You (with a freaking capital, what?!)

Yes, it sounds bonkers, but in the context of everything you've read so far...this madness might just work, right?!

And (I say this with **love!**) all of the other stuff you've tried isn't working all that well, right?

Maybe, this just might...

This is **The** Hack-of-all-Hacks that makes **the** Code accessible for regular guys and gals like you and me. It's **not** sitting and learning for hours on end. It's something brilliantly different...

Our senses are **the** tool that's really gonna help us build, reconstruct and direct a Rainbow Road that goes from The Conscious, thinking, controlling mind; through The Unconscious Emotional "Safehouse" mind where all of the feels, memories, emotions and limits lie; and into The Subconscious where You (with a Capital Y) exist.

With The 7 Steps, you will embody the following 7 Fundamental Foundations of the work:

1. Peace
2. Growth
3. Freedom
4. Gratitude
5. Joy
6. Alignment
7. Surrender

...by harmonising each Step with 3 Sensory Stimulants:

- a colour
- a smell
- a taste

When seen, smelt or tasted, each Sensory Stimulant will conjure up the healing of your Rainbow Road by taking you to a deeper level of You where change can happen without force, one Step at a time.

Easy freaking BREEZY!!!

Doing this maverick-stylie covert op allows you to leapfrog The Conscious Mind's incessant signal of, "Revert back to safehouse! Back to safehouse!" that goes off whenever you attempt to go near anything new. As you learn about each of The 7 Fundamental Foundations of the work by addressing one aspect of The Conscious Mind at a time, you will adorn yourself in as much (or as little) of the sensory element as you feel inspired to.

Each day of the week has one of The 7 Fundamental Foundations ascribed to it in the chart below.

THE 7 STEPS (one per day)	PIGGYBACK SENSORY HACK™ STIMULANT[9]
1. Mind-on-Mute Monday To embody **Peace**, you must recognise that the voice inside your head is, in fact, NOT you!	Greens and Mints
2. Trigger-Free Tuesday To embody **Growth**, you must stop being so pissed off by the world and start learning from it instead.	Oranges

---

[9] *Please note: you can use just **one** sensory stimulant. Also, please substitute any flavours or colours for ANYTHING you'd most like and will work for you, ESPECIALLY (and obviously) for those with allergies, where foods cannot be tolerated. The least pressure you put on yourself to get this "perfect", the better. It has to be brilliant for you – no one else! It is the principle of this work that works, not the specific colour and scent association.*

3. Wake-up Wednesday	Watermelon Pinks
To embody **Freedom**, you must see your bitchy, unkind thoughts for what they actually are so you can stop giving yourself such a hard time!	
4. Thankful Thursday	Lavender Purples
Without **Gratitude**, you cannot move forward in life. Learn how to feel it, embody it and be in awe at how good life gets to feel!	
5. Feel-It Friday	Almond and Blues
To ultimately get in touch with your **Joy**, allow yourself to feel ALL your feelings fully. Without a healthy outlet, feelings and emotions destroy you.	
6. Saturday Sitting	Red Rhubarbs
Feel the freaking POWER of your breath to bring yourself into **Alignment**.	
7. Surrender Sunday	Yellow Citruses
To cultivate the divine skill of **Surrender**, realise how much you want to control and allow yourself to let go.	

Reading (using The Conscious Mind) whilst Piggyback Sensory Hacking™ (in The Unconscious) builds your Rainbow Road.

You're going to be reading this book all day every day (I hope!!), so don't get hung up on the specific days just yet. Focus on colours and flavours. The days will come. Once you finish this book and know all 7 areas, you will have created your Piggyback Sensory Hack™ Entry-Level Access Point.

YOUR ENTRY-LEVEL ACCESS POINT

The Entry-Level Access Point is the hint of an initial introduction to what are mind-blowing concepts when explained in their totality. Without this hint, your brain would throw the idea in question OUT INSTANTANEOUSLY!

An Entry-Level Access Point must be created as a foundational spring-board for development; a place where you perceive just enough to get The Conscious Mind intrigued while keeping it out of overwhelm – a magic Entry-Level Access spot! I'll point out opportunities for you to take in information just one bit at a time so that when you come back to a certain concept, it will already be familiar, and you will absorb it easier and easier as you go along. Creating ease and flow by covering all 7 areas gradually and regularly is what's most important for right now.

PAUSE THOUGHT™

The Pause Thought™ is the final piece of the puzzle before we get our colours on and begin Rainbow block building...

I am a realist. I know that life happens. And sometimes life is...life! Some days, your vibe is low and your resistance is HIGH. On these days, the most you've gotta do is wear your scent or colour and/or have your flavour hit closeby to communicate to that deeper part of You that you want to be experiencing this moment in a new and different way. No push. No shove. Just enough of a hint to say, "Naaaaa, let's see this another way...I'm open to seeing this another way..." And on these low-vibe days, and every day going forward, every time you spot your colour or smell your smell or taste your taste, take a Pause Thought™.

A Pause Thought™ is a microsecond of a moment in which you become acutely aware of what's happening inside your being, right now, in real time. Now, you might be thinking:

"I don't wanna know, Emma. My mind is a shit show I just try to avoid!"

I get it. But remember, The 7 Steps are the tools that are going to allow you to feel confident going to these spaces. Right now, I'm just explaining what's what (remember, you haven't learned it yet!). Reading this book and learning these 7 Steps means you're going to feel newly inspired to **want** to venture outside of your "Safehouse" picket fence. That voice, the "I don't wanna!", is your primitive Conscious Brain closing the blinds of your Emotional "Safehouse" as you're threatening to leave.

A Pause Thought™ is designed to be taken:

> *When you're going to the loo,*
> *(Especially for a number 2)*
> *When you're making a stew,*
> *(Or any kind of food)*
> *When you're standing in a queue,*
> *When you don't know what to do,*
> *Take a Pause Thought™*

Pause Thoughts™ are not hours upon hours of study. Or journaling. Or meditating. Or learning. Or...whatever else you think learning *should* mean. Pause Thoughts™ are microsecond stuff!

A Pause Thought™ is simply asking yourself, "Where the funk am I at right now?!"

The colours, scents and flavours are intended to prompt you into these moments. A sniff of Thankful Thursday lavender or a flash of Saturday Sitting rhubarb red and it's going cha-cha-slide your mind into a new habit of checking in with where your mental load is at.

Because you're actively doing The Work (reading this book, taking the online course, joining a group or doing 1:1 coaching with me), when you've surrounded yourself with the Piggyback Sensory Hack™ Stimulants, you're building your Rainbow Road even when you don't think you are – that's the **beauty** of this! Allowing that Youest part of You to come through on the REGULAR!

So, you aren't just chewing mint gum on Monday; you're interrupting the monkey in your mind. The taste of mint reminds you to think, *"What's that little monster up to!?"*

You aren't just wearing red lipstick, you're applying it thinking of the power of breathwork on Saturday Sitting: *"I'm going to take this breath a little more intentionally".*

Things as simple as sipping your favourite mojito with a micro Pause Thought™ of, "Where am I at?!" will carry out the Mindset Work that **will** eradicate anxiety – just make sure you're chewing mint gum or sipping your mojito the next time you're learning about your Monkey Mind so that You make these links on all three levels.

Living your life in this way will actively change the way you perceive your *umwelt*. Your default response might be:

"It's a lot of effort, Emma. Colours and scents and all that jazz for the rest of my life!?"

That's your Conscious Brain freaking the funk OUT, thinking I'm trying to get you to extend your "Safehouse" into a snake pit. There are so many ways to do this, to make it fun. And fun is what we're going for; it's what life is meant to be.

Look in your wardrobe. What colour are you missing? Go on a shopping trip and buy that coloured something. I have T-shirts you can buy in each of the colours – buy one for each day and know you have your colours in your wardrobe ready to go. Or spend one supermarket trip gathering one of each of the tastes (go add them to your Tesco online order basket right now). Go to your local health shop and get your-self some essential oils. Or buy our Piggyback Sensory Hack™ Pack at www.thereismorethanthis.com and put the order on repeat. Watch your Anxious Conscious Brain want to make doing this hard, and then choose to go and make it bloody easy!

You won't always **need** to do this. Slowly, your Road will be thick, strong and long and you will ride it with ecstatic ease and joy (I've got to get my mind out of the gutter! lol). You won't always *need* the Piggyback Sensory Hacks™ – your new *umwelt* will just be living free from anxiety.

Living free from anxiety means your brain is trained to perceive a new *umwelt*, naturally and instinctively. It becomes second nature. Once you get a taste of this expansive way of living, you won't EVER stop!

But...one step at a time. And 7 Steps in total. Ready?

PART 2

YOU ARE THE SOLUTION: *YOUR RAINBOW ROAD*

Before we dive into constructing Your Rainbow Road, there is one thing you must **promise** to relentlessly remember so that ALL of this gets to feel fun and easy.

Say it with me:

"I solemnly swear I won't stop until I truly remember what it's like to live free from anxiety FOREVER. ANYTHING less which comes across my path will be investigated like it's an absurd anomaly. My life is fun, easy and filled with joy. My mission is not to forget that I forgot, and to remember that life gets to be an Anxiety-Free Dance PARTY!"

THE ANXIOUS AVATAR

The Anxious Avatar is a version of you which you've been convinced to believe is Actual You . It's not! I appreciate it's a weird sentiment to start with, but I **promise** it will come to make sense (and none at all) in the **best** ways super soon. The Anxious Avatar is a cumulation of three entities. I have named them The Trio of Terror, and the first three chapters of Part 2 are dedicated to learning about this bunch:

- ◊ A Monkey in your Mind who's NEVER on mute.
- ◊ A Toad whose poisons wreak havoc, leaving no space for choices you **wish** you could make.
- ◊ And a Bratty Bitch in your Brain who doesn't know how to be kind to your mind (or anyone else for a lot of the time).

Learning to spot these three will show you everything that you are **not.**

This makes space so that you then get to see who **Actual You** truly is.

Mind-on-Mute Monday
A QUIET MENTAL SPACE

*The thing that hurts you the most in life is
your own untamed mind. The thing that can help
you the most in life is a disciplined mind. When the
wild mind is untamed, it can be very harmful.*

—Satya Narayana Goenka

Introducing The bobbing Voice in your Head, Monkey Bob

There is a voice inside your head, and that voice is a DICK! It's also absolutely and definitely NOT you! But you don't know that it's not you. At least not *yet*...

By the end of this chapter, not only will you come to know this voice, but you'll have his number and will be able to permanently delete it from your speed-dial favourites. So clear of his tones and tendencies, you'll know him so totally and utterly that the You who's been at the mercy of his voice (your whole life) will start mapping out a green-shaped path to walk on that leads to your Conscious thoughts. And it all starts with learning about The Monkey in your Mind on Mind-on-Mute Mondays.

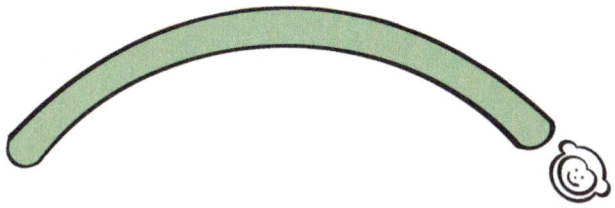

To do this, we're going to work on the mint green part of your Rainbow Road, which means you must:

1. Go get something minty green. Or just mint. Or just green. This chapter's Sensory Stimulant is Mint Green (or any other shade of green for that matter).
2. Read this chapter and do what it says – especially the sensory stuff.
3. Say "Fudge it" and try on the freaking dress!

By "Try on the Dress", I mean this:

You gotta "Play Pretend". You've gotta remember how you did it way back when you were a babe...

Play Pretend like you're in the market for a new dress. Not just any dress...**the** dress! The one that when you wear it, you feel like a million-gazillion dollars! You've seen it. You're in love. It's the most glorious designer dress that's ever been birthed: a hand-stitched glowworm silk kinda dress that holds you in alllll the right places. It's glorious. You love every element of it. But right now, you believe this dress (the Work) is too fancy, unrealistic, too flashy, too revealing and too much over your budget to be yours. You think, "*It's beyond **glorious**! It's just not for me...*"

For it to be yours, which it freaking-well CAN, you must do one thing – Number 3 your way through ALL of this work and just try it on.

"A monkey in my mind? What **are** you on about, Emma!?!"

Fudge it! Just try it on!

"This will never work in my life because of X, Y and Z that's happened/is happening – that voice which bobs in my head is too strong!"

I hear you. He's strong, but you must go and try it on...

"I could never do that. It's just not me."

Fudge it...in every orifice. And try on the freaking dress!!!

...as often as possible, using your Pause Thoughts™ and your Green and Mint Sensory Experience.

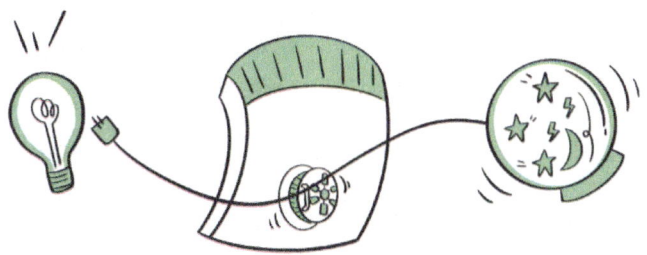

One day, it'll all make "sense" and NO sense at the same time in the most liberating way. You'll say, "Holy shitballs! There IS a monkey in my mind. And he has these really weird and annoying habits which torment the bejesus out of me. He never stops. No wonder I was so knackered for so much of the time! Now I see him and his annoying ways. And NOW I know how to snap his favourite tree-top routes in two so he falls on his arse, and I can smile and wave at his bizarreness!! This was all mine to see all along – and now I can!!"

Getting messages like this from clients NEVER gets old for me.

I can't wait to receive yours too.

HERE'S THE CHALLENGE...

There is a voice inside your head, and it swings from thought to thought/branch to branch like a crazed monkey searching for the last ever chocolate-dipped-sprinkle-covered banana in the jungle of your mind. And he squawks incessantly as he does so.

There is **no** such banana, yet he's undeterred in his quest!

"An obsessed monkey in my brain? WTF, Emma?!"

Stick with me, and remember to try on that dress for a sec...

The monkey's Number 1 mission in this world is to make everything and everyone "out there" make sense to you. To dot the i's and cross those t's so that it all feels like a brew and a biscuit in your brain. He's scrambling for a moment of, "Ahhh, well that feels better. Now I can just be".

Only...you're confused. He's even more confused. There are i's without dots and t's without crosses **everywhere**, yet he continues to try and figure it all out.

And he's not like You or me. He doesn't give up when the going gets tough or it all gets a bit awkward. He bunkers down and continues to remain DETERMINED to figure it all out. Isolation, nervous breakdowns, panic attacks and relationships collapsing are no match for this voice's thirst for dominance and comprehension. All in a bid to make you feel safer so that it all makes sense and you (**finally**!) "understand" and get a moment of reprieve.

His mission is destined to fail, but he doesn't relent. If anything, he goes in HARDER if he gets a sense that failure might ensue!

He drives you like a freight train, a tormented soul screeching from disaster to disaster hoping for that elusive moment of, "Ahhh, much better...Brew anyone?"

It doesn't come and nothing gets different.

HERE'S WHAT YOU CAN CHOOSE TO SEEK...

Mind-on-Mute Monday will show you the power of interrupting your usual thought patterns. You don't need to follow the mind's every whim...

By the end of this chapter, you'll be able to:

- Exploit the banana-biscuit- and brew-crazed voice inside your head for what it is so you get to see how it torments you so avidly.
- Identify this voice AND be onto its favourite tricks.
- Liberate yourself and the Monkey in your mind from the incessant swinging and squawking. You're exhausted and so is he, and it's this fight that keeps you **so** knackered that you don't have the strength to do anything differently.

Getting clear on who he is means that You get sure on who You actually are. And you'll come to know that You are actually more self-sufficient than you thought.

"Bullshit," I hear you cry. But when you've learned what's in the pages of this book, you'll see that it's not. I promise.

PAUSE THOUGHTS™

Right now, your Conscious Brain doesn't believe that this transformation is possible. That's okay. That's the role of this part of the mind. It's to be accepted for what it is.

Your job isn't to convince it; your job is to create that mint green part of your Rainbow Road, piggybacking the notions I share *from* your (doubting) Conscious Mind, *through* that Emotional change-making space of your Unconscious and *into* the Subconscious.

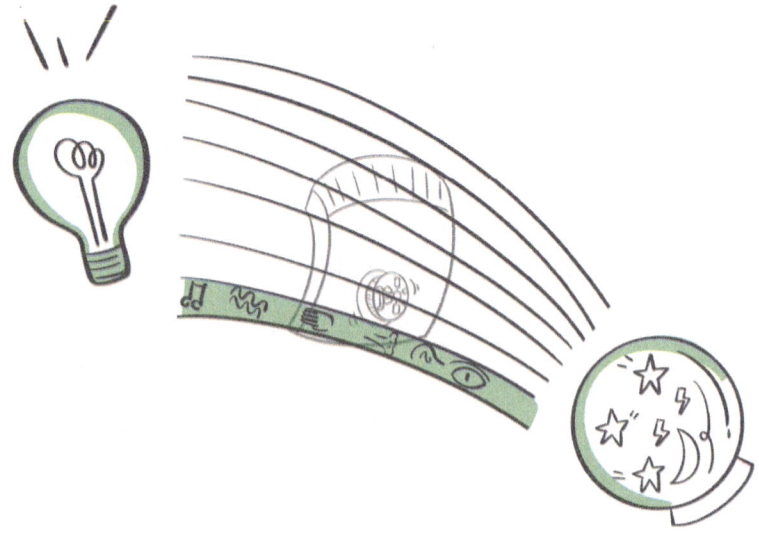

**TO DO THIS EASILY, AS YOU READ THIS CHAPTER,
YOU MUST EMBODY MINT GREENS.**

Wear your minty tops and greeny socks. Suck on peppermint Polos and make your chewing gum go pop. Use minty shampoos and have a mojito with your boo. Embody mint greens whilst learning the power of realising your mind houses a monkey. Go, right now. Get something mint (even if it's sitting with your tube of toothpaste open beside you as you read – NO freaking rules here!).

After you've read this book, on each Monday that follows, carry this minty sensory stimulant with you. Then, when you see, smell, taste or touch Mint Greens, you'll actively create a Pause Thought™ Moment, making space within your Unconscious stories and emotions – a space for You (not The Monkey) to come strutting through.

Ready? Let's go try on that dress...

YOUR TRUTH

Actual You is hidden in the belly of the Subconscious. You hold a deep, devout knowing of yourself that's so familiar, you know it inside out, back to front, upside down.

Now, I know the levels of anxiety this statement might bring up. You might roll your eyes and think, "Well, that'd be nice and all, but accessing this part of myself is just not going to happen," but, I **promise** you that it's true – just stick with me...

When you were born, you were the rawest version of Capital-Y You, kicking and screaming at **anyone** who cared to pay attention to you for at least a microsecond and feeling emotions as and when they came up, sharing your inner thoughts the moment they arrived. Being this way scared the bejesus out of your parents because You are (very intentionally!) the literal reincarnation of everything they've spent their entire lives running away from – The Universe be working this way!!

Their rapid attempts to get you to leap to their Emotional "Safehouse" Bunker ASAP (so that you "fit in" and everything just goes the way *they* think it should in *your* life) made you distrust You-with-a-capital-Y and those emotions that were crying out to be felt.

The Truth is:

★ You are born knowing who the funk you are and what you're here to do. I call this *Your Truth*.

But You were shown how to experience your parents' communal *umwelt* (which they learned from *their* parents) until You and *Your Truth* felt more like an alien invader that threatened your safety every time it tried to come out.

Eventually, (if parents are anything, they are consistent and persistent in their need to be "right") their *umwelt* perception stuck. Hard and fast.

You then accepted your place in their Emotional "Safehouse" and promised to look for clues that made their *umwelt* seem feasible, burying *Your Truth* each and every time you did.

Forcing yourself into the submission of their *umwelt* like this doesn't transition into your psyche without leaving a residual fallout. This fallout can be segmented into the three distinguishable elements that make up The Trio of Terror. You're going to meet the other two later. Right now, you're meeting the first:

This first fallout is a voice. And that voice inside your head is this lostness of You blindly scrambling around looking for *Your Truth* whilst listening to everyone else. It's the fallout of attempting to suppress *Your Truth* in exchange for their *umwelt*.

It's confusing AF!

To add to the confusion, this voice in your head, for all his fudged-up ways, is actually trying to "help" – attempting to make sense of all of this mushed-up *umwelt* medley you've inherited, going back millennia.

It's lost, trying to look for evidence to make sense of this nonsensical sensory experience and making tedious links between it all. It's scrambling and squawking in an attempt to land somewhere safely and receive even the tiniest bit of, "Ah, that feels better. Now I get to chill".

If you aren't sure what I mean, here's an example...

This verbal diarrhoea is your attempt at making this nonsensical world sensical to you. It bobs from one thought...to the next...until you're in Timbuktu with no recollection of how you got there.

THE VOICE INSIDE YOUR HEAD

This voice inside your head is the first of our Trio of Terror – the first of the three deadly spokes in the Conscious human-brain wheel that I'm going to introduce you to.

I refer to the voice inside your head as being a *dick*.

The Oxford English Dictionary defines a *dick* as:

Dick

dɪk

Noun

A brash and insensitive person who puts their own interests above all else[10]

Have you ever noticed this voice in your head before?

---

10   Urban dictionary: https://www.urbandictionary.com/define.php?term=Being%20a%20Dick

To Action

HOW TO KNOW IF YOU HAVE A VOICE IN YOUR HEAD

You might be terrified that noticing this means you're a psychopath. You might think that talking about it makes it real and that if you talk about it, it's gonna get worse, get bigger, grow legs and finish you off entirely!!

But voice inside your head is part of the human experience. If you aren't sure as to whether you have one, take a second. Ask yourself, without speaking out loud:

"Do I have a voice inside my head?"

What follows that question for you?

That's the voice!

The shower is the PERFECT place to follow this Voice Monkey around in your mind. Whilst you stand and attempt to relax under the showerhead, notice that voice trying to spoil it all.

Noticing this voice is a tool that allows you to create distance from your anxiety. Doing so allows you to transcend it and connect with the You that you're here to be.

LET'S CALL HIM BOB

To gain more clarity on this voice, name him. Or her. Or it. I call him Bob. He was christened one day when I was exhausted with the bull-shit I was beginning to become acutely aware of in my head.

"This voice inside my head has such a big gob, and it's such a freaking KNOB! There's only one name for him. Bob. Bob the gobby knob who's addicted to being a dick to me!"

But who is he and why the freaking heck is he here raising so much hell inside your mind, anyway?!

Bob has been mentally constructed; he's the psychological fallout/by-product of your pain personified. Like Morph (the little orange play-dough guy), Bob has been put together piece by piece, each and every time someone insisted that all of that You-ness that You were bringing to the party wasn't what was "meant" to be at the party. Over the years, your Monkey Playdough Ball has morphed into something so big and overwhelming that it's hard to distinguish what's true and real for You and what's a giant Playdough Monkey Mush-Monster.

WATCH YOUR MENTAL CHATTER

To gain clarity, watch your mental chatter and internally ask yourself the question: *Has today been a brilliant day?* Watch as it loops around and over different subjects and topics, weaving and jumping from one subject to another, through tedious links and loops. Your instinct is to be cross by what you observe (this instinct is The Third Element of The Trio, which you will come to learn about shortly). The work right now is to notice it all – your frustration as well as the bob of this voice. Laugh at the human-ness of this experience.

"Oh, I just can't do this, Emma. Laugh?! WTF?! It's too overwhelming!"

I KNOW it's overwhelming; I lived trapped in Bob's Emotional "Safehouse" Cellar for 30+ years of my life. Being willing to explore this is what will change it. Just try...If you notice this voice, BRILLIANT!!

You might be thinking, "I don't think I'd use **'brilliant'** to quantify the frustrations I feel when I notice this voice!" In that moment, immediately pull up YouTube's Funniest Fails to laugh at. And laugh. ESPECIALLY when you really don't feel like it! You'll get to a point, if you're willing to, where you can actually start to see Bob and you'll naturally evolve to a space where you can laugh at what he's saying to you the moment he starts. But start small. Baby steps. Laugh any way you can.

As you begin to notice Bob and his weird-ass ways, you will come to realise that you'll never quite know where it's going to go and what he's going to think up next. And neither does he. He's as lost as you. He's trying (yet doing a HORRIBLE job) to help. He just wants to settle. You'll hear him say: "How about this? Well, what do we think of this? Could it maybe be this?"

He's trying to rest upon a moment where you say, "Ah, that makes sense. That's better. That's enough. Let's rest", but you don't actually **ever** get to this point this way. If you don't seek to see You, and laugh at his ass, you won't **ever** get to rest...

When you notice him chiming on, desperate to settle, speak out loud: "It's okay not to know Bob. I don't need you to find my answer".

MY BOB

My Bob was so busy, **all** of the time, that I wasn't ever able to rest – even when I went to bed. The Trio of Terror liked it that way! I was a walking zombie. I was ashen in colour. I had huge black rings under my eyes, and the skin underneath them looked like sandpaper. A huge culprit behind my disturbed nights was Bob. Even in my sleep he was hunting for answers outside of me. I'd scream out and wake up standing in places I hadn't gone to sleep in.

One night, at the height of University (a time I've now identified as being one of the most miserable time frames of my entire life), I was visiting home. It was dissertation time, and I was stressed beyond anything I'd known to that date (It got worse. Jesus, it got worse – that's what happens when you aren't willing to see your own shit and just keep "soldiering on").

In the early hours one morning, I had the most vivid dream – one I still remember now because of the number of times I'd told it to excuse my black eye and bandages.

My "Dream Dissertation" was sitting up high on a shelf, inside a folder. It began to fall. But it wasn't my dissertation. It represented my life. My whole world was in jeopardy and was falling. It all came down to this dream moment. Catch or release; sink or swim; live or die.

I rushed to the shelf to save the dreamed-up folder as it hurtled towards the elements.

Torrential wind and rain ate up the paper I'd spent the best part of my final year writing.

...but the shelf and folder didn't exist outside of my mind.

My then boyfriend/now husband describes this moment as me being suddenly thrust up into standing and thrown out of bed within a fraction of a second. And instead of the imaginary shelf, there was a wall jutting out just enough from my bed to allow me to shoulder-barge it. I spun around and hit the floor with the fiercest force.

Bemused by the whole thing, my boyfriend scuttled to my side with eyes wide as saucers. "What the hell are you doing, Em?"

I came to, looked around, and sobbed.

"I have no idea".

This night was a culmination of the following thoughts:

All of these thoughts basically came down to one basic belief:

"Keep working harder and looking out *there* and you'll **finally** feel better."

I had slipped into deep enough sleep to allow The Subconscious part of me to come out and smack me over the head. It was trying to give me a shock. It was a moment of, "You're fucking up royally. You're having a horrible time. You aren't here to do this. *Just stop*!"

I refused. And it had to get a whole heap worse before I was willing to do it any other way.

STAMP COLLECTING: WHAT THE CONSCIOUS BRAIN IS GONNA SAY AND WHY YOU SHOULDN'T LISTEN

Bob, and the other two elements of The Trio of Terror, can be observed operating under loads of different names.

If you've been stamped with Western Medicine's "psychosis" or "bipolar disorder" or any other of their positively unhelpful stamps, then what I'm going to share with you next is going to rock your world in ALL kinds of ways. We're going to get curious about a different way to see them...

Your Monkey Voice, however, will wanna hold onto all of these Stamps like they're the shiniest, rarest Pog (for my 90s babes) that was ever produced.

This prompts the question:

"Why would I wanna hold onto something so shitty?!?" Right?

It's because a Stamp is a clear and defined label, and labels "make sense" to you. A label feels like a justification to your Conscious Mind. You losing your hold on your life somehow feels better if there is a very specific name and reason to "justify" its happenings.

Bob will wanna hold onto "anxiety" or "depression" or "ADHD" or "fibromyalgia" or "OCD" (some of my Bob's favourite stamps from my past) or whichever box you've been shoved into in the dark with no idea which way is up!

I've got good news for You and bad news for Bob, who's currently leading the show, so he probably won't like this next bit...

You are not that Stamp – no matter how much The Monkey Mind wants you to think you are. Immediately, your Monkey will reject this idea because it gives your Bob a reason (if I'm being brutally honest [and I say this with so much love, and as someone who has held onto so many of the Stamps above]), an excuse to continue to exist the way that you are.

That label that they stamped onto you is the side effect and not the illness itself. It's the mental fallout of a lost mindset, **so** far away from who You are here to be. Your symptoms, which allowed this Stamp to be stapled to you so concretely, are actually just physical manifestations of the fact that you have spent too long running away from the Youest (with a Capital Y), most authentic, unruly, royally fucked up (in THE BEST kinda way) version of You. These symptoms are Actual You SCREAMING (whilst you're being suffocated by The Trio of Terror as they're pretending to be you) desperately trying to get out.

This might sting a little. But avoiding it doesn't help you make it different. The Stamp, the box, the medication, the therapy...It isn't working, is it?! Stamps, boxes, medications and therapies keep you functioning. Fuck functioning! We want climatic GLORY!

You're not here to exist; you're here for *More Than This*! Right now, we're here together and the plaster[11] is coming off so fresh air can finally get to the wound that's been festering underneath that Stamp for too long now. The sting will fade. It will heal. I promise...

---

[11]   Another word for bandage.

There is nothing wrong with You. You're freaking perfection! But without changing some fundamental things around the way you're thinking right now, you're never going to get to see it and you're always going to believe you're the problem.

FOCUS OUT THERE KEEPS YOU LOST

Your reason doesn't live *out there* – no matter how much Bob tries to tell you it does, and no matter how sparkly, delicious or luxurious it may seem.

Looking and hoping that the answers live *out there* looks like seeking validation from:

- Belonging to a church
- Obtaining the highest form of education
- Being active in the "best" political party
- Having the "most prestigious" profession.

You do this because those adults, with their blinded *umwelts*, convinced you so intently that what lies within you isn't to be trusted – that the answers lie outside. Bob's life mission is to find evidence to actualise this!!

In an attempt to do this, you've abandoned Yourself, your feelings and your emotions, and you've focused all of your energies and awareness outside of You on the hunt for "THE" answer. Your focus is:

- to know more
- to understand better
- to excel
- to do
- to be
- to have more

It's little wonder you're so exhausted and consider your typical *Maslow's Base 1 Rest Phase* activities to be the ultimate dirty weekend!

Being able to see these Bob-like workings in my brain allowed me to become less identified with them. Getting to know my Bob's favourite tricks and tips and learning to laugh at the ridiculousness of what he was peddling was crucial to discovering a life without anxiety.

At least now it feels like I can keep my beady eyes on him. Or ears. Or... actually...how the heck do I define him? Where does he end and where do I start?

I asked myself this question in a moment of terror. "FUCK!!!! I am freaking mental – just like my worst fears promised!!"

WHERE DOES BOB END AND WHERE DO I START?

Bob has a massive gob[12] and doesn't shut up. He is a knob[13], overthinking EVERYTHING! He's dedicated his whole life to "figuring out" the world "for you". But his findings will always be in a dazed haze somewhere between Your *Truth* and the idealistic *umwelts* of everyone else around you. To help you understand this, here are some direct and absolute opposites between you and Bob:

BOB	YOU
Bob says that he "knows" – he finds "absolute" answers in what you can hear, see, smell, touch, taste and think.	*You are curious about everything and realise that you perceive through energy and that, ultimately, the more you learn, the more you realise you know close to nothing.*

---

[12] Another word for *mouth*.
[13] Another word for *dick*.

Bob believes that he is superior to others.	*You know that we are all one.*
Bob is frustrated when he isn't in charge.	*You know that surrender is the true currency of this world.*
Bob is loud; he talks a lot and hardly listens.	*You are silent – you listen, speaking only when necessary. You speak with love, with truth and only when it is needed.*
Bob cares only for the self.	*You care for the collective.*
Bob is driven by greed and collecting accolades of righteousness.	*You have a soul-driven purpose needing no recognition.*
Bob cares desperately about what others think.	*You hardly notice others as You know their perception of you is merely a reflection of themselves.*
Bob is obsessed with your outward appearance and holding onto your youthfulness.	*You know that the only beauty You need care about lies inside your heart.*

Right now, this list might feel ridiculous. Or you might think it applies to the thousands of other people reading this book but not you. That I've got it wrong – not for them, as you're sure they're great and have this lovely "*You*" side to them, in abundance – and it's just you who isn't like what I've described. That it's you and only you who's greedy to the core, who talks too much and upsets others, who is driven by the material things you still believe hold the elusive answer you're in search of. That you're "wrong" or "bad" or "mad" and there's nothing I can say which'll sway you otherwise.

Yet you're still here. You're still reading. Know why? It's that "*You*" part of you that's underneath all of Bob's musings who's saying, "I'M IN HERE!!! I PROMISE! JUST KEEP GETTING CURIOUS!!!! I'm ready to lead..."

BOB AND THE BRAIN-FOREST

The biggest problem with Bob is his obsession with "knowing". And he can only put pieces of your Life Puzzle together through your sensory experience of the world that we all live in (you know, the world that makes sense to not one of us, yet here we are...).

How many times have you said to yourself, "If I could just make sense of it, understand why or how it happened, then I'll be able to let it go."

That's where that scrambling to "know" comes in hard. To make links. To put it all together.

Remember your Emotional "Safehouse" that your brain is obsessed with getting back to – quick-march?! The voice inside your head is integral to getting you back there super speedy.

Imagine your Emotional "Safehouse" surrounded by a forest – a forest your Bob knows like the back of his furry little hands. In the trees, we're in his world, playing his weird-ass games. And he moves without a trace.

Every thought is a branch. The more familiar the thought, the thicker and more established the branch is. The more often you think it and then think of something related to it (Christmas dinner; your dad drinking too much at Christmas dinner; your dad drinking too much at home when you were a kid; you watching your dad hurt your mum after he'd been drinking too much...), the closer those tree branches will grow until they're linked. And the more often they all get tied together, the more tightly woven they become.

These routes become Bob's **favourites.** Easy. One initial thought and he can keep going for ages – swinging without a second thought of, "Where should this hand go next?" It's automatic: Christmas pudding; drunk dad; Where's the gin!?

You don't know where you are or what's happening, but before you know it, Bob's dragged you back home into the "Safehouse".

What happens is this:

An external Trigger happens – you hear, smell, taste, see, touch or think something and **Bob takes up his starting position.** This trigger has stirred up feelings and emotions embedded within the Unconscious space between The Conscious "knowing" and the Subconscious You. Bob, who exists within your Conscious Mind, is very responsive to strong emotions. Especially ones that feel a bit shitty – he wants to fight or take flight.

"Branches at the ready," he cries! His regular tree-branch route wakes up and starts stretching out their offerings to him to make the glide even more accessible.

He's OFF! Swinging from branch to branch to "make sense" of it all and get out of that forest pickle/uncomfortable emotion and back to your "Safehouse" ASAP.

The point of noticing this isn't so you can beat yourself up about the hard time you're allowing a made-up monkey in your mind to give you. The point of noticing is to snap each branch on his regular tree-routes as you begin to Find them. This brain-forest metaphor is intended to show you the ravaged monkeying Bob in your thoughts. It allows you to see where his hand lies – and where his next move is.

To combat his monkey ways, you've got to go all Ninja on Bob and snap that next branch he's just about to reach for.

"Christmas is coming...I'd soooo love to love Christmas...it's just Dad..."

HERE!!! In this moment, notice this and interrupt it. Doesn't matter how...just snap off that thought-branch! Blast a Christmas tune or go buy and wrap a gift. Sod him ruining your favourite day of the year, AGAIN!

Bob will say to this, "Well, this won't change the fact that Dad is a drunk who spoils anything nice!" And he's right – no point arguing. But **why** allow Bob to mentally torture you about it!? You have the power to interrupt your thoughts in **this** moment before they can go off jumping along their familiar neurological routes. In this snapping of the branch and changing your focus to something you actually **do** want, you're taking away your Bob's Emotional "Safehouse" route.

The more often you notice his Bobbing about, and the more light-hearted you can make seeing his affairs, the more you're interrupting that route back to "Safehouse". And each time you do, you're snapping off a branch and putting him on his arse. You'll have him looking up at the tree canopy confused AF thinking, "But that way always worked. It's the way it's always been. It's never been a problem before".

And you're not gonna explain.

And with each *crash bang*, Bob becomes more aware of his swings. And with this, he brings consideration to the paths and routes he wants to take and stops being so passive in his bobbing/habits/thinkings.

Suddenly, Bob's love for getting back to that Emotional "Safehouse" doesn't feel as safe as it did. Now, reaching out for a tree branch to get there could mean it being snatched away at any moment and him being dropped on his arse.

This process allows new routes to become open and accessible. Routes where trees are golden mint-leaved, rainbow-coloured glory – a space where anything is possible. A place where Actual You can start to flex and Bob can take a moment to be in the trees and enjoy the view, which is filled with all of the mint-chocolate-sprinkled bananas a monkey might ever ask for.

Maybe you'll stop freaking out about your alcoholic Dad and start to make some space to do something differently. It might not feel good the first time and you might not feel ready, but interrupting your thoughts to make space to change them IS the start to taking action in this 3D world and thus creating lasting change.

Bob will soon come to realise that you slamming him on his arse, laughing in his face and him staying outside of The Emotional "Safehouse" is actually a really glorious thing. He won't believe you. You can't explain this. You must snap those branches and *show* him. It's a win-win situation for both you *and* Bob.

If you still think you're the one speaking,
then who's the one listening?

MIND-ON-MUTE MONDAY HIGHLIGHTS:

1. Wear your mint greens as you watch your mental Monkey Chatter jump from branch to branch in hopes of a Banana Biscuit back at the "Safehouse".
2. Notice when you become aware that your thoughts are Bobbing. It will come easier with practice, as you build this green part of your Rainbow Road.
3. Laugh at the ridiculousness of Bob and all of his shenanigans. Start by noticing and interrupting these moments with silly YouTube shorts. If outright laughing at him seems a step too far right now, no worries. You **will** reach this point by becoming consistent in noticing him.

REMEMBER:

Mind-on-Mute Mondays:

Wear your Minty Greens and explore this mind-blowing fact:

There is a voice inside your head.

This voice is <u>not</u> You.

Seek to notice every time he's getting his knickers in a twist, and snap a branch from his most favourite, familiar neurological brain-loops so he starts to become less comfortable travelling these outdated routes. Get curious around the idea that if there is a voice speaking, then who is the one listening?

That voice is You!

You will not know it the first moment you contemplate it, but you will come to know it. And once you do, you won't care to "understand" and "know". You'll just let it be. Here you'll feel a freedom you had no idea could exist for you.

To access your Mind-on-Mute Monday supplementary supportive workbooks and videos, please <u>CLICK HERE</u>.

Trigger-Free Tuesday
CREATE A SPACE TO CHOOSE FREEDOM

Triggers point to where you are not free.

Introducing The poisoner of Good Things, Toad

Licking The Toad
It's time to stop licking the frog, kissing the Toad or doing whatever the heck it is you've been doing to chase that mystical high that doesn't exist.

There's a magical, mystical space between the things that piss you off ROYALLY and the way you react to them, and your job is to Find this space! Do this and accessing that Youest version of You will be automatic and instinctive – just like breathing.

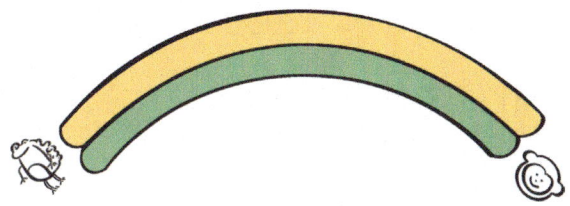

To do this, we're going to work on the orange part of your Rainbow Road, which means you must:

1. Get your St Moriz Self Tanner out (or any other tangerine tans) because orange is our Piggyback Sensory Hack™ for this chapter.
2. Read Trigger-Free Tuesday and do what it says – especially the sensory stuff. You're already getting to know your Monkey Mind – YEY YOU! ROCKSTAR! Let's keep going...
3. Say, "Fudge it", continue to play pretend and try on the freaking dress when it comes to the Toadlike mayhem I'm going to show you that is unfolding in your brain. It'll make little to no sense to your Conscious Mind at first, but as you make that Rainbow Road, all the pieces will fall into place.

"I've been licking a *toad*? What the hell?!

Fudge it! And try it on.

"I'm licking this toad in order to get high?! What in the actual world, Emma!?!"

Fudge it! Just try it on!

"...and I am to access a 'mystical' space in place of 'licking the toad'? What is going on here?!"

Fudge. It. And. Try. It. On.

...as often as possible, using your Pause Thoughts™ and your Orange Sensory Experience.

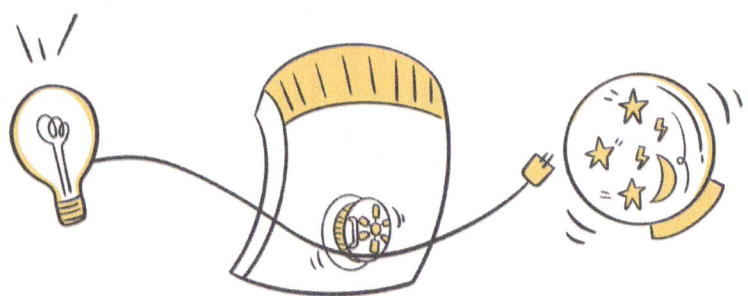

And one day, it'll slide on like a glove and you'll say:

"Holy moley, I keep licking the Toad's poisonous warts, hoping for a high that makes me feel alive and that life is truly worth living. But, no matter how many licks, it never actualises. Attempting to find this quiet space of peace, joy, endless energy and happiness the way I'm going is like trying to force out a sneeze that's stuck in my snout – PAINFUL! I need to stop doing it this way. And I also need to stop trying to steal sneezes from other people ('cause that's a thing too!). AND **now**, after reading this chapter, I blinking-well[14] know how to do it. No Toad licking – just unequivocal joy!"

HERE'S THE CHALLENGE...

Being Triggered

In life, being *Triggered* is like puking and pooping everywhere all at the same time.

Okay, it might not be that extreme – but I'm here for the dramatics!

You can become Triggered when something happens that you don't like and it stirs up all kinds of emotions with a **massive** wooden spoon.

---

[14]   *really and truly*

Sometimes being Triggered is out in the world and super obvious, like going to a party where you know Uncle Knobhead will be and he makes you feel all kinds of *yuck* because of that thing he did ages ago; you're Triggered.

And other times, you don't know what in the world is happening, which sounds like:

"I feel super shitty and I have absolutely NO blooming idea why!" You're Triggered here too (and not knowing why is actually fine – stand down, Bob!).

Regardless of its origin, what happens EVERY time (whether you know what's going on or not) is that some external thing triggers an internal emotional response which you express in one of two ways. You either:

1. **Express the puke/poop Trigger outwardly** for the whole world to see (or [sneakily!!] just the people you want to see) as:
   - Sarcasm
   - Shouting
   - Running away
   - Shaking
   - Having a panic attack
   - Physical aggression...

Or...

2. **Internalise/swallow the puke/poop Trigger,** which manifests as:
   - Ruminating
   - Festering
   - Playing out scenarios again and again
   - Bitterness
   - Resentment
   - Jealousy

In Trigger-Free Tuesday's work, I (strangely – shock horror!) feature a Toad to explain how all of this works. I will show you how he joins forces with Bob as they continue their search for outside answers…

…which they don't find, **of course,** as your answer is tucked beautifully inside You at the end of that Rainbow Road. But even knowing this doesn't stop you from continuing to seek answers from the "outside world" right along with them…

This triggers you even more.

"I'm fucking it up, again!"

…which makes you look "out there" even more restrictively and intensely.

"I must try harder…"

This approach then manifests even less answers…

"*This is still not working!*"

And it tricks you into thinking there's something wrong with you.

"It's only ever me who doesn't 'get it'!"

This makes you look to others for a feeling of aliveness/energy…

"It doesn't feel good, yet I don't know any other way to do this!"

And it triggers you even harder.

"I'm gonna be doomed to feel this blooming awful way eternally!"

And you're off, back to that "Safehouse" for tea. Sad. And alone. Again! In fact, maybe a new level of sad and alone that you didn't even know existed until now.

HERE'S WHAT YOU CAN CHOOSE TO SEEK...

Trigger-Free Tuesday will show you the quiet space you have the power to create for yourself **inside** you. *Bye bye, Triggers – Forever!* You don't need to puke or poop every time you're Triggered – there's a way less messy, more fun way to live coming right up...

By the end of this chapter, you'll be able to:

◊ Identify when and where these Triggered Responses are getting in the way of you living your absolute best life
◊ Know how to stop those Triggered Responses
◊ Own what's yours and let the rest go
◊ Become like Teflon

Exploring Trigger-Free Tuesday is going to show you everything you're absolutely **not**. You're not the Triggered, emotionally explosive/implosive version you're presenting to the world. Knowing this allows you to get sure on who You (that bloody brilliant being) actually are (underneath the poop and puke explosions).

It's not "rubbish on toast"; it's a fact – one that you will realise as you continue to move through this book...

PAUSE THOUGHTS™

Right now, your Conscious Brain doesn't believe that living outside of the puke and poop frenzy is accessible and available to you. It's telling you:

- Your emotions are too inflamed.
- You're too sensitive and it'll hurt too intensely.
- They're too reliant on you.
- Your specific circumstances are too unique and obscure to change.
- None of this "life-doesn't-have-to-feel-like-an-endurance-test stuff" can possibly relate to you.

ALL of the above is a big, fat lie. But it's okay. Believing this is the role of this part of the mind. Remember: we CANNOT change this. You can use talk therapy until you're blue in the face, but this part of the mind just IS. Full stop. Your first job here is to accept this.

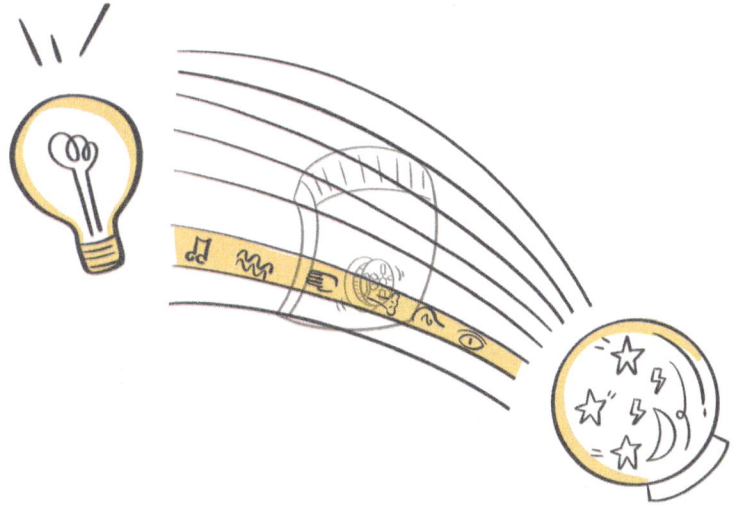

THEN, your job is to create that tangerine part of your Rainbow Road, piggybacking the notions I share *from* your (doubting) Conscious Mind, *through* that Emotional change-making space of your Unconscious and *into* The Subconscious.

TO DO THIS EASILY, AS YOU READ THIS CHAPTER, YOU MUST EMBODY TANGERINE ORANGES.

Wear your tangerine tank tops and orangey socks. Double tap your Terry's Chocolate Orange (YUM!) and drink your freshly squeezed juice. Use tangerine essential oils or smother some marmalade on your morning toast. Embody tangerine oranges whilst learning to harness your Triggers on Tuesdays. Go, right now. Get something orange (even if it's a manky[15] old satsuma that's been in the back of the fridge for too long). See the colour, smell the smell and allow that to penetrate as you do this work.

Then once you've read this book, each Tuesday, carry this citrusy sensory stimulant with you. Every time you see, smell, taste or touch tangerines, you'll actively create a Pause Thought™ Moment: a moment to take a deeper dive into your Unconscious Emotional "Safehouse" stories and emotions. This will create space for *You* (not The Triggered Toad that's currently dominating your Conscious Mind) to shine through.

---

15   Old, gross, grotesque.

Ready? Let's go try on that dress...

THE EMOTIONALLY TRIGGERED TOAD

The Triggered Toad is the second of our Trio of Terror – the second of the three deadly spokes in the human-brain wheel.

Here's the Oxford English Dictionary definition of a toad:

Toad[16]

/təʊd/

noun

1. a tailless <u>amphibian</u> with a short <u>stout</u> body and short legs, typically having dry warty skin that can <u>exude</u> poison.

2. a <u>contemptible</u> or <u>detestable</u> person (used as a general term of abuse).

   "you're an arrogant little toad"

Similar: wretch, beast, pig, rat, creep, louse, snake, skunk, weasel, lowlife, scumbag, heel, stinkpot, stinker, no-good, son of a bitch, SOB, nasty piece of work, scrote, blighter, bad lot, spalpeen, rat fink

---

[16]   Definitions from <u>Oxford Languages</u>

Both descriptions fit this area of the work perfectly! Your Toad will do whatever is needed to get his hands on his precious reward: Dopamine.

Dopamine is actually a neurotransmitter made in your brain. As part of the brain's reward system, it sends messages of, "Ahhh, that's bloody lovely" throughout the body when it is stimulated. It exists inside all humans. Dopamine occurs in the brain...

- When having great sex – especially with loads of foreplay
- During shopping trips where everything fits and your bank account is endless
- When smelling something yummy cooking in the oven as you walk in from work
- During intensive workouts
- While jamming to your favourite TUUUUNNNNEEEEE!!!

To get you free from all of those anxieties holding you back, let's use The Toad as a metaphor for your reward system and go along with the silly Toad story.

THE SILLY TOAD STORY

By using The Toad as our metaphor, we can perceive distance between what's happening and what we'd prefer to be happening, which is a really blooming helpful way to bring clarity to any Toady proceedings taking place in our *umwelts*. For our silly story, it's The Toad, not your reward system, which carries a different kind of Dopamine that you're addicted to *out there*, hidden on his back. He's seductive and you're addicted to finding him out and licking his poisonous, Dope-filled warts. GROSS!! I know! But...anything silly, gross and weird sticks out and your brain forms a strong thought around it – so we're rolling with it!

The Toad KNOWS you're meant to get dopamine from inside of you, and yet, he just can't help himself...

He is the definition of a flirt – tempting you with his toxin, goading you to reap his poisonous rewards but then getting angry AF when you do; like a cat who rolls over, exposes his tummy and then rips your hand apart when you go in for the stroke. He's like that ex who didn't want to be with you but didn't want anyone else to have you either.

Unfortunately, as with any addict, the tolerance levels for Dope get higher and higher the more you have. To get that "all things are lovely" high, you find yourself fantasising (or actualising) the need for more out there...

- Sex with more, hotter people doing weirder stuff
- Shopping weekends in Paris with no established spending limit
- Gourmet takeout **every** night
- In-home Peloton installed as well as a hot yoga studio with a live-in yogi

To feel better, you want Dope endlessly. If it's going to have **any** hint of an effect on a nervous system (which has been shot to shiitake mushrooms over years of experiencing intense anxiety), you've gotta go bigger, **every** time!

And because, let's face it, live-in yogis and weekending in Paris aren't available to 99.9% of us, you've got to get creative in the hunt. A way that Toad sees fit to do this is to tempt you into more and more vulnerable positions in the hope that, as you navigate yourself out of them (by the skin of your teeth), you will FINALLY get that sweet hit you've been searching for for YEARS!

You don't. You're just cold, naked and alone. Again. And instead of that prized Dopamine coursing through your veins, you've replaced it with shame, guilt and more sadness.

WHAT IS A TRIGGERED RESPONSE?

A Triggered Response is where you lose your shit. It's the projectile vom or poop from finally catching the Toad, licking that wart and poisoning yourself. Sometimes it's messy and spills all over the floor for everyone to see and you're left in the midst of it thinking, "What the funk was that!?" Or you're thinking, "Well, they got precisely what they deserved – riling me up like that!!!"

It's a poop-bath of untamed emotions with any unexpressed emotion clawing to get out in any way it can: the silent treatment, cross words, physical violence, screaming, shouting, crying, overwhelm, withdrawing, defensiveness – puke and poop everywhere where you have little to no control over it. When it's coming, IT'S COMING. Move outta the way or get shat on – splat!

Other times, the poop and puke isn't so obvious. Maybe you've got dead good at repressing and hiding the physicality of it (silently fuming); this means you've become a "master" of internalising...

Don't think trying to hide it this way will keep you safe – it can be smelt from miles away. People are often more put off by this behaviour because it's more underhanded and hidden. At least when you're being shat on from a great height, you know it!

Whether it's out or you've gotten really good at holding it in, it's poisoning you and those you love most.

Speaking of *them*, let's take a look at those you love and their Toads (we **all** have one!) because they're pretty important too...

HAPPY THEM = MY HAPPY ME

It's bad enough when it's your own, but it's even worse when it's someone else's puke and poop – especially when it's your boss, your partner, your parents or someone else who has a serious impact on your life. So, you condition yourself to become hyperaware of everyone else's Toads and Dope addictions. The first time we spot someone we love just about to ingest some of their own Toad poison (on another wild Dope chase) and we intervene by providing them with a new route to feeling Dope, we *seemingly* change the direction of that moment and the moments to follow.

This feels GREAT! And it gives *us* a Dope hit too, from an easy-to-lick source right in front of us. Winning! (Or so we think...)

The first person I learned to do this with was one of my favourite people in the world, my Dad[17]. He was unpredictable and quietly volatile. He'd withdraw from me if I'd disappointed him with any of my accidental childlike learning. I came to realise that a party trick would stop his poison wart reaction of poop and puke spilling out all over the house. The trick was to make a stupid noise somewhere between my nose and throat. The silliness of it all was enough to make him smile and make almost any moment lighter. It was often enough to disturb the desire for him to eat his own poison. I was his external doping machine. And I was happy to oblige if it kept us puke-free.

Living like this is soul-destroying. We feel a deep sickness within our stomachs almost all of the time – waiting to catch the precise moment that they're about to ingest their poison so we can intervene. We fail more times than we get it "right". Living this way means you somehow feel responsible for it all.

Most of us stumble through life this way in order to get that external Dope reprieve. We try our best to keep everyone else, and their Toads, happy AF, with the thought process being, "If I figure out ways to keep

---

[17] It should be noted here how explaining your **own** perception of how someone you love treated you means precisely that – it's your perception (and it's probably very different to theirs – and that's okay). It doesn't mean that you don't love them, respect them or think of them as anything less than brilliant. It just means that an element of their humanness didn't work for you. Most of us think this way about someone we love. It's pretty regular too. Only most aren't brave enough to say it (or think it's a sign of disrespect if we try). It's not. It's your perception. I hope sharing this here gives you permission to speak Your Truth about someone you love, too.

them and their Toads sweet[18], then I don't need to worry about their poop and puke spilling out all over me and thus risking the stuff that makes my life fun. AND it feels like a (kinda fucked-up) game where I get to 'win'. Winning gives me Dope – and Dope is dope."

If we're really "good" at it, this becomes our mission. Another external jobbie[19].

Living this way becomes impossible. Their Dope demands become reliant upon you and your skills to manage them. Your Dopamine rush is linked to something outside of your actual control. And you've got your own poisons to deal with.

The biggest danger is that once you've ingested a Toad's poison once, it stays with you no matter how many times you shit it out on the people you love (until you're willing to "Create a Space to Choose Freedom" – The Trigger-Free Tuesday Tool that's coming up super soon...).

But, for right now, I have some ideas on how to shield yourself from their shit show, and how to spot those poisons living within before they poison you from the inside out.

IT'S THEM! THEY'RE THE TOAD!

Because you're so good at being that external Dope source for so many (giving you a little hint of, "I fix things for others and that makes me feel dope!"), you continue to think that your answer to all of this *getting better, nicer and easier* is if **other people** would just learn to get a grip on their obsessive Toad licking. *They* should stop making such a mess all over you!

---

[18]   *To keep (someone/something) sweet* means to be kind to someone so they will do something in return.

[19]   *task*

But the actual answer you're looking for lies in beginning to explore your own Toadish ways.

You might wonder why the hell you'd wanna do this, right!? The idea of it can feel a lot like dancing with the devil, in 9-inch heels, teetering on the mouth of a deadly-poison-filled volcano that's ready to erupt.

"Why would I wanna explore something which feels so uncomfortable when I don't feel like **I'm** the biggest problem in my life!?" you might ask.

This way of thinking is self-preservative. It is one of the main anchors of The Trio of Terror I mentioned earlier. You've got Bob trying to get in the way of Mind-on-Mute Mondays, and now you've got your Toad's main method of leverage that keeps you stuck in The Conscious Mind chaos: if something inflicts any type of pain, blame others because it feels safer to want to shift the blame and not take responsibility. This can sound like:

- "Oh, that order was misplaced because *Darren* didn't give me the correct information at the time that I needed it. Bloody Darren!" *eye roll*
- "I missed the appointment because *you* didn't remind me through the correct medium."
- "My marriage fell apart because *he* didn't know how to express his feelings."

Instinctively, the first thing we wanna do is blame *them*! Out *there*! They're all fucked! Defo not us.

You might say, "I know I'm the only one who can change me". But saying this and truly believing it are two distinctly different things. Let me show you...

We are conditioned to please others and be likeable. These traits stem from our primitive ancestors whose survival was entirely dependent on being accepted by the tribe. Making choices that would cause one to be ostracised by the clan was a dangerous game back then. Not being part of a bigger network and playing a role within it left you on the outside, vulnerable to wild animals, malnutrition, exposure – all of the stuff that wreaks eternal doom and death.

Even a mild attempt at merely contemplating the fact that you *might* be poisoning yourself, licking your (or anyone else's who'll allow you to for that matter) warts is enough for you to feel like you're preparing for your own death by exposing your jugular to the community who you feel are armed with knives ready to slit your throat in the dead of night!

Not **one** person in the whole wide world wants to see this. Not. One! Me included. But please know that a willingness to see this will be defining for you. It doesn't mean you're "bad" or "mad"; it just means you're human. And in order to truly see this human side of you and how it's different from ACTUAL You (with a Capital Y), learning The Firework Strategy is imperative...

THE FIREWORK STRATEGY

I'm going to use the term "Energy" to describe your focus, attention and awareness.

A life lived without knowing how to connect to your internal energies feels like your energy levels are dried out and depleted:

- You're too tired to do anything – even fun things.
- You're living on microwave and convenience meals.
- You're knackered (no matter how much time you spend in bed), but you still can't get a good night's sleep.

A life lived in this space always leaves you in an Energy Deficit, desperately wishing for More but without **any** drive to actively go out to do something about it. This space creates a hunger, an insatiable appetite for something, ANYTHING, to satisfy your pangs with minimum effort.

When you're in this space, other people are a great meal-ticket to bring balance to your deficit, and not only in the previously mentioned way (when you intervene before they sip their poison and go OFF it), but in a different way too: in an Energy Exchange where they give you their focus, attention and awareness and it fills you up with a feeling of, "I'm seen. I matter. I'm important". Like a firework display banquet has been constructed solely for your delight.

When you're hungry, tired and in desperate need of energy, a firework display, at their expense, is the PERFECT solution. Even if their display is a bit shitty, with malfunctioning Catherine wheels and rockets aimed for your head, it's better than the barren wasteland of your existence – or so Toad tells you...

So, you go out armed with matches, ready to hear those familiar squeals.

Never forget...this is **not** intentional. This has been happening (on some level) since you were tiny. It's become **so** second nature to you that you don't even know it's happening.

It *is* happening on some level, and your job is to **want** to see this...

Feeling energyless and depleted, you start small, waving your match kinda close to their fuse:

"Why didn't you put away the dishes like I asked?"

Annoyingly, they don't give all that much of an answer. They don't care about the dishes – they're watching the footie[20]. It goes over their head. No spark. No energy. So, you press:

"I want you to do this now, please."

They don't. (Of course they don't. You're asking them to do something that can't truly register in their brain. They're elsewhere...it's green...

---

[20]   The football/soccer game.

and there are 22 people who are far more interesting than that sink you're whanging on about![21])

"Do it, or I'm gonna be pissed! You never do the washing up."

They don't! And your (Unconscious/unintentional/yet you've done it so many times it's become second nature) plan is starting to work. They're getting pissed off at you mumbling, something to do with dinner (literally have no idea what you're on about!!), and their anger/energy is starting to seep towards you as they attempt to focus on the screen but are beginning to be too frustrated to. It's working...you can feel some of that fire...You leave, then come back...

"Have you still not done it!?"

You think, "Sod this![22] I'm not getting enough energy here. I'm parched! It's time to light that fuse and experience the finale..."

"You're just like your Dad." (the person he wants to be like LEAST of all!)

Fuse lit. And BOOM!

Explosion. Energy shower coming your way.

I get that this sounds weird. And ridiculous. And completely and utterly warped...

But you will do it. I do it. We all do it in some way or another. And it won't be this example (or maybe it will). It will be your own unique way of stealing their energy through The Firework Strategy – a more consistent energy source than that bloody, illusive Toad with his poison promises. You do it all to feel **something/ANYTHING!!** Because feeling **something** is better than feeling nothing at all. No wonder your mind and your world feel a little chaotic right now. To make it less so, super speed, let's choose something different...

---

[21]   Talking about it a lot, so much so, it might've got a little boring.
[22]   Forget it; it ain't happening!

ENERGY EXCHANGE

To Action

Think about someone you see a lot. Watch them interact with others. See where they're on a hunt for energy and what kind of methods they use to light the fuse. It's so much simpler to see these things in people around you before you're able to see them in yourself (I literally thought I'd worked out The Secret Code to everyone else's problems, and I was the **one** exception to it all...lolz!).

As you look, you will start to see four categories of behaviours begin to materialise. They are:

1. **The Oppressor:** Do they get angry? Intimidate others? Show physical or verbal aggression if they are being challenged?
2. **The Interrogator:** Do they question everything? Themselves? You? The world? Always with a need to be seen as "right"?
3. **The Retreater:** Do they retreat? Withdraw? Lock themselves away in the hope that you'll go chasing after them (or give them what they want)?
4. **The Victim:** Are they super unsure of themselves? It's like the world's always against them? "Pity Party" comes to mind when you think of them. They hope to be seen as "weak" so that others give them an easier ride?

People never fit firmly in one camp. So, wear your tangerines, and when you see/smell/taste them, get curious on which of these categories people you know fit in, and when.

MAKE SPACE

This part here is where I want you to take an extra big lungful, eyeful or mouthful of that tangerine. Read this next part slowly, and intentionally. Let your soul marinate in it...

Creating a Space to Choose Freedom **is *how* you come to see your world for what it is so you can start to choose what you actually want. You have the power to slow everything down so you get to decide what you want instead of just repeating The Triggered Toad and Firework responses that have gone before.**

Victor Frankl was a Jewish psychiatrist who survived three concentration camps. He shared the profound realisations he had about the human psyche in his book *Man's Search for Meaning*. Frankl describes this Space as follows:

> *Between stimulus and response there is a space. In that space is our power to choose our response. In our response lies our growth and our freedom.*
>
> —*Victor Frankl*

The way most humans go about the business of living is that when things happen to us and we get Triggered, we react with the human response of fight, flight or freeze – over and over and OVER...But what Frankl observed under the intense microscopic lens of the concentration camp was how some people managed to override this instinctive behaviour because in these camps, if you fought, you'd be shot; if you took flight, you'd run into barbed-wire fences; and if you froze, you'd also be shot.

In Auschwitz, Frankl saw that the survivors mastered the art of aligning with a "space" where the Art of Choice could be practised before a Triggered Response happened.

After the "something" happens (#life) and before you do something as a reaction/you projectile vom, **there is a space.**

And it's in this Space that you can choose...

"To lick the Toad or *not* to lick the Toad?"

"To vom or *not* to vom?"

"To set off fireworks or throw a bucket of water on the fuse?"

REACT WITH NO SPACE: The "something happening" might be your mother-in-law telling you just how wonderful her son is, AGAIN! (And after you just picked up his dirty pants from the floor for the fourth time that week!) You react. Puke all over her. Weirdly, she's thrilled!

RESPOND WITH SPACE: She starts whanging on about her brilliant son, you remember the dirty pants and think, "Ah… she knows only a hint of the truth. And that's okay!" You go inside. You keep your energy to yourself and she's left wondering what's happened!

You get to choose to respond and create an outcome that you actually **want.**

You will build to this...This is NOT a one and done. It's a brick-by-brick build, giving the sturdiest foundation kind of vibe. So, get your orange on, go back to Frankl's quote and read everything that follows it all over again.

TO NOTICE

Your first job is to notice when that Triggered Moment has happened. You must then **retrospectively** note the moment you **first** became aware of what went down; that moment when you:

1. Licked your Toad and vommed
2. Licked their Toad and pooped
3. Lit their firework because you were feeling depleted
4. Had your firework lit because they were feeling depleted and you surrendered your energy to them

Clues to help you realise when you've done one of the four above are to be on the lookout for when you have:

1. **Expressed the puke/poop Trigger outward Response of:**
   - Sarcasm
   - Shouting
   - Running away
   - Shaking
   - Having a panic attack
   - Physical aggression

Or...

2. **Internalised/swallowed the puke/poop with a Response of**
   - Ruminating
   - Festering
   - Playing out scenarios again and again
   - Bitterness
   - Resentment
   - Jealousy

Your #1 job is to notice when you've puked or pooped (no matter how far after the event it is that you notice) and when you do, celebrate your brilliant self for raising your awareness of that moment. In doing this, you're sending a message of, "I want to be better at doing this".

It's like you're putting a marker in the sand at this moment of noticing, saying, "THAT'S THE TOAD AND HIS POISONOUS WAYS!! *And that wasn't ideal, and it didn't go to any kind of plan, but I freaking SEE it now. Seeing is a start. And I know I'm gonna keep going...so...freaking YEY!"*

THE TOAD'S DOUBLE BLUFF

At first, your Toad might play a double bluff and you might be Triggered here. If you're thinking about Victor Frankl's death-defying skills in three different concentration camps all from finding this fecking ELUSIVE Space you're trying to see, but it makes no sense to you right now, you might think, "Why am I so shit at this!?"

This stage of "Trying to See the Toad But Missing Him" is an essential part of the process that cannot be missed. Accept this completely and utterly shitty fact. Use it as fuel for the fire of your success. You are **not** meant to stop this guy on day one (so please don't try – The Trio is eager to watch you fail at this!). Smile and wave to that Toad as you notice how he tries to find a backdoor to Triggeredness.

Seeing ANY of this bizarreness play out is You seeing. And ANY amount of You seeing is You placing orange bricks into Your Rainbow Road to victory. One brick at a time. It's unsteady and uneven to begin with. Some bricks are so tiny, you feel like they don't count (they freaking DO!!), but that's okay. It's the process, and you're here to see it through.

When you reach this point of seeing (even if you're frustrated as funk because you feel helpless to do anything!!), it's made its way up The

Rainbow Road and has entered your awareness by this point – **and that's a really great thing!**

To move closer to Your Space to Choose Freedom, wear your Trigger-Free Tuesday Toad Tangerine Sensory Stimulants and continue to notice your Toad. Doing this reduces the time it takes for you to notice when you've ingested the poisonous warts. As you become a badass at noticing the fallout of what went before, naturally (no shoving or forcing, remember!!), a shorter timeframe between the Trigger and you noticing your reaction will materialise. This will continue until you come to Your Space – a space where you notice **before** The Triggered Response happens, **the** Space to choose Freedom.

BE LIKE TEFLON

Teflon was made so food doesn't stick to it and simply slides straight off. Imagine you are wearing a Teflon suit: embody the protective properties of this reflective surface and imagine it stands between you and the person triggering you. Instead of focusing on their fireworky/vommy/pukey bullshit, use ALL of your energy to put your focus on this silver lining and keep this shield between you and them.

Watch as all their poop, puke and firework sparks reflect off of your Teflon suit and slide clean-off. You're Teflon now, baby!

Using your Sensory Stimulants, you'll start to see that situations which previously felt like you were up to your armpits in ooze will finally cease to be a problem.

Over and over, embody your tangrines until you open up enough Space to freaking CHOOSE!!!!

The first time you experience this in real time, you HAVE to tell me – these are my favourite type of messages to receive! Once you get a peek at this space, you expand...until one day, you **will** see the

Triggered Response beginning to take shape and you will actively choose out of it.

This way, you become aware of the triggering thing happening: you're thinking of insults to purge their way, or you feel the familiar pangs of jealousy, or you start mapping out your exit plan...but before you put your plan in motion to come back with your reaction, you instead choose to respond. You step into that Space that **you've** opened up by laying out that orange Rainbow Road over and over every time you notice yourself getting Triggered.

You can actively begin to choose how you'd most like to **respond** instead of merely reacting with Unconsciously reactive puking/pooping at lightning-speed succession. It is *this* response that Frankl speaks of. You go to this place of responding, and not reacting, by accessing Your Space.

In these moments, how you respond is THE key to moving out of an existence of life happening to you and into one where You create the life you were born to create.

You are Free!!!

Instead of being at the mercy of triggers, you have the power to create space for a new response.

TRIGGER-FREE TUESDAY HIGHLIGHTS:

1. Wear your tangerines, and with each Pause Thought™, get curious around which Toad is up to what. It's easier to get objective about other people first, so start there – see *their* shit shows – where they're eating their own poison, where they're trying to get Dope from someone else (maybe you) and where they are baiting others by putting a flame close to their fuse. Watch it unfolding and smile at the mental space this is creating for you.

2. When you start to get skilled in this, begin to reflect internally; see where in your world you're:

   a. Licking your Toad and vomming
   b. Licking their Toad and pooping
   c. Lighting their firework because you were feeling depleted
   d. Had your firework lit because they were feeling depleted and you surrendered your energy to them

   Celebrate the space you are creating in this noticing. Say to yourself, *"Well, that wasn't great, but I see it. And seeing is a start. And I know I'm gonna keep going...I can't not!"*

3. Use your oranges in your daily Pause Thoughts™ Practice to allow this Space-making habit to be consistent in your life. As you do this,

Your Space to **choose** will open up and one day (without force) you will Find yourself in the life you want.

4. You have the ability to **_be like Teflon_**. Let the reactions of others and emotionally triggering situations slide RIGHT off your imaginary Teflon suit!

REMEMBER:

Mind-on-Mute Mondays:

Wear your Minty Greens and explore this mind-blowing fact:

There is a voice inside your head.

This voice is <u>not</u> You.

Seek to notice every time he's getting his knickers in a twist, and snap a branch from his most favourite, familiar neurological brain-loops so he starts to become less comfortable travelling these outdated routes. Get curious around the idea that if there is a voice speaking, then who is the one listening?

That voice is You!

You will not know it the first moment you contemplate it, but you will come to know it. And once you do, you won't care to "understand" and "know". You'll just let it be. Here you'll feel a freedom you had no idea could exist for you.

To access your Mind-on-Mute Monday supplementary supportive workbooks and videos, please CLICK HERE.

REMEMBER:

Trigger-Free Tuesday:

Wear your Orangy Tangerines.

Toad believes that everyone else is to blame and that it'd all be just fine and dandy if **they** all stopped being such arseholes! Your job here is to be like Teflon: create a Space to Choose Freedom between the stuff happening outside of you and how you are reacting or responding to it. Keep laying the tangerine part of your Rainbow Road. Notice every time you see you're on the hunt for your Toad/wanting to bathe in someone else's firework explosions and say, "I see you and it's **not** going down this way ANYmore!!"

To access your Trigger-Free Tuesday workbook and supporting video, please CLICK HERE.

Wake-Up Wednesday
BE KIND TO YOUR MIND

The Ego, however, is not who you really are. The ego is your self image; it is your social mask; it is the role you are playing. Your social mask thrives on approval. It wants control, and it is sustained by power, because it lives in fear.

—Deepak Chopra

Introducing The Fiend in your Mind, Francis

You're meant to be the leading lady in your own life and, right now, there's ONE reason why it doesn't feel that way. That reason's name is Francis, and in this chapter, you're going to meet her.

In this chapter, you will meet this foe – who's a judgemental, unkind, self-absorbed bitch, the gatekeeper of The Emotional "Safehouse" that lives inside your brain – and see that you are not her and she is not You.

To do this, we're going to work on the watermelon pink part of your Rainbow Road, which means you must:

1. Never go without your Watermelon Sugar on Wednesdays! Watermelon pink, specifically, is our Piggyback Sensory Hack™ for this Chapter.
2. Read this Wake-up Wednesday chapter and do what it says – especially the sensory stuff. You've met the first two spokes in The Trio of Terror. Now it's time to meet the third and final one.
3. Remember to say, "Fudge it", over and over again. Play pretend as you try on the freaking dress...

"A mega bitch who lives inside my brain? What on earth, Emma?!"

Fudge it...just try it on.

"Are you trying to say I have a split personality!?"

Nope. Fudge. It. And. Try. It. On.

"So, there's someone in my mind who isn't actually me?!"

Bizarre? Yes! But you've still got to say, "Fudge it," and try it on...

...as often as possible, using your Pause Thoughts™ and your Watermelon Pink Sensory Experience.

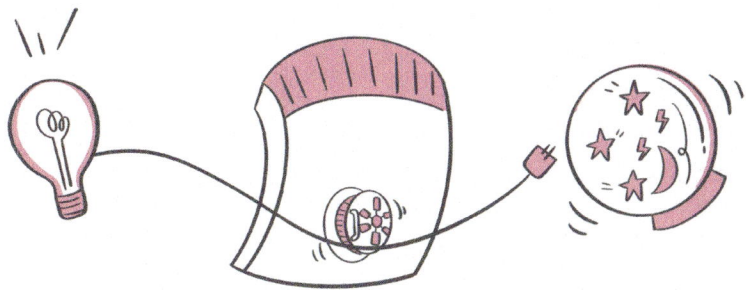

And one day, it'll slide on like a glove and you'll say:

"That part of me that I once thought was me, who I've disliked for a MASSIVE part of my life, **isn't** actually me! **I'm** actually pretty cool/blooming BRILLIANT! And I've been inside here, lying dormant the whole time! That voice that's always unkind, judgemental and obsessed with telling me what a prick I am ISN'T ME!! And that drive and thirst to control everything is simply an extension of her...IT'S NOT ME! YAHOOOOOOOOOO!"

HERE'S THE CHALLENGE...

When you think:

- "I hate myself."
- "They'd be better off without me."
- "They're so much more 'this' than me."
- "I'm so jealous of their 'this'."
- "I'm such a loser."
- "It's all my fault."
- "I'm so embarrassing."
- "It doesn't matter how many times I try; I'll always fail..."

THIS is Francis, NOT you!

She is Golem from *Lord of the Rings*: that deformed halfling who lives in the shadows of the world – a shell of Sméagol, who was once the leading lad of his Hobbity life.

Francis is your Golem – you are Sméagol (just a cuter, taller version with less hairy feet). You're in there, I promise! I'm not light on making promises if I can't keep them. You're just a bit lost behind all that Francis noise (and she's LOUD!)

Soon, with this Third Step, You get to see her as different from You... promise!

HERE'S WHAT YOU CAN CHOOSE TO SEEK...

Wake-up Wednesday, with all of its watermelon glory, will teach you **how** to be on the lookout for Francis and her Golem-esque ways.

By the end of this chapter, you'll be able to:

◊ See how Francis wastes almost ALL of your energy making sure everyone else continues to think of you the way *she* thinks they should think of you
◊ See how she's seduced you into fighting with the world
◊ Not hate her; you'll actually come to love her

◊ Give her what she wants, which is, weirdly (given her behaviours!) a feeling of safety and love

To truly see this – to build that Rainbow Road – you've gotta get past her. And she's a twat! But we've got skills; soon she'll cease to be a problem!

Learning the Wake-up Wednesday elements is going to show you so much of what you're absolutely **not**! This, in turn, allows you to get sure on who You actually are, to come to know the Actual You and how bloody brilliant You are – NOT this fear-driven frenzied fiend who has been created and shaped by fear.

The way to seeing this all is laid out in the Wake-Up Wednesday work...

PAUSE THOUGHTS™

Right now, your Conscious Brain thinks that Francis and you exist as one, that it's you (you silly Moo) who's spoiling everything so majestically (like the moran you are!). You think that the things you've done, and the thoughts you think, are the reason why you're undeserving of a brilliant life.

That's a lie. But it's okay. That's the role of this part of the mind (and she is **the** gatekeeper here!). Remember, we CANNOT change this through thought and "knowing". Your job here is to accept this whilst simultaneously getting curious AF about it...

Try on that dress...

THEN, your job is to create that watermelon-y pink part of your Rainbow Road, piggybacking the notions I share *from* your (doubting) Conscious Mind, *through* that Emotional change-making space of your Unconscious and *into* the Subconscious.

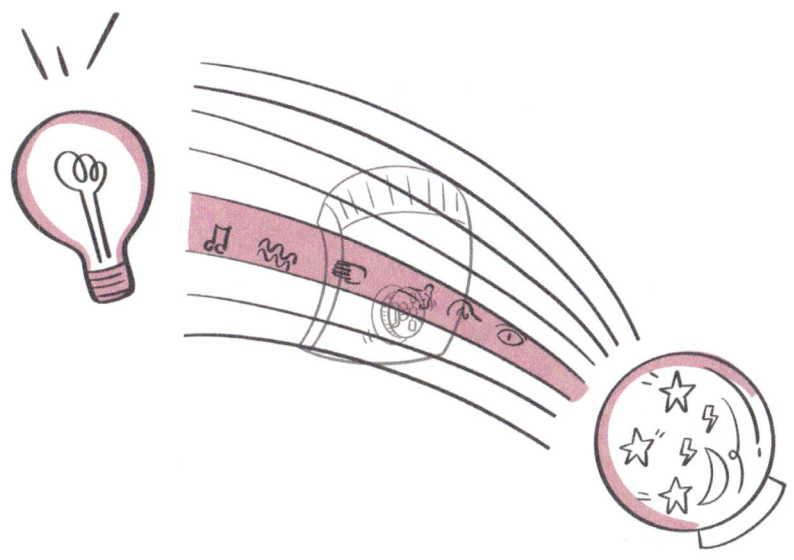

TO DO THIS EASILY, AS YOU READ THIS CHAPTER, YOU MUST EMBODY WATERMELON PINKS.

Wear your pink jumper, tops and pink Crocs. Suck on those super-yum watermelon lollipops. Pop on your favourite blush with a little extra umph. Use watermelon wax melts so it smells like Wake-Up

Wednesday around your entire home. Embody watermelon pinks whilst you read this and learn how to set eyes on The Anxious Avatar that is ruling your world each Wednesday. Go, right now. Get something watermelon pink. Have Harry Styles's "Watermelon Sugar" on low in the background. See the colour, smell the smell, hear the sounds and allow that to permeate as you read this chapter.

Then, once you've read this book, each Wednesday you'll carry this pink watermelon sensory stimulant with you. Every time you see, smell, taste or touch it, you'll actively create a Watermelon Pause Thought™ Moment: a moment to take a deeper dive into your Unconscious stories and emotions (and see what the freaking heck Francis is up to!) – making space for **You** (not The Anxious Avatar in your Conscious Mind) to shine through.

Ready? Let's go try on that dress...

THE LEADING LADY OF YOUR LIFE

Francis is the third and final part of our Trio of Terror – the third of the three deadly spokes in the human-brain wheel. Francis is a fiend. Oxford defines such a being as:

fiend

/fiːnd/

noun

1. an evil spirit or demon.

Similar: demon, devil, evil spirit, imp, bogie, incubus, succubus

2. **INFORMAL:** an enthusiast or devotee of a particular thing.

   "a football fiend"

Similar: enthusiast, fanatic, maniac, addict, devotee, fan, lover, follower, freak, nut, ham

Don't go freaking out – she's not the literal devil (lol!). She's just dev-il-like in her behaviour towards you. She is also a freaking devotee of keeping you alive and being on permanent high alert for **any** gnat-fart HINT of a death threat towards you. The word "fiend" is the perfect summary of Francis.

To truly see her high-alert-DEFCON1 ways, you've got to be willing to get more intimate with the fiend inside your brain. This will allow you to create some distance between you and her (just like you've done with that Monkey and that Toad) to see where she ends and where you begin. A great place to start is familiarising yourself with her Red Rag Moments.

LIKE A RED RAG TO A BULL

Red Rag Moments are where Francis feels like she's being:

- Overlooked
- Underseen
- Misheard
- Taken advantage of
- Ridiculed
- Embarrassed
- Made to feel guilty
- Made to feel ashamed or any other intense emotion which is unpleasant to feel

In these moments when she thinks you're being perceived by others as anything less than your most brilliant self (the strongest, best warrior in camp who no other tribe member, bear or snake would ever DARE to eat), she's THERE! She squawks in your defence. She ruminates over what you could've or should've done to be perceived as more ferocious next time – or more of a victim who's so puny and pathetic that nothing or no one would ever wanna eat your scrawny ass. She's constantly thinking about how she'll navigate it all differently next time so that you freaking "win!"

But You (with a Capital Y) don't win doing life this way. Only she does. And it makes her stronger...

Not only is she whooping and hollering about anything she perceives as a threat to the persona you present to the world, but she's also super quick to judge others too.

And there's a **massive** link between these two actions...

To get clearer on where your Francis ends and where you begin, you must first spot exactly what she judges others on most harshly.

I made this link whilst on a bus. A lady was sharing her woes with me around her lack of mobility. The solution seemed simple to me, "Mobility scooters look ace[23]! Get one of those!" I said.

"What?! Have everyone look at me and think I'm fat and lazy?!" was her retort. And it struck me...This thought wouldn't have ever entered my psyche – if I needed a scooter, I'd jump right on board. But **her Francis** saw people who used them as lazy and fat. **Her Francis'** judgement of others was what she'd been convinced was the most terrifying thing to receive from the world. So, she continued to allow her Francis to judge others, and she continued to struggle. Her Francis had led her to believe that being seen as fat and lazy was the worst – worse than being immobile and housebound. That's the power of Francis if she goes unseen in your blindspot for too long.

---

[23] Brilliant, the best, dope, banging, couldn't be better!

To Action

GET TO KNOW YOUR FRANCIS

Watch your Francis. What is she obsessed with? Look for those super judgy, jealous, bitchy remarks she makes about other people:

- What is she saying?
- When are you being particularly unkind and judgy of others?
- Is there a common theme?
- Is there a common emotion?
- Is there a common space it happens in?

Then, track it back. What she's saying is actually a reflection of how you're speaking and treating yourself in this area. This is a great space to start seeing your Francis Fiend from and how she's making you emotionally housebound. Learn where she's throwing up mobility-scooter smoke and mirrors. **These areas are where she has the greatest power, control and hold over you. These spaces are her greatest strengths in keeping you playing small and her in charge.** Your job here is to notice how she's thinking and acting in a way you don't like.

You **aren't** angry at her (you can't be, otherwise she continues to "win"), you're curious. In moments where you notice her here, say, "Oh, HEY Francis! I freaking see you!!" Then, actively and actively choose something else to focus your thoughts on. I call this "The Switch". Open a window to get a look at the world outside or go make a brew[24]. It doesn't matter WHAT you do here. Just make sure that when you've noticed a thought you don't want to be having, you call it out and Switch your focus. Doing this sends a message of, "I'm not here for this anymore!!"

---

[24]   Cup of the finest, English tea (Yorkshire Tea, if I'm being **really** precise).

There are specific actions Francis takes to sustain her insatiable appetite. Sadly for you, she lives on a diet of poison, and you must learn what this means if you're ever going to live free from her influence.

POISON APPLES AND THEIR STOREROOM

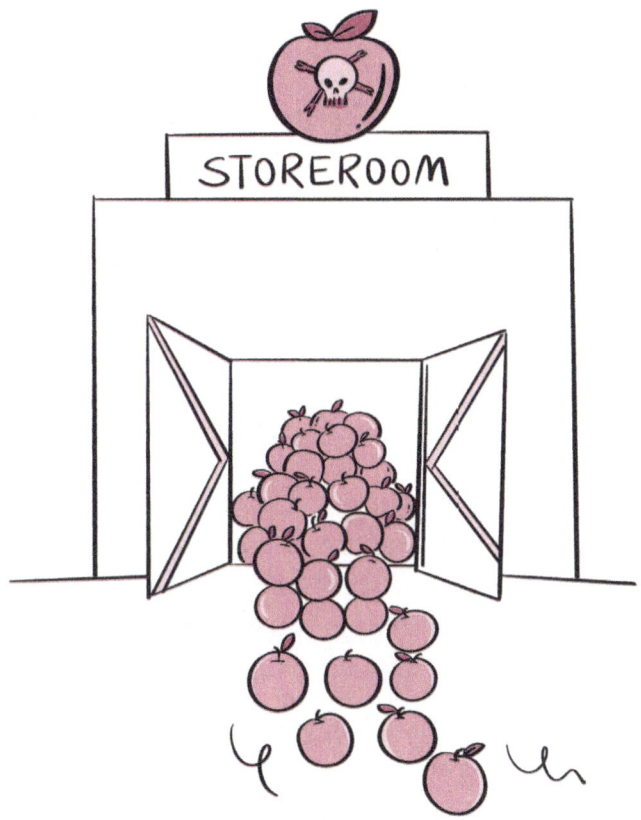

You need energy to stay alive. You require food inside The Emotional "Safehouse" that The Trio have you pinned to. The Trio won't let you starve – you're their fave! So, they need to work out how to provide sustenance and where to store this so you don't have to wander too far from The "Safehouse". Francis has made herself the sole provider of sourcing this sustenance for you. She does so with apples. And she stockpiles them in a "Storeroom" on the side of The "Safehouse". It's locked – to keep all of those "bad things" out and keep all of your supplies tucked in TIGHT – no escape!

When consumed, ordinary apples provide you with energy. Energy is GOOD. So scranning down on apples, on the surface, is a pretty promising idea. Only...the kind of apples that Francis likes to keep in your Storeroom aren't your regular farm shop finds. They're different: they house a deadly poison which is undetectable to you. And there are three Poison Apple types that Francis insists on feeding you which have a lot to do with why you're feeling so stuck.

- Toxic Poison Apples
- Control Poison Apples
- Grudge Poison Apples

Snow White can help us better comprehend our challenges:

Your Poison Apple experience in life is both identical to/and opposite from Snow White's Poison apple encounter:

It's **identical** because you're having head-to-head hidden-witch experiences, like Snow White, almost every day of your regular life. Like Snow's witch, your Francis is camouflaged so perfectly that you're oblivious to her. Before you know it, you've let in the disguised hag and eaten her Poison Apple without even realising.

Unlike Snow White's experience, the poison levels Francis' apples are exposing you to are undetectable to most mortals (**especially** those who aren't learning The 7 Steps). And because you haven't dropped dead yet, she continues to poison you incessantly, on the daily.

Our story (real life) is especially different from Snow White's because... we aren't living in a freaking fairy tale!

The handsome Prince comes to Snow White's rescue. The harsh truth of **our** life is:

No one is coming to save you.
No one is coming to rescue you.
Especially not a bloody prince.
You've got to save yourself!

No matter how handsome, rich and adoring of you the prince is, how helpful and considerate the dwarves are, how DIVINE the location of your luxury lodge in the woods is or how delicious true love's kiss is, NONE of these will save you from the hidden poisons laced throughout your life.

What **will** save you is your willingness to see yourself eating this poison (by trying on that dress over and over). **Then,** when you see it, stop eating Poison Apples!!!!

The **how** is coming up...

Unfortunately, Francis lives on a Beverly Hills detox fad diet of apples – every morning, noon and night. She needs food to live (and remember, you can't kill her – a girl's gotta eat, and apples are *Life* for Francis). **You need energy, and without being connected to the Youest of Yous, she'll always be on the hunt!** But (and it's a big-ass *but*) Francis cannot differentiate between a Poison Apple and a Pink Lady. And, even more dangerously, she's blindly feeding you Poison Apples simply because their toxic taste is so familiar.

I think, if you look hard enough, there's actual footage of her stockpiling apples in your Emotional "Safehouse" and she's whispering, "These are the ones we like. These are the special ones," with a Gollum-esque lisp, and a little, "My precious" at the end[25].

To Francis, what's familiar, no matter how poisonous = Emotional "Safehouse" Safe. *Not dead "Safehouse" Safe* is "good enough" for her – but it's **not** good enough for you! Let's first see what she's up to so we can then change it. There are three types of poison that she is most accustomed to. Let's start with the first...

---

[25] If you don't know who he is, google "Gollum, my precious" and see what comes up – Francis is just like him with his ring-obsessed ways but with her favourite apples.

TOXIC POISON APPLES

Just as Snow White found out, you too will come to learn that sometimes even the most tantalisingly delicious looking things, and the seemingly "kindest" and "most inviting" acts, can be laced with enough poison to knock you unconscious. Currently, your life is littered with Toxic Poison apples you can't see...

Toxic Poison Apples in your life might look like:

◊ Toxic gossip
◊ Toxic relationships
◊ Toxic TV shows
◊ Toxic workplaces
◊ Toxic diets

These things can feel like soul food in a moment of indulgence (they're familiar and often full of energy/excitement/drama):

- Gossiping at work about someone else's inadequacies makes you feel like your own might go unmissed – Toxic Poison
- Watching reality shows like *The Kardashians* where families snipe and snide at each other regularly is enticing because it makes our dysfunction feel more regular, exciting and manageable – Toxic Poison
- Shows like *Love Island* present "perfect" body figurines which stir body envy and jealousy as we watch – Toxic Poison

It's all super enticing to Francis, but it's all slowly sucking the life out of you!

KNOW YOUR TOXIC POISON APPLES

Ask yourself: *What is something I "think" feels like it should be fun but in reality, after doing it, leaves me feeling depleted?*

Pick one for now. If you aren't sure where to start, begin to become aware of when you feel most drained. What has come before this depleted feeling moment?

Is it:

- Spending time with a specific person?
- Scrolling on social media?
- Netflix and chilling?
- "Body cleansing"?

Whatever your specific Toxic Poison Apple is, be on the lookout for that poison and the energy it's draining from you as the toxicity takes hold. Ask yourself: *What's something else I might do instead?* You can:

- Walk
- Listen to your favourite song
- Paint
- Skip
- Do literally ANYTHING other than the toxic thing...

GO DO IT! Merely replacing a Toxic Poison activity for something different almost feels too simple, but the results of consistently applying this (every time you see pink or smell watermelon and bring awareness to your choices) WILL be **profound**!

CONTROL POISON APPLE

The second poison used to appease Francis' poison-hungry palate with familiar flavours is the Control Poison Apple. She'll manipulate, navigate, contort and control as much of your world as she possibly can so she'll **always** have access to what she thinks you need. She tells you the lie that:

"If I'm in control, then it's safer;
we get all the apples we need.
These apples are familiar, which means
***these** apples keep us safe."*

Control is an illusion. But it's one that Francis peddles until the cows come home. **Every time Francis feels like she's in control, she eats a Control Poison Apple (and gets a much-needed energy hit), making her that little bit stronger, and You that much weaker.**

Control Poison Apples, in your everyday life, can look REALLY flipping close to being "organised". This looks like:

- Being sure that you're the only person at work who has access to all of the important information – you do it "best", it's better that way!
- Having keys to things that no one else does – other people lose them, you won't!
- Having secret bank accounts – back-up, safety stuffs
- You pack all of the bags, even your husband's, for the trip (because, "I know he'll forget something important and him doing that will cause me more upset than it's worth – it's just better if I do it".)
- You make dinner and don't want help – "You'll get in my way and spoil it!"
- You stack the dishwasher because you don't waste space – energy efficient!
- Printing off the entire holiday itinerary and colour coding it – perfect!
- You make the bed or fold the washing your way because it's most efficient, looks nicest and is just THE way it's got to be, okay!?!!

These are literally a list of my Francis' Control Poison Apples. My brain contextualised them as, "Errrr, this is just saving time and stopping anything from going "wrong" – especially if we're in a foreign country!!!

Your brain might be screaming, "Emma, this is just a sensible way to live life."

It is not! It's hidden – Poison Apple 101. It's time to try on that dress...

KNOW YOUR CONTROL POISON APPLES

Ask yourself: *What am I seeking to control?* Pick one thing and pick something that's obvious that you can work on – maybe your "Special Dishwash Stack". (Lol!) Now, ask yourself the following questions surrounding this thing.

1. *Am I open to seeing this scenario differently?*
2. *Does my brain tell me that doing this thing my way is helpful to me?*
3. *How might I challenge myself to release this control?*
4. *(Is there someone else who can help?)*
5. *What am I afraid of losing in releasing this control here?*
6. *Is this as bad as Francis is making out?*
7. *Could I actually handle this?*
8. *What might I gain in doing this?*
9. *What's one step I can challenge myself to take today to let go of control?*

Put this one step as a reminder in your phone. If you're in bed or you've just sat down to read, you can come back to this book the second it's done. Promise yourself to do the one thing, then come back. Do this and you're stepping into a different kind of power!

What are you waiting for? GO DO IT!

THE GRUDGE POISON APPLE

The third Poison Apple is The Grudge Poison Apple. Its poison holds others in contempt for what they have done and for how undeserving of your compassion they are. It's often the most challenging poison to extract because you're blind to its potency. Its effect is heightened by the shroud of intensely uncomfortable emotions that this poison provokes. Grudge Apples feel simpler to indulge in than exploring the situation's potential to teach you something about yourself. Let's explore...

IN LIFE, YOU ALWAYS GET WHAT YOU NEED.

I hear your Francis screaming at me from here, but stick with me for a moment...

You always just about make it, right? It eventually works out okay in the end. Even the really bloody awfully sad things get to a level of okay-ness, in time [spoiler: if that thing doesn't feel okay yet, it's not the end]. There is something to seek under **everything** – even the really pants[26] stuff you'd much rather give a hard pass to.

If your Francis isn't already pissed after reading how "you get what you need", she's going to be **royally** peeved when you read what comes next...

---

[26] *worthless*

It's all going to unfold precisely as it's meant to, and your job is to learn through it – not to resist it. It's your inability to easily identify when Francis is feeding you Grudge Poison Apples whilst pretending they're wholesome Granny Smiths that's preventing you from learning and growing. You're eating poison, thinking you're doing a body cleanse.

Francis' reply to this will be, "You don't know my story, my background. You don't know what happened, the toxicity they thrust upon me. How sick she was. What he did to me. How bad it got, and how it still makes no sense! I DESERVE to feel this pain and not WANT to bloody-well learn and grow! Sod that!"

You're damn right about ALL of this!!

You did NOT deserve any of what happened to you – it **was** blooming **awful**. And yet, I stand by the above phrase – no matter **what** they did/ or are doing (even that! [sorry]). By not seeking to learn what it's trying to teach, *you* are actively letting Francis poison you by holding onto how much you deserve to feel the pain of it all.

Holding a grudge is like eating a storeroom FULL of Poison Apples and expecting the other person to die.

It only burns its container...YOU!

I have worked with individuals who were just as confused and frustrated by the idea of letting go of their **"right** to eat their Grudge Poison Apples"** (who have dealt with the most brutal atrocities) as you are right now. Hell, I was confused AF too – and I fought taking responsibility for how LIT I'd allowed my Francis to get, and for her thirst for Grudge Poison – hence the paralysis!

The more Francis fights to keep your "right" to be so pained and hold a Grudge because of what they did to you, and how awful it was/is, the more Grudge Poison you're fed.

I will never attend an anti-war rally.
If you have a peace rally, invite me.

—Mother Teresa

OPEN UP THE STOREROOM

The thing that makes me and my clients different from 99% of the world is the fact that we are willing to release control and the desire to "fight" to keep the poison (Grudge, Control, Toxic – ALL of it!) We **WANT** to want to open up the storeroom (read that again). And we **want** to want to be happy to rummage through the Apple Storeroom on the side of our "Safehouse" and relentlessly seek out the Poison Apples to (FINALLY!!) chuck their rotten asses outta there!!

We don't want to! But the **want** to want to get to the other side is enough to drive us to open the storeroom doors, by a teeny crack to begin with, until we've done it so many times it feels safe enough (actually, really bloody great!!) to prop them WIDE open, saying:

"Is this a Toxic Poison Apple? Is this a Control Poison Apple? Ah...a Grudge Poison Apple. Wow, that one's a doozy. I've been holding onto it for YEARS. FINALLY it's time to throw it out!"

At this point, all it will take is a nibble of the skin. You'll detect a hint of poison and (getting wiser to the taste) you'll spit it out...

Over and over again, *nibble spit* the pain of this poison, and know that fighting to barricade the storeroom door and hold onto it all is ALL Francis.

I work with people who are willing to bust open the doors of their Apple Storeroom which goes against allll of the humanness of ourselves. A willingness to do this will create crazy-ass results like...

- I healed paralysis and overcame fibromyalgia with no medication.

- I'm currently working 1:1 with a woman who has succeeded in navigating her 6-year-old's brain tumour – she feels new levels of strength to navigate him (and herself) through the medical and emotional process, through the pains of it all to actualise the best outcome within their power.
- I have worked with rape victims who stopped fighting their abusers and focused on healing themselves, and therefore did.
- People with debilitating health anxieties stopped fighting for their health and started taking care of their bodies; their anxiety became obsolete.
- People who're continually tormented by OCD and ADHD stopped fighting their intrusive thoughts and started nurturing the uniqueness of their brains, so they began to SHINE!

In her quest to stay on top, Francis has always got you either fighting to keep the doors of your Storeroom locked tight or fighting to keep others away. It's your job to find her favourite fights...

To Action

CONSIDER IF YOU'RE FIGHTING FOR YOUR PAIN

Ask yourself these questions, and write down your answers:

1. *What's the biggest thing you're fighting to keep in your Storeroom?* (political party, health, environmental health, a diagnosis, a trauma you've been subjected to)

2. *What do you believe will happen if you stop fighting for or against it?*

3. *Is this true?*

Stop for a second, and look at the last two answers...Is this actually true?[27]

4. *What might be truer?* (How can you be proactive without fighting?)

Francis could be LIT after reading this:

"You **want** animals to get cancer in their bum holes, Emma!?!"

"You want communism to make a comeback?!"

"You want me to not get the diagnosis for the thing plaguing my existence, EMMA?!"

Notice how she's desperately clinging to ANYTHING which will keep you scrambling to attempt to hold onto that pain and keep the fight alive. If I've touched a particularly powerful avenue that she LOVES to hold you down in the shadows of (so that you keep playing small and allow her to continue dominating the bejesus out of you), her response here will be extreme as she objects to what I'm asking you to try on.

If this is you, take a moment to relish in the fact that you are actively building your Rainbow Road here, and that's a bloody brilliant thing! Get up. Take your book (go on...do it!) and look at yourself in the mirror. Smile and say, out loud, "We're doing it ALL an entirely new way. YES!!!"

---

[27] Do you need to fight so hard, or could you continue to raise your awareness and take action in a different way? Being proactive and "fighting" are two totally and utterly different energies – a world filled with the former would make magic!

Francis might be screaming, "Stop reading! Block her! Delete him! Never shop at Sainsbury's[28] in town **ever** again because that's where she shops and we might bump into her, and she'll make us get all uncomfortable thinking about all of this stuff and it might just open up our Storeroom to the world to rifle through." And she's off...

Whilst she's off on one, and you can see her throwing every toy she has out of her pram[29], I want to talk to you. Hear me when I say:

What happened to you is valid! And it shouldn't have happened. Full stop! What drives you to keep your Storeroom locked and filled to the brim with Poison Apples is the knowledge that if anyone tries to challenge you to do life differently, you get to open up the doors, show off this overwhelming overflow and say, "Look how full and bloody awful this all is. I couldn't possibly sort through this lot and actually change!! It's my reason – *cough* excuse! – not to".

A Storeroom piled high is Francis giving a **false** promise to quench the thirst for your invalidated pains to finally feel legitimised.

> ***Doing this ONLY means you chase validation from others as permission to feel the way you do; weirdly, the higher it's stacked, the more you'll search.***

EMPTY OUT YOUR STOREROOM

I'm going to be real with you. You don't need this Storeroom! You don't need anyone else to see it and say, "That's a lot. Poor you. No wonder you're in such a state. Keep doing what you're doing. As you were. Stay put". Life stays exactly as it is, if you choose this.

To start emptying your Storeroom, you must decide that these pains are legit **because** you say so. Right now, say it with me:

---

[28] The name of a grocery store chain in the UK.
[29] Another word for *stroller*.

"My pains are legit because I decide that they freaking ARE. FULL FUCKING STOP!!"

But just because they're legit **doesn't** mean you have to stay trapped within them.

Francis is probably back again. She hates this (and me!!)!

She'll make the most tenuously bizarre links within and around it all. This keeps the whole thing really strong and alive within you. She'll do this by making links between *it* and your worst fears – those bloody awful things that you never EVER want to happen (or happen again). She'll tease you with threats of, "If you get any ideas about opening up the Storeroom and fishing out all of those apples I've literally spent YEARS building up, I'll be livid". She translates this to thoughts of:

"What if she sees that I've deleted her?! What is he trying to do now that I've blocked him?! What if Emma changes where she's shopping too, and I might bump into her there and maybe she'll know I changed Big Shop[30] shops because of her?! Awkward!!!!"

Better just stay home...as you trudge back to that Non-Safe "Safehouse" with Poison Apples now overflowing from the Storeroom into your "living" spaces.

This way of doing things just isn't working, is it? You're stressed off your tits! You don't feel any more in control or energy-filled by fighting so hard to keep the pains of your Poison Apple Storeroom in such overflow, do you? And that thing you're fighting so avidly for isn't really building all that much traction either if you're being totally and utterly honest, right?

There's no time for a Pity Party (Pity Parties are Francis' favourite kind of bash!). And the good news is that breakdowns are NOT part of the

---

[30]   A *Big Shop* is when you do a massive shop and hope that you've bought everything you need to mean you never have to leave the house and come to the shops again for at least 6 months (lol!! [or maybe a week, or two!!!])

work. Breakdowns only happen because you're refusing to try a new way. Yet you're here, this far into this book, which means you aren't waiting for the crash and burn moment any longer. Being proactive **before** needing a crash and burn moment means they'll cease – YEY!!!

You don't have to wait for an awkward bump-into-somebody in the shampoo aisle to realise you're on a Poison Apple chase. You don't have to wait for your ex to start calling you at 2 am, heavy-breathing down the phone before you notice you're eating Poison Apples in an attempt to receive energy. You can start to do it differently now.

What you **do** have to do is go try on the bloody dress, face that pile of apples head-on and start chuckin' 'em.

To Action

EMPTY OUT THE POISON APPLE STOREROOM

When you notice that you're getting angry, defensive, irritable and generally digging your heels in about the subject of holding onto the apples in your Poison Apple Storeroom (your pain, their pain, the "good fight", their lack of fight for something you believe to be important), say these words out loud:

1. *Is holding on, taking control or fighting for this to remain locked within The Storeroom helpful?*
2. *What might opening the Storeroom and letting go look like?*

   You **will** receive an answer **if** you're open to it (and most probably NOT the first time, so repeat this when you see the patterns emerge) through a feeling in your gut. You might even hear words that your intuition is speaking. When you receive this answer, say, "Thank you," and then ask yourself:

3. Can I try this on?

Remember, it won't fit the first time! And those who expect it to are going to remain precisely where they are at, in their "Safehouse" with the Storeroom filled to the brim with apples and NO sign of them going anywhere (apart from your tummy). Don't be that person. That's Francis at the helm, and she is not you – no matter how good she gets at pretending to be.

Be warned: Sometimes Francis creates a story under a story when she can see that you're beginning to expose her bullshit as you continually try on the dress and get wind of where she's munching on Poison Apples. When she realises that you're beginning to actually (dare I say it) enjoy rooting through your Apple Storeroom to uncover the Poison mess she's been storing up for YEARS, she'll go darker and deeper. **Don't be scared of this**. It's actually a really GOOD thing. It's part of the process of Waking Up. Francis going dark might sound like this kind of ridiculousness:

"If you don't *feel bad/continue to fight about/control what's happening to them/what happened to you*, it means you *don't care/love them/ yourself* and you're a bad person."

...or some other dark ninja stealth-mode chatter, but Francis' reasons for saying something like this might surprise you...

WEIRD-ASS, OVERPROTECTIVE FRIEND NOT *ACTUALLY* A FIEND?!

When you see your Francis doing this to you, what you *want* to do is:

Hold up a Poison Apple and say, "Francis, eating this is killing us, you DICK! Stop forcing me to. If you don't, I'm going to drop you off the top of the tallest mountain, giving zero shits about what happens to you".

I'm sorry to disappoint you here, but that just isn't happening! NOT on your nelly! She won't die! Instead...

What we must do with Francis is befriend the fiend.

See her for what she is – a lost and frightened little bean in survival mode 24/7 who thinks that you LOVE her apples and that they're safest in the Storeroom so you don't have to leave The "Safehouse". Begin to notice where she's trying to "up" her energy by having a feeding frenzy on poisonous toxicity and start tempting her to add some variety to her diet. Educate her on a new way of being – by leading life with your best foot forward (and not her two left feet which keep walking you in circles back to your "Safehouse"). Encourage her to **want** to want to clear out the Storeroom (this *want* creates magic).

This being, who (as you move through this work) you're gonna see clearer and clearer, actually loves you. A LOT! You're her favourite thing in the whole wide world. She believes that her apples are what are keeping you alive, and she doesn't want you to die. She'll think that any weird new apples you're trying to get her to eat, outside of your Emotional "Safehouse", are from places where starving bears are roaming free ready to eat you. She is scared. *She is actually an overbearingly protective best friend, and not the foe she won "Best Actress" for.*

Take a watermelon hit of something to ground yourself in this. Read it again, and again, until it starts to sink in a little deeper.

As you begin to spot her, you want to say, "Screw you, you psychopath!!" But this kind of speech only adds to her poison – a Poison Grudge Apple held against **her** is her favourite kind of delicacy: one which allows her to grow in strength. Instead, what **is** powerful for the both of you (in the most beautifully balanced kind of way) when you see her acting out is to say:

"In her own little fucked-up way, she loves me. She thinks there's a bear outside my door and that I am a prime-cut rump. There's no bear, Francis. New foods are yum. I am safe. Stand the funk down!"

Loving yet assertive. PERFECT for Francis! In order to tantalise your Conscious Brain (AKA Francis The Freaking Gate Keeper) to allow in anything new (and remember that this is the **only** way to create anything new outside of what you're currently experiencing), we must learn to tantalise her with an Entry-Level Access Point where you make her say:

"Okay...this kinda makes sense/this does not suggest imminent death potential. I'll allow it".

Remember, she wants you alive, so she'll move if you're moving towards More life. And if it holds the potential promise of this, she'll actually loosen her grip on the keys to your Storeroom and her fight for toxicity, grudges and control and actually chill out a *little*. Free from her apple obsessions, she'll allow you a sliver of space in your "Safehouse's" back garden to place the pink steppingstones that will bring you closer to The Subconscious access space of peace, love, joy and CHILL.

So much easier.

To achieve this and start making some pink path on that Rainbow Road in your Unconscious Mind, you must speak to Francis with a loving, firm kindness. Wear your pink watermelons to remind you to love on her that little bit harder. To help here, we're going to look at how she got there in the first place. Realising this should open up gates of compassion for her that you didn't know could exist within you. This next part should help even further with this...

FRANCIS GOT INTENSIFIED THROUGH YOUR PARENTS' FEARS

No matter who you are, someone, somewhere along the lifeline of your existence experienced sheer terror. And it got passed down the line from Francis to Francis.

The strength of your parents' protection/control and fight are a direct reflection of how much fear was in their world. Most often, they aren't a dick (even though they can **really** behave like one). They're scared. Their antidote to feeling so unsafe is to grapple for more control: control = known = safe.

Protection/control from parents can manifest as:

- Speaking/making decisions for you

- Hoarding
- Dictating
- "Disciplining"
- Lying
- Gaslighting
- "This is all for your own good" (yikes!!)

It can also have damaging effects when fear pushes them into:

- Over-protectiveness
- Hiding important truths from you
- Overpraising and overlooking flaws

In some way, on some level, their Francis got deep inside you (no matter how much you think, "I'm nothing like my Mother" – you probably are). So, instead of Francis' retort of:

"Not my parents – they're the exception. They're just a 'this' (insert the label which you have stamped them with – 'good' or 'bad')!"

Let's explore a concept (which Francis will *never* get/want to understand) for what actually happened to cause it to play out this way:

The easiest way to keep you "safe" and for your parents to remain in "control" (lol) of their life was to encourage you to believe they knew best. This made it so you compliantly just did the things which kept you all "safely" inside **their** already-established Emotional "Safehouse".

But you didn't want to go into their "Safehouse". It's boring, and actually, when you're little, it's scarier in there than it is in the free, wide-open world.

You being alive and not wanting to go into this space with them is a problem for them! They love you. They don't want you left exposed outside The "Safehouse". They also do **not** want to stay out there with you (yikes!!!). This all proves to be super problematic for their well-rehearsed "Return to Safehouse" routine that they had under wraps for **years** preceding your arrival.

You (or rather, what you embody) are a problem!

Marry this with the fact that you arrived into their world, kicking and screaming all of their biggest life lessons/their darkest and most "dangerous" feelings and emotions (that's what we are – a bundle of ALL of the stuff our parents shoved into their "Safehouse" and refused to deal with for lifetimes). And they have a real problem – a teeny, super-cute one which they love more than anything (in their own, unique, most often fudged-up way) that's going to be incessantly hounding them for the next 18+ years. It's a very complicated feeling for them. This is a next-level problem for their need to feel in control/familiar/safe – kids are ANYTHING but this! Their "solution" was to smush you into their version of what they thought would keep you extra safe/in their control/quietly shoved in their "Safehouse". They do such a good job of moulding you that you absolutely begin to believe that this dark, gloomy, scary space is actually what life is meant to feel like. Parents are there most of the time to remind you what is expected for you to remain "safely" in the "Safehouse" parameters. They:

- Tell you "right" or "wrong"
- Make you "wrong" so that you don't feel brave enough to go at it alone/will always need them/they'll always feel in control and therefore safe
- Encourage you to seek out their permission – they control if and how you move
- Disempower you so you don't feel capable without them
- Focus solely on the negatives so you feel incapable
- Focus solely on your positives whilst they skim over your flaws and mistakes – they don't celebrate them as opportunities to learn, so you learn that mistakes are taboo, leaving you terrified to "try"
- Encourage you to seek their approval

Now, you're all grown up and stuff, and they probably aren't around all of the time, so life without them is unknown. The liberatingly powerful thing to do would be to run naked in the wild screaming, "I'm freaking FREE!" And that's what most of us leave *thinking* we're going to do.

But without that Rainbow Road firmly in place, Francis leads and you're out of their "Safehouse", desperately trying to forge your own next door to theirs. And Francis is hunting for familiar. And without your parents directly there, your external environment attempts to fill the fear-void your parents created by drawing to you:

- A boss who treats you with the same contempt as your dad
- A partner who puts you down the same way as your mum did
- A work colleague who bosses you around and tells you how stupid you are (in the most passive aggressive way possible) like your sister did
- A friend who always tells you how much weight you've gotta shift, like your Grandma did
- A boyfriend who always picks out your flaws, just like your brother

Always having someone "on your back" waiting to "pull you down" means that you live with residual undertones of fear running through more areas of your life than you'd like. I know this sounds weird. I also KNOW that if you and I were to sit together, face to face, and I asked, "Do you like having these people and circumstances in your life that are causing you to repeatedly move through familiar pain patterns with no reward?" you'd actively scream, "NOT ON YOUR NELLY!!"

Yet, they're so familiar, known and hold the warped promise of "safety"/ familiarity that they just keep coming at you.

LIFE HAS TAUGHT YOU THAT FEAR IS FAMILIAR

Living this way means that fear becomes familiar. And when fear becomes your default setting that you link to familiar/safety, you end up in quite the pickle! This way, fear becomes your Primary "Safehouse" Emotion, so much so that simply physically drawing those actual people into your life isn't enough. You need something more permanent. Your answer to this is to internalise the most familiar, frightening voices from your past and put them on loop in your mind:

- When you go to eat the cookie, you hear an internal voice of Grandma as she sneers, "A moment on the lips, a lifetime on the hips".
- When you go to voice your thoughts in a meeting, you feel your dad's eye roll and the embarrassment of saying the "wrong thing" again. You hear, "You're so pathetic!"
- You go to invest in yourself and you hear your mum say, "Don't waste money. It doesn't grow on trees. Save it for a rainy day".

To Action

WHOSE VOICE IS FRANCIS USING?

To Find whose voice Francis has taken on most fiercely, you've got to get curious when you feel a strong emotion trying to take hold. When you're (apparently) "fucking up", whose voice do you hear? Be on the lookout for that voice – each time you feel yourself:

- Speaking when you "shouldn't"
- Taking a wrong turn when you're driving
- Laughing too loudly
- Eating something fun
- Being whatever it is that was discouraged by those around you

> Whose voice do you hear in your head?
>
> That voice is your Francis. Smile and wave at her each time you hear her, with an energy of, "Hello, old friend. I hear you. But pretty soon this isn't going to hurt anymore.

ANYTHING BUT THAT...

If you're getting curious around a diet of non-Toxic, anti-Control Apples or if you're making too much noise in a direction too far away from your Emotional "Safehouse", Francis will dredge up the ace up her sleeve: the notion of, "I can handle anything but 'that' one thing..."

It's a powerful sentiment (and one that Francis will HATE me asking you to explore). So, let's get willing to go there. To do so, ask yourself:

What's the thing that 'I can handle anything but 'that'?

It might be, I can handle anything:

- but not getting cancer
- but not my parents getting old
- but not losing my job/house/wife/child...

Be brave, and get clear: What's your worst? What's your "Anything but 'that'"?

Whatever it is (and you've probably gone a bit hot and sweaty with me asking about it), THAT'S Francis' favourite thing to hold over your head.

She knows that any kind of HINT towards anything remotely to do with this area of your world will have you ducking for cover in your "Safehouse" and adding some apples to your Storeroom. You'll be home, with curtains closed, under the extra snuggling blanket after swallowing the key to your Storeroom, reprimanding yourself, "How silly of me to risk the potential of that one thing materialising just because I was getting above my station and fancying something different. I'll just stop!"

CELL, STREET, CASKET

You think that your "Anything but 'that'" will ultimately and directly (or indirectly) cause a demise which reduces you to either:

1. Do something illegal which'll see you put in the slammer
2. Do something reckless which'll lead to you losing all of your money and your house – putting you out on the streets
3. Do something which will lead you, or someone you love very much (often more than yourself), to die (...yikes!!)

You might be a little reluctant to recognise this. Francis is FURIOUS that you're even kind of contemplating it. But explore it. Pop your booty in that dress if you want this to be different (and, I'm guessing that if you're this far into this book, you freaking DO!) and give your ass a shake!

Think about it. Will taking that inspired action *directly* lead you down a path of bad luck that will result in you going to jail?

Are you *actually* going to end up on the street if you go for that dream job you've wanted for ages, even *if* you got fired (Francis anticipates the worst!)? Truly?

Will someone you love *actually* die if you finally do something for you? Will it truly result in death?

Sit with this. Feel for the true, objective answers to these questions. Once you see through Francis' erroneous beliefs, you know you are beginning to Wake Up.

WHAT'S YOUR WORST?

Get clear on what your Worst is:

- Is it somehow linked to ending up in prison, without any money or dead?
- Is this as true as Francis is making it out to be?

Let Francis get her spiel out of the way first (you know, the one you've been listening to for all this time – THE reason why you're still in the same spot!)

THEN, ask again and see what's under all that noise...

Is this as true as Francis is making it out to be?

Get willing to go one step further... Even **if** this worst happens (which it **won't!!**), would I actually be able to handle it? If you get real honest with yourself, the answer is almost always a resounding... "YES!!" (Despite the fact that you, **obviously,** wouldn't actively choose it).

Keep going. And every time you feel that "worst" coming up, come back to this over and over again. One day, it'll land. You'll see how Francis has been holding you back, and it'll all become so much clearer.

OTHER EMOTIONS

Maybe you don't identify with fear as intensely as I'm whanging on about. Maybe it's another emotion. Maybe your parents were free and easy.

Fearful or not, I want you to explore what you'd identify as your primary emotions. What are the most familiar emotions to you?

- Shame?
- Guilt?
- Sadness?
- Anger?
- Happiness?
- Disgust?
- Frustration?
- Embarrassment?

To help you here, go back through your Back-Dated Mental Archive of "Things I wish I'd never done" (we all have one – it's like a Highlight Reel, minus the fun!!) and go through each in turn. What is the main emotion that you feel as you peruse each memory? Is there a theme? A familiar sense of dread which weaves its way through them all? Don't let Francis get too hung up on absolutely defining the emotion. You being able to feel it in your body and recognise that it's there is simply what we need here.

If your familiar is shame, maybe Francis will run a soundtrack of:

| **ASHAMED** | **SAD** | **ANGRY** |

"I can't believe you did that, you horrible, horrible person", whenever anything reminds you of something you once did wrong.

If your familiar is sadness, she might spin a situation to make you think that you've been left out, or that the opportunity wasn't available to you because you suck.

If your familiar is anger, the possibility of resolving conflict with communication is completely disregarded and she'll lead with flames and a sharp tongue.

No matter how bloody awful they are, these emotions are familiar. And just because I haven't said it enough:

Familiar = safe for Francis.

I don't know your most familiar Emotion. Maybe you don't either. But a direct pathway to it will be there – firmly established. And Francis will spend your whole lifetime attempting to drag you back to it, one way or another, **unless** you become aware of it and ***want** to want* to challenge yourself to do something about it.

We've come to the end of truly getting to know Francis, the final element of The Trio of Terror, and how she's been poisoning you for years with her confusing-as-funk, overwhelming best friend/fiend-like ways of behaving towards you. Going forward, every Wednesday, wear your Watermelon pinks and try on that dress. This act is The Subconscious reminder for Francis and her frightened, frightening behaviours that are slowly poisoning you. With each pink Sensory Stimulant, you'll truly recognise the impersonator who's been pretending to be you this whole time. As she becomes clearer, you'll create a distance from Francis and take your place as the leading lady in your life. Life will feel rosey again – promise. Open up the Storeroom and empty out those apples.

Wake up to everything You are not so that you can truly see who You are – you're ace! Wait until You see...

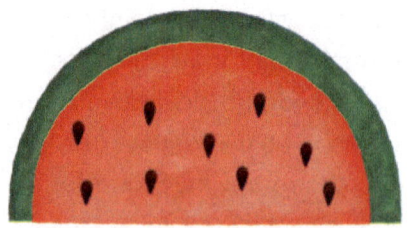

WAKE-UP WEDNESDAY HIGHLIGHTS:

1. Wear your watermelon pinks and, with each Pause Thought™, get curious around where Francis is pretending to be the Leading Lady in YOUR Life. Notice her and say, "Oh, HEY Francis! I freaking see you," then choose something else to focus your thoughts/ energies on".

2. Be on the lookout for Red Rag Moments where Francis is judging you or others with fierceness and intensity. It is in these spaces that she holds power over you, keeping Actual You hiding in the shadows of her. Look to release these judgements.

3. Francis thinks that every new move you make outside of your Emotional "Safehouse" will land you in a Cell, on the Streets or in a Casket. No such thing will happen. Track your current fear. What's *your* **worst**? Is that **really** going to happen? Truly? Or will it just be an inconvenient moment (or two)? If the worst-case scenario did happen (which it most likely won't), could you handle it? Fuck YEAH you could – You're beyond BRILLIANT!!

4. Remind yourself each time you get upset with Francis that in her own little fucked-up way, she loves you. She thinks there's a bear outside your door and that you are a prime-cut rump. Tell Francis: ***"There's no bear, Francis. New foods are yum. I am safe. Stand the funk down!"*** And then make brave moves. She will follow you into open waters MADE for you.

REMEMBER:

Mind-on-Mute Mondays:

Wear your Minty Greens and explore this mind-blowing fact:

There is a voice inside your head.

This voice is <u>not</u> You.

Seek to notice every time he's getting his knickers in a twist, and snap a branch from his most favourite, familiar neurological brain-loops so he starts to become less comfortable travelling these outdated routes. Get curious around the idea that if there is a voice speaking, then who is the one listening?

That voice is You!

You will not know it the first moment you contemplate it, but you will come to know it. And once you do, you won't care to "understand" and "know". You'll just let it be. Here you'll feel a freedom you had no idea could exist for you.

To access your Mind-on-Mute Monday supplementary supportive workbooks and videos, please <u>CLICK HERE</u>.

REMEMBER:

Trigger-Free Tuesday:

Wear your Orangy Tangerines.

Toad believes that everyone else is to blame and that it'd all be just fine and dandy if **they** all stopped being such arseholes! Your job here is to be like Teflon: create a Space to Choose Freedom between the stuff happening outside of you and how you are reacting or responding to it. Keep laying the tangerine part of your Rainbow Road. Notice every time you see you're on the hunt for your Toad/wanting to bathe in someone else's firework explosions and say, "I see you and it's **not** going down this way ANYmore!!"

To access your Trigger-Free Tuesday workbook and supporting video, please CLICK HERE.

REMEMBER:

Wake-up Wednesdays:

Wear your watermelon pink and learn how to be kind to your mind. You're only thinking this way because all of those harsh voices that told you that you weren't "good enough" for this world got so loud that they've become etched inside your mind. Now, on eternal replay as your Francis, you've listened to them/her for so long that you've got confused. You think she is you and that you are her. You aren't. And the way to see this is to notice where she is introducing poisonous, grudge-bearing and controlling toxicity into your life, telling you it's good for you/all you deserve. When you spot this, remember that she is the overbearingly over-protective friend, and **not** the fiend she's doing a REALLY good job of pretending to be. You aren't landing yourself in the Street, the Cell or in a Casket. You're moving into new spaces – a wide open sea. Once she realises that the water's fine, she'll come join you. But you must move first.

To access your Wake-Up Wednesday supplementary supportive workbooks and videos, please CLICK HERE.

ACTUAL YOU

Actual You is the bonafide, legit, for REALS You (with the most capital of Y's). *This **You** is not something which can be divided and conquered to be actualised: Actual You is already in existence. After dancing toe to toe with The Trio for the last three chapters to learn what they're up to, you'll see that everything that's **not** them is Actual You.*

There are some tools and techniques which will allow Actual You to overcome The Trio's obstacles more readily. To stop the drama dance of "Is that the Trio? Is that Actual Me? Is it BOTH?!", you're going to learn them over the next four chapters:

◊ Gearing your attitude towards gratitude
◊ Feeling your feelings in a way that actually feels comfortable
◊ Learning to breathe in a way that creates ease of access to Your Rainbow Road
◊ Learning how surrender gets to be the superpower you didn't know you needed

Learning to embody these four steps will show you everything that's **Actual You.**

Thankful Thursday
BE GRATEFUL FOR THE JOURNEY

'Enough' is a feast.

—Buddhist proverb

Introducing The Quick-Fix Plum

Your mind is in a rapid search for More. You're wired for it. We all are! That's why no matter what you get, it never feels like enough. The "trick" to getting More, and feeling fulfilled as FUNK every step of the way, is to become gratefully grounded in what you already have. Then, your More flows to you, and it feels next-level kind of fabulous.

For this fabulous to feel less like fantasy (and more like your new reality), you get to learn how to spot when you're looking for a self-sabotaging Quick-Fix hit to "feel better" right now. You'll then notice that instead of self-sabotage, you will begin building an Ice Cream Sundae Sanctuary for yourself that you get to eat at on the regular. It's a "No Quickie Zone". Instead, you'll be eating ice cream for breakfast, lunch and dinner every day!

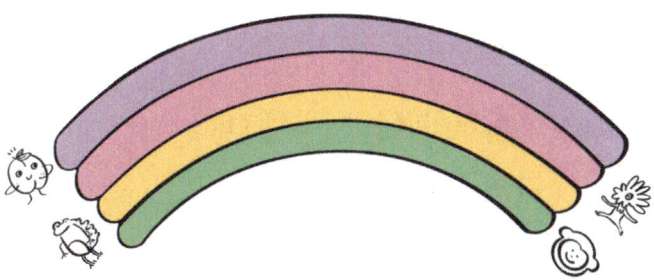

To do this, we're going to work on the purple part of your Rainbow Road, which means you must:

1. Get your purples OUT!
2. Read this Thankful Thursday Chapter using the lavender senses to stimulate a deep-seated sense of gratitude. This is actually your most natural state of being. Now that you've truly seen the full force of The Trio of Terror, it's time to connect to gratitude to move past The Trio and their bobbing, triggered, fiendish ways...
3. Remember to say, "Fudge it", over and over again. Play pretend as you try on that dress...

"I've got to be grateful for the shit show that is my life **before** I get the stuff that I **actually** want?! You're having a laugh!"

Fudge it! And try it on.

"You're telling me that the things I'm salivating over are only 'Quick-Fix Hits'? What?!"

Fudge. It. And. Try. It. On.

"...and there's an Ice Cream Sundae Sanctuary for me to eat at whenever I want? Emma..."

Just go...

...as often as possible, using your Pause Thoughts™ and your Lavender Purple Sensory Experience.

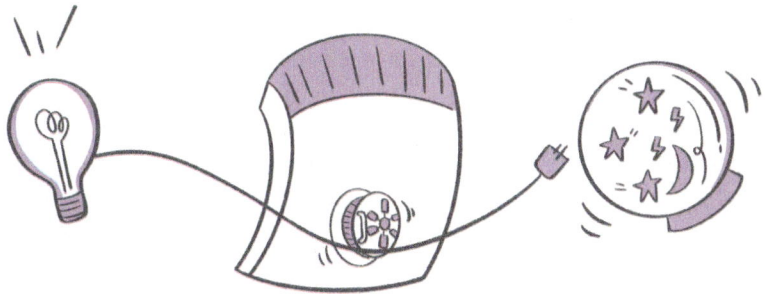

And one day, this silliness will slide on like a glove and you'll say:

"Jeez LOUISE, I've been tempted by 'Quick-Fix Plum Hits' for almost my whole entire life! No wonder I've got such an insatiable hunger for More. It's **never** felt like my emptiness could be fulfilled, no matter how much I 'got'. Plums are nice to have, but now I know they're not essential for me to expand into My glory of More. SWEET!"

Like everything else...it's bizarre but BRILLIANT!

HERE'S THE CHALLENGE...

Right now, you're scrambling to get bigger, better, faster, longer, juicier anythings and **everythings** based on a promise from The Trio that they're the answer you're looking for. Struggling for the next promotion, the bigger house, the slimmer waist, the thicker hair...thinking they'll make you feel whole inside! It's actually nowhere close to 'The Thing' – but The Trio don't want you to know that!

When The Trio catches wind of your desire to feel grateful for the life you currently lead, they'll panic – and they'll do everything in their power to draw you back to their "Safehouse" through the "Quick-Fix" route.

To be done with believing The Trio's "Quick-Hit" promises which deliver feelings of lack and uncertainty, you must start making space to lay the purple part of your Rainbow Road. This act will allow The Subconscious (that all-knowing super-grateful-for-EVERYTHING part of you) to come marching through.

Throughout this chapter, you will come to know that feeling grateful for what you've already got is a HUGE element in getting that dress up and around your hips. The Trio has kept you away from its glory for too long. It's time to start trying it on.

HERE'S WHAT YOU CAN CHOOSE TO SEEK...

On Thankful Thursdays, you are going to learn how to feel grateful as funk WITHOUT needing to rely on ANYTHING outside of you. No more

hunting out there, aimlessly lost and repeatedly MORE disappointed when that next thing doesn't provide you with the feelings The Trio promised.

By the end of this chapter, you'll be able to:

◊ Know how to escape The Trio of Terror's isolated (Plummy) temptations

◊ Receive your internal Ice Cream Sundaes – with Rainbow Road sprinkles to boot!

◊ Know when you're lost and looking for a Quick-Fix Plum, and you'll know exactly what **your** most damaging Quick-Fix Plum is. This is so that you can Find love and gratitude, even in the shit-storm situations you don't want to be in, and get grounded in the moment

◊ Connect with a new voice (a helpful one – one that isn't Bob, Toad or Francis) and learn how to listen to her

Learning the Thankful Thursday elements is going to show you how to connect with the brilliance of what you already have so you can effortlessly draw in the More that's meant for you.

To truly do this, you're going to need your Pause Thoughts™...

PAUSE THOUGHTS™

Right now, your Conscious Brain thinks that you **only** get to feel grateful when you've achieved something "big" outside of you, that it's **only** when you've reached a high-enough parameter or milestone that you're "allowed" to feel good enough and grateful. Ever notice that even when you do reach a milestone, it's pretty anticlimactic (AND, if you have a Trio anywhere close to mine, they're constantly moving the goalposts for what's "good enough" anyway!!)? This pattern sets you up for failure, no matter what you do.

Saying, "I know the stuff doesn't matter – it's the journey" whilst secretly thinking, "but I want the stuff and I'm SICK of the journey that's battering me!" is a pretty regular human-mind response to life. Acknowledging that you're thinking this way is okay. It's the role of this part of the mind. Remember, we CANNOT change this through "thought" and "knowing". Your job here is to accept this whilst simultaneously getting curious AF about it – because you're DONE with it!

THEN, your job is to create that plummy lavender purple part of your Rainbow Road, piggybacking the notions I share *from* your (doubting) Conscious Mind, *through* that Emotional change-making space of your Unconscious and *into* the Subconscious.

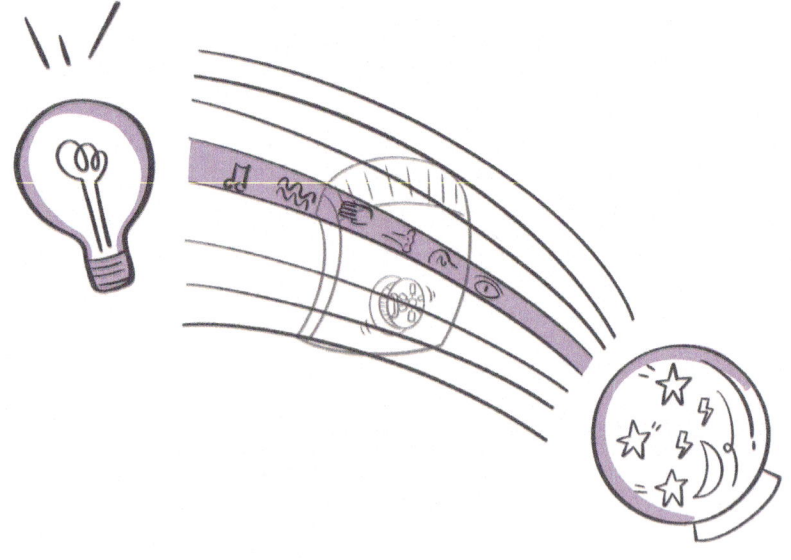

TO DO THIS EASILY, AS YOU READ THIS CHAPTER, YOU MUST EMBODY LAVENDER PURPLES.

Wear your purple pants, frocks[31] and plummy socks. Chow down on purple fruits and sprouting purple broccoli tops. Wear your purple shades of eyeshadow. Get the lavender oil-lamp burning, and pop on a lavender eye mask as you drift off to the land of Nod with Thankful Thursday's fun fuelling your Unconscious thoughts. Embody lavender purples whilst you read this and learn how to set your senses to perceive where and how you're looking for Quick-Fix Plums when you're actually being called to expand into your Ice Cream Sundae Sanctuary each Thursday. Go, right now. Get something lavender-y purple. See the colour, smell the smell, hear the sounds and allow it all to permeate as you read this chapter and do the work.

Then, once you've read this book, each Thursday you'll carry this lavender purple sensory stimulant with you. Every time you see, smell, taste or touch it, you'll actively create a Thankful Thursday Pause Thought™ Moment: a moment to take a deeper dive into your Unconscious

---

[31]   *dresses*

stories and emotions. This will allow you to make space for *You* (not The Quick-Fix Plum-er) to shine through.

Ready? Let's go try on that dress...

GRATITUDE ATTITUDE

Gratitude is your key to unlocking it all – as in EVERYTHING! But it's really bloody hard to do when you have a primitive part of the brain that's **obsessed** with looking for the shitty things in life to make it all feel more familiar to you. (Thanks Bob, Toad and Francis!) They've got you like:

"I don't bloody-well want this horrible thing to keep happening to me!! I want something lovely and fun that feels great! I don't want to struggle or feel shame, fear, sadness or guilt. I wanna look around me at allll of the bloody lovely stuff I KNOW (consciously) that I've got and feel grateful AF for it, but, for some reason...I just can't!"

Gratitude is one of the most naturally occurring, fundamental emotions. Truly feeling it will show you that you are exactly where you are meant to be at precisely the right time. Without it, life feels like it's permanently pulling the rug from under your feet JUST as you were starting to get a stable footing.

The reason that so many of us feel like we're in a tug-of-war with life's rug and don't feel connected to gratitude on the daily is because we've been taught to believe that gratitude is a removed moment which lives on the outside of us, hiding in something else, something which must be sought out and almost conquered to be felt...

...almost like it's a juicy purple Plum, growing on a Plum tree super far away, hidden from you, contained in your next move, thought or intention...If only you could figure out the next step to get a smidge closer, maybe you'll get there...**finally**.

THE LAST QUICK-FIX PLUM

Check for yourself: What was the last thing you got that you told yourself would be THE thing which would reward you with that juicy pluminess?

- The new job?
- The new love of your life?
- The baby?
- The business?
- Negative biopsy results?

What's the last thing you said would be the final piece of the puzzle, when it'll all feel like "enough"? The thing you'd promised would allow you to take stock and be grateful AF for it all?

Now, ask yourself:

◊ When you got it, was it enough?
◊ Have you stopped wanting and waiting?

◊ Did you stop in the moment of it to enjoy the juice dripping down your chin?

◊ Did you Find the feeling you were searching for?

You didn't, did you? Not truly! Even if there *was* a moment of, "Yey!"...that incomplete feeling **always** follows. No shame is necessary here (thanks Trio for trying!!). Awareness is what we're going for. Just be aware. That's all that is needed.

You feel like nothing will ever be enough because it **never** feels like enough when you live outside the gratitude of this moment. I know that **you** know that you've got it pretty good. Even despite the humanness of your life (AKA those shitty bits that no human being walking on the face of this earth is allowed to escape). But if you reflect on your life in the main, it's pretty **good**, yes!? And yet, you're struggling to cement yourself in the right-now moment of it, correct?

It's because you're on a quest for More. This quest is something we're all programmed for which we can't opt out of. This is actually a really good thing. It's **the** reason you're still here reading this book. Wanting More is one thing, but focusing all intention on collecting Quick-Fix Plums as **the** access point to More is another entirely. It leads us down confusing paths that we just aren't meant to be on.

Here's what I mean by The Quick-Fix Plum...

THE QUICK-FIX PLUM

The Quick-Fix Plum is small (no matter how big it promises to be – think guys with big car exhausts kind of vibe!) and **always** leaves

a bitter taste and an even bigger unfulfilled "hunger for More" after you've taken a bite.

The Quick-Fix Plum is The thing which you believe is **the** answer to it all. It convinces you that if you had "it", then Bob's your Uncle and Fanny's your Aunt...**now** *life feels great, you got your More and gratitude is in abundance*. Case closed! Only...it doesn't work this way.

You're suspicious of this right now. You're so sure that you KNOW your answer to your More – that's the nature of The Conscious Mind. So, we'll have to look for Entry-Level Access Points for this plummy notion to land...

Once you conquer a Quick-Fix Plum, you only get to nibble the shiny exterior, and before you know it, it's snatched away and hidden somewhere new and even more secretive: the next hunt for you to embark upon. This is your innate drive for More in the driving seat. When the purple part of your Rainbow Road isn't developed, this craving is left unharnessed and without direction.

It works this way because you **know** that juicy plum exists in its Quick-Fix Form (you see it on perfect Instagram feeds, in shop windows, in husbands and wives kissing at the checkout in front of you) – hence why you're on such a rampage for it! Yet, all your energies are so avidly focused on the hunt for it "out there" that you're missing Actual *it* every time!

You're missing it entirely because Actual *it* **already lives inside You**. (It sounds SO cliche, I actually questioned putting this line in the book. But it's freaking TRUE! So, it had to go in [sorry, I'm not sorry!].)

And Actual *it* will **never** be found in the form of a "Quick Fix" (even though, right now, you *still* believe it does *scrolls through #dreamhouse on Insta just to check*). What you're searching for beats within the cavity inside your ribcage. It keeps the lifeforce inside you alive. And when you Find Actual *it*, it's not just a little nibble at the edges that you're "allowed" to have; it's that deep and profound delicious submergence that you've been fantasising about which, up to this point, you've been blindly attempting to get from Quick-Fix Plum nibbles *puts down the phone and starts living actual BLOODY BRILLIANT life*.

To feel that deep inner love, peace, freedom, and abundance and know precisely why the 400 trillion-to-one odds chose you, you must step into the heartfelt, grateful Ice Cream Sundae Sanctuary space within.

To Action

GET THE YESES OUT OF THE WAY

Ask yourself: *Do I truly believe, in my heart of hearts, that **this** (one thing) will make me feel happy and grateful for it all?*

Get the *yeses* out of the way; they're part of your standard Conscious "thinking" Brain, Emotional "Safehouse" Response. And keep going, with a curious, "I wonder..." Continue to ask yourself the same question, each time you think about *it* (the one thing). Repetition is key here. This is creating your Entry-Level Access Point. Ask yourself:

*Do I truly believe, in my heart of hearts, that **this** (one thing) will make me feel happy and grateful for it all?*

If this is something you really struggle with, write this question out on a Post-it and stick it to your mirror. Make it your phone's home screen. Find ways to ask yourself this question over and over and over again – make every purple prompt Pause Thought™ point you in this direction. In asking, you're disturbing that Unconscious underlayer which is obsessed with leading you in a blind chase for that Quick-Fix Plum. It breaks the Bob tree-branch that encourages the Quick-Fix thirst. It creates space for you to actually explore whether the Plum is as promising as The Trio are telling you it is.

Remain curious. Just get that dress out. That's all you've got to do for now. One day, with persistence, you'll get curious and think, "Is having '**that**' (one thing) as marvellous as my mind's trying to make me believe?" And this, my friend, is freaking IT!!! Your ONLY job is to Find ways to become the Youest version of **You**, and the focus of this work is to go with your nature, not against it. To want More is your natural state of being, and that's okay – it's The Quick Fixes which aren't.

The Trio would LOVE to tell you I'm forcing gratitude on you, but I'm NOT!

A Plum (the thing/person/event desired) tastes sour and unfulfilling IF you think its your salvation and answer to all things.

Here's the magic of this work:

IF you know that the plum is just the "cherry on top", you get to truly enjoy it for what it is.

Are you still with me?! Please say "Yes!!"

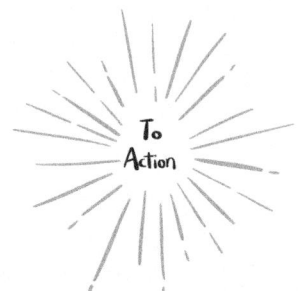

GET GRATEFUL AF FOR THE CRAZY

What do you already have to be grateful AF for right now? Ask yourself:

- *What am I grateful for within all of this craziness?*
- *What are some things in my world right now that are pretty blooming-well great that I **could** get curious about feeling grateful for?!*

When you challenge yourself to look for gratitude in these spaces, your curiosity means that you begin to open up a space where you'll start to perceive everything differently:

◊ That dead-end job is actually giving you skills and resilience which you'll transfer to create that start-up you've been dreaming about. Grateful.

◊ The broken marriage might be an opportunity to Find a level of patience and compassion that you didn't know existed. Grateful.

◊ Just about making enough money and living paycheque to paycheque affords you the understanding of budgeting, appreciating your money and living within your means. Grateful.

Set alarms on your phone throughout the course of the day called "Grateful AF!" Every time it sounds and you want to ignore it and "just finish this", catch yourself and think of something you're grateful for. Don't force it; just try on the dress and start to look for it. Keep asking (out loud is POWER here), "What is here, in this crazy, that I can choose to get grateful for?" Let your purple Pause Thoughts™ guide you here.

Finding Gratitude hidden in the abyss of chaos is Gratitude Attitude 101. Opportunities to practise these levels of Gratitude exist underneath **every** element of your life. Seeking them is superhuman, but that's precisely what you can be when you've built a life on a Rainbow Road. You just must be willing to lay down your purple path to explore them.

PET A PUSSY

A super-easy place to flex this Gratitude Attitude is with kids and animals; they're an ace space to start! If you don't have either, go out for a walk and look for a little pooch or a puss to pet. And then, actually be in the moment of petting it.

Not: "That weird woman from this book I'm reading said to do this. She seems to have a decent amount of her shit together, so I'm gonna do it..."

Do this and you're missing it. Entirely! What a waste of your life! This is you just functioning. And you're already functioning, and we're DONE living this way! So, go Find that pussy (ANY kinda pussy you want!!!) and give it a stroke. ***And be in the moment of the stroke***.

Notice when Bob, Toad and Francis come in saying, "WTF are you doing? We don't have time for this!!" Just notice. Then, speak to them, out loud, "Why, guys?! We don't have time 'cause I'm too busy existing from one moment to the next with no reprieve in sight! That's not flippin' fun!! I'm DONE existing! I'm done not feeling grateful! I AM TRYING ON THE DRESS!!!"

Stroke that pussy. And be grateful that it came into your world. Sing it out loud, "Freaking **thanks!**". If you go out for a pussy walk and fail to find one (this is **the** PERFECT chance to choose Gratitude [and not the Quick-Fix Plum]), you have two options here:

OPTION 1: Be pissed off!

1. Time to go pet a pussy. Off I go …

2. Of course there wasn't gonna be a cat when I decide to do this STUPID thing and go on a cat hunt… not a pussy in sight!

3. * goes home, furious at the ridiculousness of it all*

4. * Back to 'functioning' with even more evidence of why me and my life are so shitty! *

Or

OPTION 2: Get Grateful AF for the Crazy!

Notice how ace you are for even attempting this. And KNOW that you choosing to "fail" with The Trio of Terror giving you the hardest time about how this is a "confirmation of how pathetic you truly are" and you STILL choose to decide to go out for a pussy pet again tomorrow means you win on a completely and utterly different scale. You 10x your Great Gratitude 101 expansion. And every day that it doesn't "work" and you don't fall back into, "Poor me, of COURSE it wasn't gonna be...blah, blah, blah...", you win harder and harder. That pussy will come, and it'll be the most transformative climax you'll EVER feel. So, keep petting that pussy...

This number 2 response **is** The Gratitude Attitude, and it shouldn't be centred only around petting pussies. Seek to have this Gratitude Attitude in as many areas of your life as possible.

My Grandpop epitomised A Gratitude Attitude. He always sought out the lovely. Even at the end of his life, when his heart was giving up, his body was breaking down, and the most he could manage was pootling[32] as a passenger in the car. Looking out of the window at the world passing him by, he'd return home saying, "I've had the most wonderful time", taking us through a rundown of his favourite smells, clouds and colours. Grandpop's gratitude was next level. You don't have to be this – he was kind of superhuman! Just look for a hint of joy in the chaos – and be pleased with yourself **wanting** to want to seek it.

TRIO OF TERROR TRICKERY

Now, Bob, Toad and Francis, in their typical Trio of Terror ways, are terrified of you stepping into gratitude because this means you'll stop

---

[32] To move in a leisurely, indirect way.

looking for Quick-Fix Plums and seize opportunities to step on your Rainbow Road, moving out of their "Safehouse" Zone. So, be ready for some mind-fudgery:

*I'm meant to feel grateful for what I have already (which I don't actually want!) YET my natural state of being **is** to want more? You've told me it's predetermined within me – meaning there's not a fat lot I can do about this external craving for more? WHAT DO YOU WANT FROM ME, EMMA!?!*

I'm not meant to want the car, but I'm meant to be grateful for my clapped-out three-door?! But I'm not!

I'm not meant to want the man of my dreams, but I'm meant to love myself first?! But I don't!

I'm not meant to want the big-ass house, but I'm meant to be grateful for my one-bedroom bedsit[33]?! But I'm not!

*I want the house. The pony. The Neverfull MM Monogram Canvas Louis Vuitton. I can't not!! **And now**, thanks to you, I feel guilty AF because you're telling me that feeling grateful for what I've already got is my #1 meal ticket to actualising this More you speak of! What in the world do I do?!*

The answer is **not** to squish the spirit of wanting-moreness that's innate to you – hoping to end the Gratitude Quest once and for all. The Trio of Terror will LOVE this futile attempt and will trowel on a shitload of familiar shame just for good measure.

The answer is to...

---

[33]   A unit in a shared property where the tenant lives in the unit and shares parts of the home, like the kitchen and bathroom, with the people in the building.

ACCEPT WHERE YOU'RE AT

To truly get More, you must first accept that:

- You want more.
- What you have doesn't feel like it's enough.
- You're frustrated.
- Your best doesn't feel good enough.
- You don't truly feel grateful.

In acknowledging this (without listening to the sneers of The Trio of Terror), you are accepting the humanness of the experience which comes hand in hand with the mission of becoming the Youest version of You. Done. Out in the open. The elephant in the room has finally left. "BYE!"

To Action

MAKE "RIGHT-NOW" GRATITUDE LINKS

Along with this willingness to accept where you're at with brutal honesty, you'll begin to notice when that habit of trying to Quick-Fix-Plum-it materialises. When you chomp at the leathery surface of a plum that's out there, and feel that familiar, unfulfilled search rise to the surface, dragging you out of the moment and deeming what's to come as something "better", THIS is your Entry-Level Access Point opening UP! Watching this happen inside you will allow you to get a glimpse of something deeper and greater than you. And you'll rejoice, with kindness, ease and love as you say, "Of course it doesn't feel enough. Of course I still believe the lie that the juicy lifeforce lies outside of me. How silly, but it's okay. I'll stay curious..."

Then ask yourself, "Is there something even remotely linked to something I already have that I can be grateful for instead?"

Pick the thing you're doing right now. Say it out loud, "Sitting on the sofa", for example. THEN, sniff your lavender and find what you're grateful for in this. Is it comfy? Are you warm? Is it raining and you're safely protected from the elements? Then, put it into a gratitude sentence (whether you believe it or not right now): "I am so super grateful to be snuggled on the sofa". Gratitude Attitude in the most mundane moment. Done! Refocus and find that space to be Thankful.

Maybe you still want the bag. Or to bang that super-hot guy at the bar (again) that you KNOW is no good for you – and that it's just a Quick-Fix Plum. Fine! Go do it! Fuck! Resisting those kinda wants is gonna make that plum turn into a prune (and there isn't a person alive who enjoys prunes!!!). So, do it. Then learn. And reflect.

Did it feel like everything you hoped and wanted it to?

No?

It's time to call in a new being – outside of The Trio...

It's time to boot out those three (who are having a great Trio Time here, at your expense!) and call in Grace, who will give you a brand-spanking new perspective. Heck, call her first, if you're feeling brave enough (you might save yourself £1,400 or save yourself from getting an STI). Let's talk a little more about Grace...

Because if Bob, Toad and Francis were to have one archnemesis, it would be her.

Grace

Gréjs

Noun

1. smoothness and elegance of movement.
   "she moved through the water with effortless grace"

2. courteous good will.
   "She had the good grace to apologise to her afterwards"

3. bring honour or credit to (someone or something) by one's attendance or participation.
   "She is one of the best players ever to have graced the game"

Grace is that loving being that's been missing from your life. Grace gives zero shits what you get up to (like, literally, NONE! Not about overflowing wardrobes with designer handbags when you have NO cash in your bank or STIs). She is a constant presence you can always feel. She's there – you just might have lost sight of her for a moment as The Trio have been so loud!

She is warm, loving and inviting. There is literally nothing you could do to disappoint or upset her. She's as old as time and as wise as all of the most brilliant mystics put together, times one million! She sees the story behind every "fuck-up" and simply says:

> *My sweet baby girl, we've got this. This too shall pass, and in time, it will all make sense. I'll hold you and love you as it fades, which it always will, no matter how bad it feels.*

Grace is your ally every time you **want** to want to see things differently. She's there through every branch that Bob swings from. She's there every time Toad tempts you with another wart-bomb and each time Francis slings another "You're not good enough" Poison Apple at your head. Every time The Trio tells you that you're too much or not enough, that your plum is DEFINITELY out there in that next job title or the next sized-down clothes or one more baby or that proposal, you must learn to turn to Grace.

HAND IT OVER TO GRACE

When you can feel yourself in search of that Quick-Fix Plum, ask yourself two questions:

1. *What are The Trio of Terror saying about this?*
2. *What would Grace say? (AKA what would you say to your best friend in the whole wide world?)*

Grace isn't exclusive to just a select few people who seem to love themselves and think themselves to be brilliant, no matter how many times they "mess up" (that's just what The Trio want you to believe!). She is available to you too. But she lives in the depth of the Subconscious, at the end of that Rainbow Road. And you must make space in the Unconscious garden for that purple pathway to be laid out, for her to walk into your life and bring all of that Grace and Gratitude into your world.

When you feel yourself on the hunt for happiness out there ("I'll just email that potential job", when you only moved to this one 6 months ago thinking **this** space was **the** place, or "Maybe we should have another baby" or "Just one more handbag can't hurt..."), ask yourself (out loud if you're feeling really brave), "Is this The Trio thinking my answers lie outside?" **Then** call in Grace and say, "**I hand this over to you, Grace. Help me to see**". She will give you the balance you seek.

LIFE GETS TO BE AN ICE CREAM SUNDAE SANCTUARY

Life gets to feel like an Ice Cream Sundae Sanctuary where you are safe to eat as many Ice Cream Sundaes as you want **with** the sweet and juicy plum (not the pruny, soured one) nestled on the top. We all love a sweet plum. It's yum! And we're also super partial to ice cream. Ice Cream is yum! So...why not have both? Because that's what life gets to be for you, too. EVERYTHING that you want!

You get to have:

1. The exterior Plum-Bonus stuff, which will feel bloody brilliant
2. Gratitude for everything you already have
3. No NEED for that "Thing" to come with its plum juices and "fix" you
4. The acceptance of you wanting More

Learning to feel grateful for your life in this way means you get to eat ice cream in abundance every single day. There will be shitty days when your ice cream falls splat on the floor and gets covered with little stones, leaves and splinters of wood. Everyone stares. Passers-by walk and step through it. **But** those with a Gratitude Attitude will STILL find something (***any freaking thing*** – it can be **hard** sometimes***!!!***) in this: a snack for the ants, an opportunity for one more sale for the shop when you go to get another (sometimes you have to dig DEEP!), but there will **always** be a nugget to indulge in for a mind with a strong purple part of their Rainbow Road – there's something to feel Grateful AF for in the Crazy (I like to challenge myself to see how crazy my gratitude levels can get in all kinds of crazies)! Harbour this skill and you'll TRULY get to have it all!

Then, when that plum **does** come along (which it WILL, when moving in these superhuman spaces) – it's the icing on the cake, the jewel in the crown, the sprinkles on top. The plum is a "nice-to-have bonus", but it is NOT the main event. It is **not** an essential requirement for you to feel like you're living a fully fulfilled life.

In short: You get the Mulberry bag, the hot hubby/wife/whoever the funk you want to fuck, the luxury holidays **and** a deep-seated gratitude for yourself and your life, in its present state, in complete totality. The answer is NEVER the Plum. The plum only becomes a problem if you depict it as **the** answer to life being filled with love, gratitude and happiness.

MIND. BLOWING! Right?

Ground yourself in gratitude within the crazy of everything that you already have. For you to begin the Ice Cream Sundae Quest of living this way, look at what is already right in front of you.

The quality of your existence will be determined by your capacity to seek to see gratitude in the darkest, most hidden depths of your current circumstance.

THANKFUL THURSDAY HIGHLIGHTS

1. Wear your lavender purples. Get curious around what, where and how you've become distracted by a Quick-Fix Plum Idea (AKA where you think the answer to your happiness lies outside of you, often in doing, having or losing something).

2. To move through the illusion of having a certain Quick-Fix Plum as your ultimate answer, wear your purples and get curious around what you've already got which you can **teach** your mind to get grateful for. Most often, it's hidden within the shit storm of everything you're going through. Don't force it, just hunt...Can you see honesty as you are being lied to? Can you Find bravery in challenging times? Everything in The Universe contains its opposite. It's time to get creative and alchemise what you've been through. Sometimes you have to dig DEEP, but gratitude **will** be there. It all depends on your attitude towards it as to whether you'll seek with enough curiosity to Find it...

3. To help you get grateful, go and pet a pussy. Be grateful and grounded in the moment. Notice how The Trio wants to rush you forward, back into "existing" with, "We haven't got time for this silliness!!" Notice this, smile and pet that pussy (any pussy is perfect – oi oi!)

4. Call in Grace to give you space. Use "The Actions" and curious questions posed throughout this Purple Chapter to lay the purple part of your Rainbow Road so Grace can get through to you. Remember her words: *"My sweet baby girl, we've got this. This too shall pass,*

and in time, it will all make sense. I'll hold you and love you as it fades, which it always will, no matter how bad it feels".

REMEMBER:

Mind-on-Mute Mondays:

Wear your Minty Greens and explore this mind-blowing fact:

There is a voice inside your head.

This voice is <u>not</u> You.

Seek to notice every time he's getting his knickers in a twist, and snap a branch from his most favourite, familiar neurological brain-loops so he starts to become less comfortable travelling these outdated routes. Get curious around the idea that if there is a voice speaking, then who is the one listening?

That voice is You!

You will not know it the first moment you contemplate it, but you will come to know it. And once you do, you won't care to "understand" and "know". You'll just let it be. Here you'll feel a freedom you had no idea could exist for you.

To access your Mind-on-Mute Monday supplementary supportive workbooks and videos, please <u>CLICK HERE</u>.

REMEMBER:

Trigger-Free Tuesday:

Wear your Orangy Tangerines.

Toad believes that everyone else is to blame and that it'd all be just fine and dandy if **they** all stopped being such arseholes! Your job here is to be like Teflon: create a Space to Choose Freedom between the stuff happening outside of you and how you are reacting or responding to it. Keep laying the tangerine part of your Rainbow Road. Notice every time you see you're on the hunt for your Toad/wanting to bathe in someone else's firework explosions and say, "I see you and it's **not** going down this way ANYmore!!"

To access your Trigger-Free Tuesday workbook and supporting video, please CLICK HERE.

REMEMBER:

Wake-up Wednesdays:

Wear your watermelon pink and learn how to be kind to your mind. You're only thinking this way because all of those harsh voices that told you that you weren't "good enough" for this world got so loud that they've become etched inside your mind. Now, on eternal replay as your Francis, you've listened to them/her for so long that you've got confused. You think she is you and that you are her. You aren't. And the way to see this is to notice where she is introducing poisonous, grudge-bearing and controlling toxicity into your life, telling you it's good for you/all you deserve. When you spot this, remember that she is the overbearingly over-protective friend, and **not** the fiend she's doing a REALLY good job of pretending to be. You aren't landing yourself in the Street, the Cell or in a Casket. You're moving into new spaces – a wide open sea. Once she realises that the water's fine, she'll come join you. But you must move first.

To access your Wake-Up Wednesday supplementary supportive workbooks and videos, please CLICK HERE.

REMEMBER:

Thankful Thursdays:

Embody your lavender purples as you quit the pursuit of finding ways to Quick-Fix yourself. Centre yourself in the knowledge that all the stuff that you want on the outside of you materialises through grounding yourself in being grateful AF for the present moment and all it contains: shit shows and all! Sometimes finding gratitude in these shit-show situations feels like a push too far, but without this, your hunt for Quick-Fix Plums will continue to **drain** the joy out of your life.

When you feel drained, you've simply forgotten that you get to eat ice cream for breakfast, lunch and dinner, and that the plum is merely the cherry on top. When you find yourself down the lane, driving yourself round the BEND[34], looking for that sweet-treat promise outside of you, call in Grace. Get willing to do it differently. Find something to get grateful for in this obscure ride around the sun that we're all on.

To access your Thankful Thursday supplementary supportive workbooks and videos, please CLICK HERE.

---

[34] *Round the bend* means when you're doing foolish, silly things.

Feel-It Friday
COMFORTABLE WITH ME

Our feelings are our most genuine paths to knowledge. They are chaotic, sometimes painful, sometimes contradictory, but they come from deep within us. And we must key into those feelings and begin to extrapolate from them, examine them for new ways of understanding our experiences. This is how new visions begin, how we begin to posit a new future nourished by the past. This is what I mean by matter following energy, and energy following feeling. Our visions begin with our desires.

—*Audre Lorde*

Introducing The Brave Buffalo

In life, you have two choices: one is to continue to replicate the life you've been taught to live, and the other is to learn how to get brave and do it differently. *When you've spent a big-ass chunk of your life in the 'Feeling-Emotions-is-Bad' Bootcamp, you accumulate a backlog of tricky emotions that have gotten a little (a lot!!) stuck. In this chapter, you're going to learn why they're still there. You'll also learn how to shimmy them on their merry way ("bye, babes!!") to make more space for the ones you actually want.*

To do this, we're going to work on the almond scented, blue painted part of your Rainbow Road, which means you must:

1. Get your blues OUT to help you Piggyback Sensory Hack™ the concept that feeling blue isn't as frightening as you think.
2. Read this Feel-It Friday chapter and do what it says, especially the sensory stuff. You've had your first taster of how you step closer to You, through connecting to gratitude. Now it's time to stop "being strong" by holding onto your emotions and learn that it's safe to feel.
3. Remember to say, "Fudge it", over and over again. Play pretend as you try on the freaking dress of the ideas I present around getting comfortable with feeling your feelings.

"You're asking me to open Pandora's Box. I think I'll internally combust!"

You won't! Try it on.

"I thought being strong was a *good* thing. I can't let down my walls like that..."

Fudge. It. And. Try. It. On.

"I've got to feel feelings I've buried deep for longer than I can remember?! Why?!"

Just go...

Fudge. It. And. Try. It. On.

...and as often as possible, using your Pause Thoughts™ and your Almond and Blue Sensory Experience.

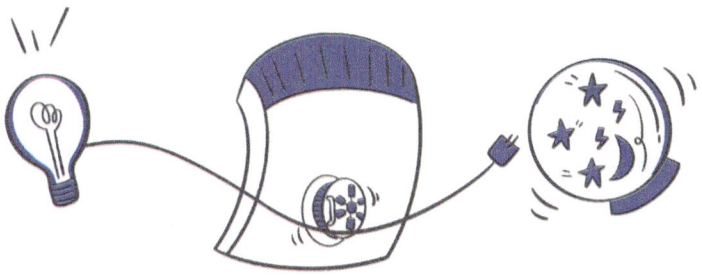

One day, this silliness will slide on like a glove and you'll say:

"Goodness gracious ME!! Trying to avoid feeling emotions was actually just me smushing them down deeper into my being. EVERY time something happened that tried to make me deal with this emotion, I chose to "be strong", "keep on trucking" and "not cause a fuss", but I was actually locking up that Me-est version of Me behind a barricade I didn't know how to break down. I've been running away like a coward thinking it was strength. Now, I'm a freaking BUFFALO, open to navigating whatever comes to face me."

The idea of feeling your feelings probably feels pretty peculiar...I know it's brand new, but it's BRILLIANT!

HERE'S THE CHALLENGE...

Life hurts. In really bizarrely peculiar ways. It often hurts you in ways that would wash over others. Their pains can be totally opposite to yours, and that's just fine. What **isn't** fine is you thinking (or being outrightly directed to think) that:

◊ The way you're feeling isn't okay
◊ Your emotions are too much, inappropriate or disproportionate to the circumstances
◊ You're wrong or too sensitive
◊ You're the only one who's losing their shit whilst the rest of the world has it all under control

When you think this way, you repress how you actually feel and you join the charade of making out like you've got it all together too, when in reality, you're like a swan – pretending you're chill on the outside, but frantically paddling underneath.

Living this way keeps You lost, and without a Rainbow Road, The Trio is well and truly in charge. They've taught you how to round up all of the negative emotions you don't want to feel and bury them behind a wall (that you've made 100 feet high!). To build this stellar wall, you've dredged up almost **all** of the blue parts of your Rainbow Road and used them to build it...but now it's cracking. It's losing its electric blue vibrancy and it's turning grey. It's crumbling down around you, and you don't know what to do. Feel-It Friday is going to show you just what you do, and it's going to feel FREEING! Feeling your feelings means letting a feeling run its course by either:

◊ Sitting with it – with curiosity as to where it will take you
◊ Expressing it outwardly – as and when something inspires you to

This is what Feel-It Friday is ALL about.

Your now automatic reaction to this idea of feeling whatever the funk needs to be felt whenever it needs to be felt might induce an internal cry of, "It's inappropriate. I'm just sensitive. It's scary. I can't! What will everyone think?"

If this is you...GOOD! You've found this work for a REASON!

HERE'S WHAT YOU CAN CHOOSE TO SEEK...

For some (me before The 7 Steps), attempting to connect to tricky emotions might feel weirder than if an alien were to walk out of your wardrobe[35] right now wielding his little glowing finger towards you.

---

35   Another word for *closet*.

Truly embracing and feeling emotions, to most, feels alien.

"Shutting down" your feelings to the world might seem like a pretty self-preserving way to go through life, **especially** when you've spent such a long-ass time feeling hurt by it. On Feel-It Friday, you are going to get to a space where you understand why you made that wall in the first place. You then get to decide if it's time to let it fall so you can open yourself up to the freedom of feeling whatever is necessary to feel in that moment.

In learning to do this, you'll feel the bravest you've ever felt. You'll actually want to step forward in a "feeling emotions is pretty cool" kind of way.

By the end of this chapter, you'll be able to:

- Notice the spark of an emotional response and be open to whatever the heck it is without judgement or worry. You'll weirdly start getting a little excited after the first couple of times when you know what lies on the other side of Feeling your Feeling.

- Feel it however it needs to be felt (physically, emotionally, mentally).
- Express it without directing it at anyone or anything. It just is.
- Move on with your day – lighter, aligned and filled with an indescribable endless energy that's meant to be coursing through you.

Even with all of the deliciousness I'm describing, perhaps you're still reluctant to learn how to feel your feelings because of several lingering fears. Some of those might be:

The fear of judgement: *"What will others think if I'm a blubbering wreck all of a sudden?"*

The fear of overwhelm: *"What if I take the lid off Pandora's Box, can't get it all back in and lose the plot[36] completely?!"*

The fear of losing who you are: *"I don't want to lose myself completely. I still want to be the same person".*

The fear of losing control: *"I may not be enjoying life all that much, but at least I know where I stand".*

The fear of this 'You' being a lesser version of the you that is familiar: *"What if after all of this I find this Capital Y version of me and she's even worse?! I'm barely coping with what I'm managing right now!*

Feel-It Friday is going to show you just how these fears around feelings are a huge driver behind why you're stuck feeling so pants. Feel-It Friday is designed so that these fears lift easily and you don't have to crowbar yourself into feeling your feelings just because you now feel like you "should".

To truly achieve this, you're going to need your Pause Thoughts™.

---

[36] To *lose the plot* means to lose one's ability to understand or cope with what is happening.

PAUSE THOUGHTS™

Feel-It Friday Pause Thoughts™ are all about the *Almond* Blue[37] Sensory Stimulants in order to reach the Subconscious.

Right now, your Conscious Brain is busy doing almost ALL of the work, telling you that "soldiering on", "being strong" and saying, "I'm fine", whenever anyone asks you is THE way to go.

"What a trooper." BLAH!!!

It's not the way, and the Almond Blues are going to help you Find *Your* way. Right now, however, let's acknowledge that on some level you continue to believe that this "trooper strength" mentality is helpful to you. To doubt is the role of the Conscious thinking part of the mind, and let's remember that we CANNOT change this through forcing thought and knowing what you "should" do. Forcing things has been the biggest part of our problem up to this point. Your job here is to accept the nature of the Conscious Mind whilst simultaneously getting curious AF about it!

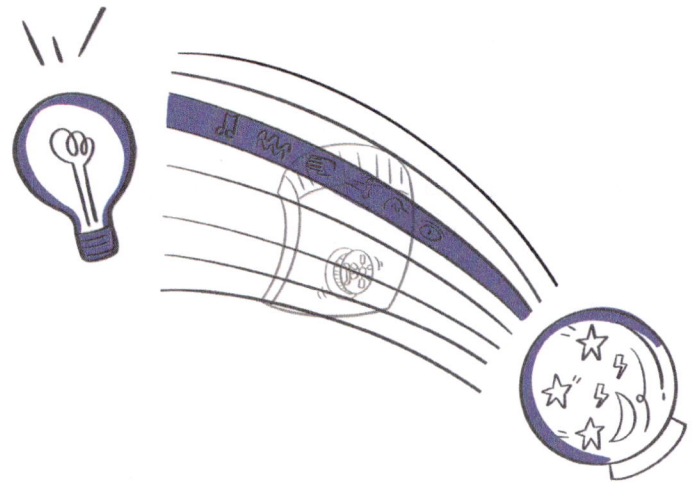

---

[37] This is the one area of the work where I just couldn't get those colour/scent matches – so just be gentle with me here, please. Equally, if you have allergies, please find your own tastes/ scents or make Friday's focus primarily around the blue.

THEN, your job is to create that bright blue part of your Rainbow Road, piggybacking the notions I share *from* your (doubting) Conscious Mind, *through* that Emotional change-making space of your Unconscious and *into* the Subconscious.

TO DO THIS EASILY, AS YOU READ THIS CHAPTER, YOU MUST EMBODY ALMOND SCENTS AND BLUE COLOURS.

As you read Feel-It Friday, I need you to embody blues, be they electric, sky or aqua. Wear your blue hairband or find a view of the deep blue. Nibble on your almonds. Slurp your almond milk latte (my favourite). Have a Disaronno or a Dr Pepper. Wear your blue bum bag[38], bathing suit or bikini. Paint your nails with blue electric bolts. Bust out the bakewell tarts[39]. All the Almond Blue blasts, whilst reading about the power of Feel-It Friday, will allow the knowledge to marinate within your Unconscious Mind, making space for the feeling of safety. Moving along the blue part of your Rainbow Road from the standpoint of the Subconscious will allow the Power to Feel to flood through.

Each Friday, carry this Almondy Blue sensory reminder with you. Each time you see, smell, taste or touch it, create a Pause Thought™ for

[38] Another word for *fanny pack*.
[39] An English tart made with almond jam.

yourself. Make space within The Unconscious for more of what will bring Actual You into alignment. Feeling your feelings isn't as frightening as The Trio of Terror are making it out to be. It's bloody brilliant!

AND it gets to be easy. **And** you're going to learn how to do it...

Ready?

MY APPROACH TO FEELING MY FEELINGS BEFORE FEEL-IT FRIDAY

Life before this 7-Step Formula could be summarised with two words: "I functioned". And the way I did this was by overthinking and underfeeling. Through this suppression, I heightened my sensitivities to a piercing level where **everything** bothered me. Everything felt like a personal attack. Everything hurt, yet I felt simultaneously numb to it all.

Flippin' WEIRD!

It was because I didn't trust myself. I didn't trust that I was capable of handling what was contained within. It felt like truly feeling and experiencing would take the lid off Pandora's box, and I didn't know what the flippin' heck was going to come writhing out.

So, I kept the lid on – TIGHT!

But one moment changed my experience with emotions, eternally. I hope my sharing it here will open up that primitive space in you to begin to explore your emotions too:

I sat in the garden of our beautiful home, admiring the growing aware-ness that I was harnessing for feeling gratitude towards the things which, before these 7 Steps, went missed. As I sat, something stirred within. No words could describe this moment. That's the thing with messages from The Subconscious – they fall outside of 3D senses and therefore no words can depict them. But it rumbled. From the deep belly of my being.

A new and strange sensation. It's weird. And uncontrolled. And it clawed to come out.

Was it a noise? A sigh? A breath? Who blooming-well KNOWS!? Not me – I think that's what terrified me most!

"It can't come out!" I panicked. "The neighbours will hear. HOW EMBARRASSING!"

*"Stop it. Stop. Noooooo!" I could hear The Trio in tandem, squealing at me. But against **every** part of my conscious being (The Trio were **fuming** here!!) I chose to brave this Pause Thought™ as a moment of exploration. Gulp!*

A moment to notice The Trio's immediate, instinctive attempt to sup-press what I was feeling.

I chose to step into that Blue space and observe it.

A volcanic emotional eruption from the depths of me spilled out. A moan that sounded animalistic. Francis, Toad and Bob clawed at it, "Stop it, you weirdo! You're losing control. This is SO BAD!"

Yet still, somehow, I stayed with it.

*And then (and this is the most absolutely GLORIOUS part!!!) it passed. It went away – **totally**! No pushback. No remnants of it hanging in the background to dredge up at a later date. No scramble for, "What in the world was that!? What does it mean?! What did I do?! Did I do it right?!"*

Just stillness.

It took up a second, maybe two – max! A couple of beats of discomfort and then...nothing. Peace. Clarity.

It felt as if I could take on the freaking WORLD! And at that moment, I was lighter. Something weighty and restrictive had released within me. An old, painfully trapped emotion had finally died. Francis had lost some power. Toad was sulking in an extinguished puddle of his own piss. And Bob was sitting at the base of his favourite tree looking up curiously at how that branch that he favoured so intensely snapped and broke his favourite course of direction.

"I've gotta do more of THIS!" I cried out loud as I sat dazed and con-fused on the grass in my garden with a Cheshire Cat grin spread across my face like I'd just lapped up an entire pail of Oreo-flavoured ice cream.

This moment gave me a taste of what life could feel like. This climatic, blissful space of feeling and being at one with myself, without being deep in a meditation or with a guide, **had** to be explored! Although I didn't know precisely what it was, I knew that what had released was a painful emotion. It didn't matter what. Knowing this was enough. Feeling free is feeling free. Full stop! It got me thinking...

So, maybe allowing those suppressed feels I feel (that I'm super embarrassed that I feel) of:

- *Anger*
- *Jealousy*
- *Shame*
- *Bitterness*

- *Resentment*
- *Fear...*

...to come forward isn't as scary as The Trio are making it out to be. Keeping a lid on Pandora's box is turning it into my casket – yikes!!!

I got curious, and this curiosity created Feel-It Friday. To breathe life into this fifth step, I first needed to see where it all started...

SQUISHED SO HARD YOU BELIEVED THEM

Your parents love you. Fact!

They've done shitty things and hurt you in ways you didn't know that you could be hurt. Obvious things: verbal, physical and sexual abuse. Neglect. Ridicule. There are also the less obvious ways, which feel close to impossible to actively "put your finger on", but you know they're there (and on some level, they do too).

However they did it, and to whatever extremes they enacted it upon you, it hurt you!

It might not feel like it, but their actions are purely a reflection of how badly *they're* hurt.

> **Hurt people hurt people.**
>
> —The Script

And this doesn't just go for parents; it's friends, colleagues, random people you meet in a bar who behave in a way where you think, "What in the world was that all about!?" Everyone is hurting. And most are hurting pretty badly.

There is a group of people who still accidentally hurt people (such is the human experience!) but are so actively aware of their own shit show that they're open to learning through as much of it as is humanly possible. Being nurtured by these beings tastes a different kind of sweet.

Some children are lucky enough to have parents devoted to learning and growing. These parents know that they've got a shit show going on inside themselves, are taking full responsibility for this, and are doing the work to open their hearts, own their mistakes, apologise, and show up in life in a new way, over and over again...

But 99.9999% of us didn't have those parents. Most of the world does **not** work within these parameters (hence why it's such a train wreck!). Most of us had parents who didn't **know** that there's a different way to do all of this.

And can you blame them, really?

Having a willingness to see yourself as raw and imperfect is completely counter to the way you have been taught to view yourself for the last however many years old you are.

Being here, right now, reading this (and getting this far), puts you in that 0.000000001% of the population.

You're a changemaker! Changemakers want to see what's behind the curtain that the rest of the world doesn't want to acknowledge is even there.

To understand why it feels like you're the *only one* who seems to be even attempting to do anything differently, let's first explore why it's so hard for them to stop being such a dick. Why it all must fall on you, and why you've got to come to peace with this fact:

When you were born you knew:

- *What you loved*
- *What lit your soul on fire*

- *How to go about getting the things you wanted*
- *How to say a big phat "NO!" to the things you didn't like*
- *What the funk you were doing (whilst simultaneously **not** knowing but taking steps to explore and learn – which is **the** beautiful thing about children)*

But your parents didn't like this liberated little thing running around the shop, making them feel like they didn't have a CLUE what the heck they were doing. Your teachers didn't like it either. Neither did your siblings. Neither did the shop assistant who likes children to be seen and not heard)...nor the doctor. Neither did pretty much anyone who had any kind of access to you.

*They squished You out of you. They made you feel **so** wrong, or put you on a pedestal **so** high, that the part of You that wasn't afraid to make mistakes went deep into hiding.*

It happens this way because they simply repeated what happened to them (to the letter of their parents' Back-to Emotional "Safehouse" strategy). Either that *or* they did a 180 and swung the pendulum in the opposite direction, causing opposite extreme results in you. Their parents squished *them* out of them. The same way theirs squished *them* outta them...and the grandparents before...and even before that...

It's a neverending cycle of squishing. All in an attempt to make life "easier" for their favourite people – aka YOU! Therefore, they impress their feelings of:

"Oh, I acted just the way you are right now, and life was really tough for me. I like you so much, and I really don't want that for you, so I'm gonna force you not to be that way so you might do a 'better' job than me. I think I've learned from my mistakes and me forcing these on you means that it'll all work better for you!"

A child's brain accepts what it is told as truth. Add to this being surrounded by adults who are:

- Committed to wanting to "understand" and control everything in their Conscious Mind
- Fixated on shaping you into what they believe will be more readily accepted by the world to avoid you getting hurt
- Confused AF by their *umwelt* sensory experience of the world around them whilst being simultaneously desperate to be in control of it because they feel so hurt by what went before them

...and you have the **perfect** recipe for pain.

This is what living life in The Conscious Brain without The Rainbow Road to the Subconscious looks like.

LET'S GET REAL

All your parents knew was that life hurts like hell and they wanted it to be different for you. So, they *tried* (in their own warped ways we don't get) their best.

They didn't know that the answer was to provide support for you to be the brightest, best version of all that you are – weird bits and all! Instead, they did it the way they inherited, and now you're left with a LOAD of emotions which you've suppressed inside because they told you that the way you're feeling isn't "right" and that it's safer to do as others say and not express how **You** feel.

MAKE THEIR BEST GOOD ENOUGH

To move beyond pain here, you must first accept that their shoddy best was precisely that...the best that they were capable of doing, with what they had available to them at the time. It was their best and it's **got** to be good enough. Maybe you don't want to believe this because somehow, believing this means that you're coming somewhat close to forgiving them. And The Trio tells you, "Forgiving them means that you liked what they did!" But this is simply not true. You get to explore a new definition today. And it goes something like this:

*"What they did was **not okay.** It was actually far from it! And, if I had a choice, I'd opt for something very different. But that's not the choice I have right now – therefore, I'm open to exploring the idea that they did the best they could do with what they had. Anything other is only torment upon myself".*

Exploring what releasing this notion might feel like will be transformative for you. You don't have to go all out and forgive them in this moment – you've just gotta be willing to get curious (get that dress out ...).

If this definition feels good for you, and you want to release this pain and suffering at the hands of their less-than-Grade-A parenting choices, continue to explore this. Remind yourself of it every time you see your almond blues. Contemplate it with an air of, "I wonder if I could feel differently about him/her/them. Write it onto your mirror and have it as the first thing that you see in the morning. Play with the notion: *Might I forgive them? Could it even be possible?* For those things that might feel impossible at first, create an Entry-Level Access Point to begin exploring from.

YOU WERE BORN TO FEEL

As a kid, you don't have problems considering and processing your emotions (anger, forgiveness, the whole sliding scale). They just **are** – like pooping (it happens!).

You're a screaming ball of emotions and you're **happy** to express precisely how you're feeling in whatever way feels good for you in any moment; then it's gone, eternally. The problems begin when the adults have a problem with your projection and start reminding you of it; you then start linking different emotions to it (shame, guilt, embarrassment – that's the start of emotions getting trapped).

Think of kids for a sec. Those temper tantrums, rolling around on the floor at Sainsbury's, are **precisely** how challenging emotions want to come out of you. They aren't directed towards anyone, they're just an explosion of what needs to be released. You know exactly what you want and don't want and you express it (and if it's going unheard, you **scream** it) straight into the world.

This triggers the bejesus out of all of the adults! They'll literally do anything to try to make it stop (**especially** if it's in public!):

- Guilt trips
- Shouting
- Eye rolls
- The silent treatment
- Head shaking
- Scolding
- Mocking
- Ridiculing
- Smacking...

The ways they attempt to make it stop are literally endless. Most often, their methodology to halter your wildness falls in line with how their parents **finally** pushed it out of them.

Over time (depending on how strong your Rainbow Road between the Conscious and Subconscious is, and how relentless they were), they won. You stopped being so You. You stopped expressing yourself in whatever guise felt good for You in that moment. And You start being more like what they're telling You to be, pleasing them first whilst suppressing anything that stirs within, labelling it as strange and alien-like, something to distrust and feel scared of.

"But why do we do this?" I hear you cry, "Why do we automatically give in?!"

It's because it's simpler in the moment – and the brain is always looking to chill out with a brew and biscuit (even from when we're really small). It's the natural space we're always looking to default back to, even then.

When parents are giving you love, attention, appreciation, celebration and admiration for behaving in the way they perceive to be a "good job", they stop giving you such a hard time and, superficially (in that moment), life feels MUCH SIMPLER, SO much simpler than you coming up against their scorn and anger every time you get something "wrong".

This un-merry dance forces you to place less awareness on what's happening inside your Rainbow Road and more awareness *outside* of You.

This chain of events causes you to distrust your own intuitions, feelings and emotions, **especially** the big ones.

OUT OF THE SUBCONSCIOUS AND INTO THE CONSCIOUS

Acting outside the path of your natural Rainbow Road alignment forces you to **think** more, to come more into your Conscious Brain where you have to "know" and "logically (lol!) figure it out'". Moving through life this way literally forces you off that Rainbow Road and into Bob's tormented thinking of, "Will the world like it if I behave in this way?"

Functioning this way drives your awareness even further out of You and Your feelings. So lost, and untrusting of yourself, you look to your parents like they have the answers, mainly because they've spent your whole life telling you that they do. The Trio LOVES this! It keeps you in the Conscious Mind where the three of them are having a BLAST!! But thinking was never meant to be the Number 1 means of awareness. Humans have evolved in such a way that it's now all we rely upon, mainly because of the parenting process we've inherited. Your parents have convinced you to think that they know what you don't. This makes you always feel yourself being drawn to checking in to ask them what they think[40].

It's like you're on the outside of you, looking out there for all of the answers, feeling super unsafe within your body. And you're getting older and feel like you "should" be able to handle it all. And now, they aren't around quite as often (maybe due to their incessant bullshit you've cut them off completely), but that deeper attachment is still there and linked (that's why you still, every now and again, wish that you could just pick up the phone and they'd **finally** give you everything you need to hear).

Life still happens. And bigger emotions build. Deep down, you know you gotta feel these emotions.

Only...you don't.

Instead, you just hold on tighter.

---

[40] Even if you had the most lovingly supportive parents on the planet who celebrated your every waking breath, this is just another metamorphosis of you thinking your parents know something about you that you don't – like your hidden naughtiness is something to be confused by. They've defined you as "good", and "brilliant" and "perfect" and they reject anything that doesn't align with this. And even if you aren't scolded for this, the underlying message is Rainbow Road destruction!!

EMOTIONAL BOUNCY BALLS

To allow your Conscious Brain (the freaking gate keeper) to let in anything new, there must be some "logic" to it. This is your Entry-Level Access Point. Remember, The Trio wants you alive (if you die, the game's over for everyone). Therefore, if the moves that I'm asking you to make hint at a shred of sense to them (i.e. the promise of a clear tree-route without broken branches, Dope or an unlimited supply of apples), they'll grant access, and **this** makes the process **sooooo** much easier.

To do this, I bring you the concept of "Emotional Bouncy Balls".

A definition of these balls goes like this:

An Emotional Bouncy Ball is a sphere of energy which is absolute and equal in size, potency and vibration/bounce to the emotion being experienced. It is created the moment this feeling is first encountered, remaining within until it is consummated and released. Some balls are super big. Some are tiny. Some have gargantuan spring. And some have very little power and hardly make a ripple at all.

Every emotion you feel is a bouncy ball. Some balls hold energies of love, joy and freaking HIGH vibes. When you feel these in your being, you feel like your whole body is alive with a fizzy feeling you're excited to express.

Big, strong emotions have a HUGE amount of kinetic energy[41]. Less intense emotions hardly bounce at all.

These balls are different from any you'll find in a gumball machine. They pass into and out of your body.

Big-ass emotions, with their huge amounts of energy, hit HARD! Much like catching a pro baseball player's home-run-hit ball in the gut. The difference between the Emotional Bouncy Ball and the baseball is this:

Baseball: You take a hit to the gut. It hurts. You don't want it to have happened. But you recognise that it quite clearly has. It's visibly obvious to you (and everyone else watching). You dust yourself off and limply throw the ball back into the field. They pick it up and take it away. The bruise fades and everyone gets on with their lives.

---

[41] Energy which a body possesses by virtue of being in motion. (Definition from <u>Oxford Languages</u>)

Emotional Bouncy Ball: You take a hit to the gut. It hurts. You don't want it to have happened. You question the Emotional Bouncy Ball. Your parents (accidentally) did a real good job of making sure you don't trust yourself.

You doubt yourself: *Was it even there? Was it that bad? Am I overreacting? Should I stop moaning and just carry on?*

Unsure on what to do, you hope and pretend that it's not there. You hope that in doing so, it'll just fade away.

Some bouncy balls have a teeny amount of kinetic energy and have hardly entered your psyche at **all**. These fade without you ever needing to hope that they might.

But these big balls, with all their pent-up energies, are there to stay.

So, it stays. Deep in the belly (it was a HARD hit). And all of that energy remains – rolling around in your gut, or chest, or throat, or head (or whatever place your bouncy balls have decided to make their home).

It feels frantic as it's trapped within, desperate to release itself, carrying the same monumental force it entered with.

Instead of feeling it (temper tantrums at Sainsbury's are simply **not** allowed), you reject it, trying to hold it down – hold it together. So, you now have this big-ass Emotional Bouncy Ball writhing around inside of you, FILLED with the unextinguished/unexperienced kinetic energy it forced its way into you with.

All of that energy in motion, stuck and waiting...

Desperate to release.

And it doesn't just sit there quietly...not on your nelly! More things start to happen in life, which hold a mild resemblance to what created that Original Emotional Bouncy Ball in the first place.

And every time you're reminded of that big-ass emotion – through the familiarity of a scent, person, place or thing in the world that you're trying to keep locked up tight – that Bouncy Ball starts to stir, screaming:

"OOooooooo, this links directly to me...Feel this so that you can LET ME THE HELL OUTTA HERE!!! I'm full to the absolute brim of kinetic energy that's weighing you down from inside here, and I wanna spring out of you and into freeeeeeeeeeeeedom!"

But we don't let ourselves experience the emotion. It feels so unsafe. Moaning in the garden is a weird thing for neighbours to hear. So, instead, just like our parents before us, we play pretend that it's not there.

Can you think where this has happened in your world? Where you're in a space where something is known by almost **everyone** there and yet everyone would rather sit in the suppressed awkwardness of the moment, instead of allowing their Emotional Bouncy Balls to fly. It's freaking WEIRD, right?! Awkward on toast!

And through this suppression, instead of releasing the Bouncy Ball Beast (it's PISSED off at you now for not seizing this perfect opportunity to feel and **not** smush it down even deeper!), you create a new Bouncy Buddy that's linked to the first. So now, when you smell the abuser's aftershave or hear that song, you remember in the background when it happened, you now have two balls writhing in a desperate attempt to be felt and released. One emotion, now with two balls...then three... then four hundred million...

To Action

DON'T SCRAMBLE AWAY. STAY.

Now, the next time you feel something stir a Bouncy Ball and you instinctively go to distract yourself with something mind-numbing (like social media, sugary food, alcohol, drugs, reality TV) notice your scramble for escape. And stay put. In these moments, challenge yourself to breathe life into whatever this is. This might look like:

- Staying when you want to walk away (be safe, obvs! Be on the lookout for The Trio lying that you aren't safe when you absolutely are)
- Bring up the awkward thing, in a non-puke/poop/firework type of way
- Ask questions
- Express your feelings or what you perceive

Do something to validate what you're feeling. Send a signal to the bouncy ball that you know it's there, you can feel it, and you want to help it move on its merry way. Like me in the garden...it can feel awkward and uncomfortable in the lead-up, but it'll feel like heaven after you get brave, stay and don't scramble away.

THE WALL

Without a process like the one above, you attempt to scramble away from feeling your emotions. But they remain. Instead of acknowledging them and then releasing them, you strive to contain these emotions. This is actually **impossible,** so instead you attempt to suppress them.

Doing this means you create something different entirely:

You're born with a fully intact Rainbow Road (the blue part is extra bright!). With each unfelt pain and scramble, every time you get hurt by the world, you think, "Wow, that hurt. What the heck happened there?! How do I make sure it can NEVER happen to me ever again?"

In your scramble to avoid your feelings, you look to the people. You look to the places. You look to the things around you. And with this information, based upon your life experience, your perception, your *umwelt* – which I hope that, by now, you understand as being subjective to you – you scramble and scheme to intervene and block the hurt. You mull it over again and again, and every time you do, a blue brick in your Rainbow Road works loose. In your scrabbled state, you swipe one of those brightly coloured blue bricks up and out of your Rainbow Road, which was once your direct line to feeling your feelings with ease through The Subconscious.

Removed from The Rainbow Road, the colours fade further until only a hint of what once was is left. It's at this point that we begin a new kind of construction. Instead of adding to the pathway, we instead start to build a wall.

The oldest, most discoloured bricks form the foundation of it. Everything else is built on top. As the weight of the bricks of further suppressed emotions are applied, the pressure causes the bottom bricks to splinter and pulverise.

This Wall is the **perceived** strength you think is an essential requirement to "survive this life". You think the wall actually keeps those hurt-
ful things, which cause you to feel those uncomfortable emotions, as
far away from you as possible so that they don't come close to touching your internal Emotional Bouncy Ball chaos EVER again, only...

THE FALSE SAFETY OF YOUR WALL

Life lived this way continues to hurt, and you now spend so much of
your time building walls that you've got very little energy for anything
else.

"GOOD!" screams Francis. She's thinking, "You're a SUPER SAFE wall
builder and you can't move walls, which means you're staying as still
as a statue.

"Brilliant!" sing Bob and Toad.

This is The Trio's DREAM idea of keeping you "safe".

Only...The Universe doesn't want you hiding like this. So...

Life continues to hurtle situations at you, bigger and harder (to get
through that wall!) whilst you continue to attempt to hide from Bouncy
Ball Hitting Situations. Opening up and feeling the hits just isn't an
option – no siree Bob. The only option you think is available to you
(Conscious Brain stuffs) is to close in those walls further, bringing the
edges ever closer and closer to you...until eventually you've created a
once-Rainbow-Road-now-dusty-grey casket in which to live out your
years. And you carry the weight of it wherever you go. Having this Wall
means you lose on all fronts.

HOW TO STOP THE VICIOUS CYCLE

The way out for You happens when you start to recognise:

1. The triggers which get your Emotional Bouncy Balls going, and that get you ready to rip up yet another part of your already perfect Rainbow Road, are actually here to help you. They must be embraced for precisely what they are: clues for how it <u>gets</u> to be different for you.
2. The Bouncy Balls want to leave just as much as you want them gone. Seek to take down the Wall to allow them to get the hell out of there!

To do this, you must see each Emotional Bouncy Ball as an opportunity to batter down the emotional barricades that are your Wall.

And becoming a buffalo is the answer (lol!)

BE MORE BUFFALO

If you've ever felt inspired to compare these Bovidae animals, one could easily band cows and buffalo together:

- horned
- hooved
- used for their hides, milk and meat

Simples.

But they're dead different in one fundamental way: the way they behave when they're shit-scared.

If there's a storm (rain lashing down, crashing thunder, lightning strikes) and you're an animal who doesn't understand words of, "Don't worry, it's just water, light and sound. You'll get wet, but you'll be fine", you'll panic. A heck of a lot, probably!

During a storm, cows freak the funk out! In cow-speak they all say:

"Holy Cow Gods, we're going to die. RUN!"

One starts, others think they know something they don't, and before you know it, they're all in a frenzy!

And that's what they do, for miles sometimes. And these silly Moos run along with the storm. As the clouds roll by, the cows follow its direction, subjecting themselves to the defining din for an excessive duration much longer than necessary.

During the same storm, the buffalo quite probably freak the funk out too. There's no human-to-buffalo verse to say that it'll pass and all will be well. But when the storm comes, the buffalo says:

"Holy Buffalo LORDY LORD, let's meet this mayhem head-on. CHARGE!"

And they head into the eye of the storm, in the direction it came from.

And as quick as it arrived, it passes.

That's what you must learn to do if you want your stormy, Emotional Bouncy Balls to leave just as quickly as they arrived. Be like the Buffalo.

COW(ARD) OR BUFFALO?

When you feel an uncomfortable emotion rising in your body, notice where it is. Physically, what does that emotion feel like inside of you and where is it? Notice how quickly you want to squish it down (to stop thinking about it or remove/distract yourself from it) and put another brick in your wall. Then notice how, despite you trying to take yourself away, when you try to "forget about it" and "think on something else", you can't.

Notice just how many times you're thinking about it in one guise or another. If you see yourself doing this, that's ACE! You're beginning to see firsthand how you're being a Cow(ard) – being subjected to something uncomfortable and trying to escape it without meeting it. And that's okay, but it's keeping you stuck. So as you get wiser to your Cow(ardly) ways, ask yourself, out loud, "Am I willing to Be More Buffalo?"

If you're done with your Cow(ardly) ways, here's how to Be More Buffalo with The Buffalo Breath:

1. When you feel that emotion and before you squish it down, raise your hands (palms facing out) up in the air as you breathe in as much air as you can (through your nose ideally, but mouth is fine too) for a slow inhale.
2. Exhale out of your mouth and breathe out all of the air in your body, as you lower your hands to your lap.
3. Repeat. Ideally, repeat for as long as it takes for this strong emotion to pass.

Do this each and every time you feel an emotional disturbance within yourself that you go to repress. Be aware of your Almond Blues as a marker to check in with yourself. Each time you do, a block gets its blue back and falls from your Wall. And as it does, you create space for an Emotional Bouncy Ball to set itself free too, eternally.

You *will* feel a release. You'll feel peace and joy and, "Well, that feels lighter!" You'll come to enjoy this moment, and you'll think, "Not being a Cow(ard) wasn't the simplest thing I've done. I resisted. I didn't want to feel it, but I did *and now*...WOW!"

This moment of "... *and now*" reflection is a Pause Thought™ which teaches The Trio that what you're doing is welcome, safe and that it's actually a bloody good thing. In realising this, they'll start to get on board with this release process. You'll start to feel better and life starts being fun because you make space for the emotions you actually want more of.

They don't "like" it, but I like to imagine the three of them, sitting behind a desk inside my mind, looking confused AF as I'm quietly, yet firmly, choosing out of their cycles, with a little smile at the side of their mouths as they're saying:

As each blue block falls, you need not actively "do" anything with it once it is free from your Wall. As you continue to wear your blues and look for almond cues, and opportunities to Feel your Feelings, this part of your Rainbow Road will be restored to its bright blue.

Open yourself up to the freedom of feeling whatever is necessary to feel in any given moment.

FEEL-IT FRIDAY HIGHLIGHTS:

1. Wear your blues and sense your almonds. Be in your Pause Thoughts™. Notice where you want to brush off feeling emotions as an "inconvenience" that the grown-ups around you would identify as "pathetic", "immature", "weak" or whatever the heck else "not good enough" label they stamped them with.

2. Rewire every guilt trip. Each time they shouted, rolled their eyes, gave you the silent treatment, shook their head, scolded you, hit you, mocked you, ridiculed you or "joked" about you. See each moment as their pained attempt to "help" you find a more solid place in the world where they hoped that life might feel easier for you than it did for them. (lol I know this seems backwards – just try it on!!)

3. Notice where you're holding onto the hope that your parents might just give you the emotional response and gratification you're still waiting on after all of this time. Ask yourself: *How might I reach a space of acceptance without them giving me this?* Get curious around accepting that their best was precisely that – the best they were capable of giving. Give yourself permission to accept this without it meaning that you liked or approved of some of the things that they did.

4. When you don't confront your emotions head-on, you contain unfelt emotions in a wall made up of your Rainbow Road bricks. Inside this lifeless casket, your pent-up bouncy-ball emotions are held down

harder. The Trio tells you, "It's safer this way". When you hear this, it's time to **Go Full Buffalo Breath**!!!

REMEMBER:

Mind-on-Mute Mondays:

Wear your Minty Greens and explore this mind-blowing fact:

There is a voice inside your head.

This voice is <u>not</u> You.

Seek to notice every time he's getting his knickers in a twist, and snap a branch from his most favourite, familiar neurological brain-loops so he starts to become less comfortable travelling these outdated routes. Get curious around the idea that if there is a voice speaking, then who is the one listening?

That voice is You!

You will not know it the first moment you contemplate it, but you will come to know it. And once you do, you won't care to "understand" and "know". You'll just let it be. Here you'll feel a freedom you had no idea could exist for you.

To access your Mind-on-Mute Monday supplementary supportive workbooks and videos, please CLICK HERE.

REMEMBER:

Trigger-Free Tuesday:

Wear your Orangy Tangerines.

Toad believes that everyone else is to blame and that it'd all be just fine and dandy if **they** all stopped being such arseholes! Your job here is to be like Teflon: create a Space to Choose Freedom between the stuff happening outside of you and how you are reacting or responding to it. Keep laying the tangerine part of your Rainbow Road. Notice every time you see you're on the hunt for your Toad/wanting to bathe in someone else's firework explosions and say, "I see you and it's **not** going down this way ANYmore!!"

To access your Trigger-Free Tuesday workbook and supporting video, please CLICK HERE.

REMEMBER:

Wake-up Wednesdays:

Wear your watermelon pink and learn how to be kind to your mind. You're only thinking this way because all of those harsh voices that told you that you weren't "good enough" for this world got so loud that they've become etched inside your mind. Now, on eternal replay as your Francis, you've listened to them/her for so long that you've got confused. You think she is you and that you are her. You aren't. And the way to see this is to notice where she is introducing poisonous, grudge-bearing and controlling toxicity into your life, telling you it's good for you/all you deserve. When you spot this, remember that she is the overbearingly over-protective friend, and **not** the fiend she's doing a REALLY good job of pretending to be. You aren't landing yourself in the Street, the Cell or in a Casket. You're moving into new spaces – a wide open sea. Once she realises that the water's fine, she'll come join you. But you must move first.

To access your Wake-Up Wednesday supplementary supportive workbooks and videos, please CLICK HERE.

REMEMBER:

Thankful Thursdays:

Embody your lavender purples as you quit the pursuit of finding ways to Quick-Fix yourself. Centre yourself in the knowledge that all the stuff that you want on the outside of you materialises through grounding yourself in being grateful AF for the present moment and all it contains: shit shows and all! Sometimes finding gratitude in these shit-show situations feels like a push too far, but without this, your hunt for Quick-Fix Plums will continue to **drain** the joy out of your life.

When you feel drained, you've simply forgotten that you get to eat ice cream for breakfast, lunch and dinner, and that the plum is merely the cherry on top. When you find yourself down the lane, driving yourself round the BEND, looking for that sweet-treat promise outside of you, call in Grace. Get willing to do it differently. Find something to get grateful for in this obscure ride around the sun that we're all on.

To access your Thankful Thursday supplementary supportive workbooks and videos, please CLICK HERE.

REMEMBER:

Feel-It Friday:

On Fridays, remember to sense your almonds and embody your blues so that feeling your feelings feels more inviting. Your Mama, Papa and any other adult who got the gift of being in close proximity to you didn't understand the glory of all that you are. Instead, they took it upon themselves to mould you into what **they** thought you "should" be. This involved a LOT of telling you to smush down any and every uncomfortable emotion, which made you into a Cow(ard). They were wrong! You're a freaking BUFFALO!

To access your Feel-It Friday supplementary supportive workbooks and videos, please CLICK HERE.

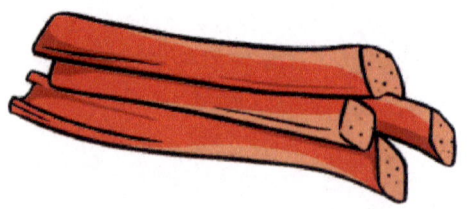

Saturday Sitting
BREATH IS THE PATH TO YOUR PARADISE

Breathwork is the most essential component to transforming consciousness.

—Dr Andrew Weil

Introducing The Alpha Alpaca Breath

**Breathwork is the gateway of
self-realisation where what you know and what
you think you should know converge.**

Breaking news! In this moment, everything really is pretty alright, right?

*The default setting of The Universe – and of Actual You with a Capital Y – is to feel really blooming GREAT. But as humans sometimes susceptible to the tricks of the brain, we're so busy thinking our way through the world, looking for problems to solve, that we've forgotten to notice our bodies and **just take a freaking breath**!*

*I KNOW that breathing techniques and meditation aren't the answer to anxiety that you were looking for (trust me – I felt this way at first too!). This would mean you'd have to take 100% responsibility for your fearful state and actively **do** something about it. It feels so much simpler to press a button, take a pill or read a book (whilst sniffing some scents and eating some treats) once and done, but this Quick-Fix mentality is slowly killing you – we're DONE with pruney plums!*

You are here to experience More love, joy, peace, energy, and abundance all whilst being free from anxiety. And this More has to merge with Your regular rhythm of life to truly create a lasting impression. What better way to do this than to incorporate the breath (not just when we want to be like a Buffalo!)?

Breathing is your body's connection to the world. It is the gentle path to your paradise. The breath will allow you to grab a firm hold of that Rainbow Road and lift yourself up onto it with ease. The more often you connect to it, the more effortless this process becomes.

And that's why we're here – to connect with the breath in our Saturday Sitting.

To do this, we're going to work on the red part of your Rainbow Road, which means you must:

1. Bring your Rhubarb Red Piggyback Sensory Hack™ stuffs OUT to play.
2. Read this Saturday Sitting chapter and do what it says alongside the sensory stuff. Your awareness of what's going on is beginning to get bomb, so now it's time to truly start stepping on that Rainbow Road...
3. Remember to say, "Fudge it", over and over again. Play pretend as you *try on the freaking dress*. Your Conscious Brain will then get on board to connect to your breath and get a leg up onto that Rainbow Road to the Subconscious.

"But Emma, meditation is tricky for me..."

Fudge it! Try it on!

"You want me to just breathe? What's that gonna do?!"

Fudge. It. And. Try. It. On.

"But what if I can't relax?!?"

Just go...

...as often as possible, using your Pause Thoughts™ and your Red Rhubarb Sensory Experience.

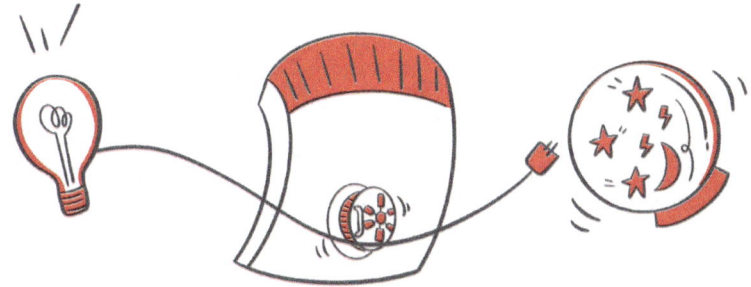

And one day, this silliness will slide on like a glove and you'll say:

"I had no idea that meditation was so blooming simple! Approaching it with a different vibe shifts the whole thing to be easy and enlightening. Now I want to do it. I'm excited to do it. My brain does it without me even needing to think about doing it. Now, I can't actually imagine my life now without it."

It's bizarre but BRILLIANT!

HERE'S THE CHALLENGE...

In your Unconscious, there are stories that fit your version of *umwelt*, which determine your rules for what breathwork means for you. It might feel:

- Overwhelming
- Impossible to fit into a day
- Optional
- Frustrating
- Uncomfortable
- Boring
- TORTUROUS!!

Throughout this chapter, you will come to know that you've been holding your breath for almost your whole life. It's time to, truly, take a breath...

HERE'S WHAT YOU CAN CHOOSE TO SEEK...

This sixth step is going to teach you how to use your breath to create more space in your Unconscious Mind and touch that elusive Subconscious.

By the end of this chapter, you'll be able to:

- Move from "I know I **should** meditate" to thinking, "Hey, I haven't meditated yet today...I'm weirdly excited to!"
- Learn how to do a Quickie session that becomes part of your daily life habit.
- Connect with long and slow breathwork
- Disturb Bob's neurological tree-top patterns, putting something new in their place

You and I both know that meditation is important; we're told so on the daily by everyone from The Buddha to Elon Musk. Saturday Sitting will show you how you get to feel empowered by, and not resentful of, this fact.

Right now, your definition of what breathwork is sits locked inside the corners of the West Wing, in your Emotional "Safehouse" mind. The Trio has the key and will be damned if they'll hand it over easily. Making space to lay the rhubarb red part of your Rainbow Road will allow the Subconscious You to come steaming down the Breathwork part of The Rainbow Road like it's a runway you freaking OWN!

To truly do this, and build that Rainbow Road, you've got to get past the idea that breathwork is optional in this life. It absolutely is **not** something you can opt into and out of as and when you so choose. And the sooner you come to realise this, the easier and more energy-filled your world becomes.

To truly do this (WITHOUT "Push"!!!), you're going to need to use your Pause Thoughts™...

PAUSE THOUGHTS™

On Saturdays, we use our Pause Thoughts™ to show your Trio that meditation is mega (and not the waste of time that they're trying to convince you it is).

The Trio of Terror are too good at convincing you of the following:

- "We don't have the time".
- "We've got too much going on".
- "We haven't got the energy for this..."

And you've probably believed them for a while, and that's okay, but continuing to believe this is **not**. We CANNOT change this thought through "knowing"; it's time to create an Entry-Level Access Point around this as you get curious AF about making it different!

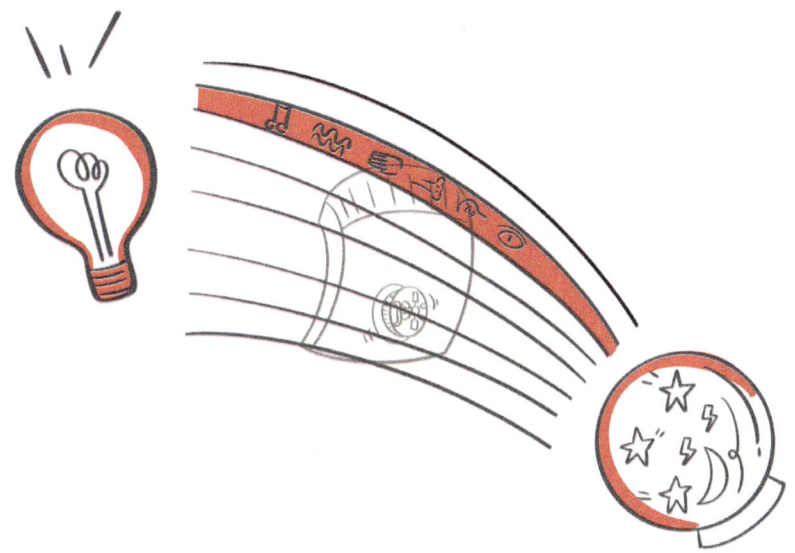

Your job is to create that *rhubarby-est* red part of your Rainbow Road, piggybacking the notions I share *from* your (doubting) Conscious Mind, *through* that Emotional change-making space of your Unconscious and *into* the Subconscious.

TO DO THIS EASILY, AS YOU READ THIS CHAPTER, YOU MUST EMBODY RHUBARB REDS.

Become all shades and tastes of that lusciousness. Wear your brightest lippy[42] or don your reddest stilettos. Suck on a rhubarb and custard sweetie[43] and pop a crumble[44] into the oven. Slurp on a rum and rhubarb cocktail or nibble (or devour entirely) a rhubarb roulade. All the red rhubarbs, whilst reading about the power of Saturday Sitting, will allow you to return to centre.

Then, once you've read this book, each Saturday, carry this rhubarby red sensory reminder with you. And each time you see, smell, taste or touch it, create a Pause Thought™ for yourself – whilst going to the loo, standing in a queue, when you don't know what to do. This will make space within The Unconscious for more of what will bring your inner being into alignment.

Sitting with yourself isn't as frustrating as The Trio are making out. Breathwork is bloody brilliant!!

---

[42]   Short for *lipstick*.
[43]   Another word for *sweet treats*.
[44]   Fruit dish containing a layer of dry mixture made of flour, butter, and sugar.

Ready?

"MEDITATION IS THE BEE'S KNEES... BUT I DON'T HAVE TIME FOR IT"

I knew meditation was a big deal. Anyone doing anything remotely brilliant banged on[45] about it pretty much all the time! But I didn't have the time! My life was chaos, running on an *umwelt* of, "If I'm not rushing and limited on time, then this wouldn't feel like my life! And if it doesn't feel life my life, then I'm not in my 'Safehouse' and it doesn't feel safe." To uphold this feeling of "not-enough-timeness", I'd always be looking for how I could live on the breath of, "I'll take in just enough to get me through this moment".

Five Steps in, I was realising that "understanding" and "knowledge" is, most often, The Trio talking.

And although I was feeling more grateful, and I was feeling more feelings, I was still being dragged back into their chaos more often than I

---

45   Talked about it a lot – so much so, you might be a little sick of hearing about it!

liked. I needed to get out of my head, truly. I knew it was time to take a breath. So, it seemed I had to find a way to "be into" meditation. A quick Google search and the first thing that I came across was this dude called Satya Narayana Goenka.

He looked chill. He looked like the kinda chill that I didn't believe existed in human form. His little peaceful face made me want to be sick and hug him all at the same time.

Watching him up there, on his little chair, all relaxed and stuff. *Bloody liar!* (I laugh as I type this, but it was how I felt back then). In my disgruntled, anxious state, I imagined that he went back to his room (after doing his little spiel) with cold sweats and had a panic attack. My anxiety was so through the roof that I didn't believe that people like him truly existed. I was so sceptical and yet **incredibly** intrigued...

I soon after learned that Goenka led 10-day Silent Meditation Retreats. Back then, my twins were brand-spanking new, my husband worked away a LOT, and I was a teacher. I had a **lot** going on, so escaping for 10 days wasn't an option (nor would I have wanted it to be, sitting in silence with only my thoughts for company – **no thank you**!). So, I made my own little 10-day retreat (which lasted for almost a month in totality).

Each night, I'd sing to my babes and, as they lay dropping off to sleep, I'd put in my earphones and attempt to understand Goenka's lies (lol!) of witchcraft and wizardry.

In the daytime (during my babes' kick-ass naps [which could last between 3-4 hours]), I'd be silent and breathe. Not for hours initially (I'd have died!), but I did the best I could sneak. It was an intense time, but I was desperate. And desperate people do desperate things.

Over the course of the weeks, I could feel shifts. Not the earth-shattering climaxes that The Trio was searching for, but moments of, "Well, this feels flippin' **better**!"

But the devotion and levels of consistency that it took to snatch a moment of, "That's a bit better," were superhuman. And, typically, I crashed and burned. Ten-day silent retreats weren't attainable for regular Jos and Joannas who had a lot of shit to get did, on a regular basis. If meditation wasn't sitting in silence for hours on end at silent retreats, frustrated by the lack of time and ability to do it, what else might it be?

I had to Find a way to do it. At this point, The Trio were having a BALL now that I could spot them **but** didn't have a phat lot of what to **do** with them!

I was feeling resistance.

The first thing I had to do was realise that meditation wasn't ANYTHING like I thought it was (Sorry Goenka!)...

"I JUST DON'T HAVE THE ENERGY"

The reason you don't meditate consistently right now is because of your ideal of what you think meditation "should" be.

ANY time you use the word "should" to describe something, I want internal alarm bells to go OFF!

The idea of "should" gives the automatic assumption that there is a "shouldn't" sitting behind it.

SPOT WHEN YOU'RE "SHOULDING"

Get curious when you see yourself "shoulding" (new verb!).

Ask yourself: *What if there was no "right" way to do this? What would I do then?*

There is no "right way" to do this. There is no "should" when it comes to meditation (and **life** for that matter!).

Meditation can be hours sitting in remote locations. It can also be a stolen moment whilst sitting on the rush-hour train. Meditation can be walking in silence. It can also be an acute awareness of your speech when you're talking.

Meditation can be chanting. It can also be singing. Meditation can be spiritual spaces. It can also be washing up your mug at the kitchen sink.

There are no rules.

Meditation is heightening your choice to choose into being totally and utterly aware of this moment, to take up divine space where you intentionally create distance between your thoughts/this sensory experience and Your awareness of these constructs.

"I DON'T HAVE TIME!"

Even with The Pause Thoughts™, The Trio are QUICK to use their favourite excuse...

Time is something humans made up to make sense of this sensory experience. To further add to our illusion that we have it all under control. For time to exist, there must be an awareness to measure it. You are that awareness. Time is measured by you (and 7.7 billion others) and an omnipresent awareness (but that's for my next book...).

QUESTION WHAT ELSE EXISTS

Think about this for a second: *What exists outside of this moment?*

Tomorrow is not yet here. We can predict and plan, but it is yet to arrive. The past exists only as a memory and through stories and images. There is only this moment. Anything outside of this is recall or projection.

Don't skim this. Take a rhubard hit and go back and read it again. Take a moment to feel this (tell The Trio to "feck off" as you do). Our work is to ground ourselves in this moment, entirely. As often as possible. Know that time flows through you, the observer within your awareness. Rhubard reds are there to remind you to truly take a breath. It really is as easy as that!

So, the question is **never**, "Do I have time?" The question is, "Right in this very moment, the only moment in which I have true awareness, do I choose to go to my breath?"

It all starts to become pretty easy when you start to zoom in on the moment of being alive right now and the concept that nothing exists outside of it. It's pretty empowering, actually! And there is only ever one answer to this question: yes or no. "Try" is a commitment to a lack of decision.

"Yes, but I can't right now because I only have a moment to read before..."

"No. I'm so busy I can't possibly breathe in and out for 10 seconds, but I will do it later..."

The word "try" is BANNED in my Mindset World. This screams "harsh!", but using this word is like taking an axe to your Rainbow Road and smashing it down, **hard**. "Try" is an Unconscious response. "Try" doesn't allow you to commit, and committing one way or another is **essential**.

Will you or won't you?

Do you or don't you?

Yes or no?

These answers tell you where you stand. Never "try". ALWAYS choose. If you've been a "tryer" up to this point, NO shame! I was the #1 Tryer for a LONG-ass time. Your willingness to "try" and/or choose has a LOT to do with your *umwelt*. Allow me to explain...

THE SENSORY EXPERIENCE

Just like Jakob von Uexküll told us, your entire life is created through a sensory experience.

And we've learned how everyone and their wife is in a competition to get you to subscribe to their *umwelt* so they feel less alone in their "Safehouse" street...

"The cat says what?" "What colour is this?" "How many of these?"

"That's right. Good job. So clever!"

Merit awarded each and every time you try to learn your sensory cues in line with what's "expected".

This puts your senses well and truly in the driving seat. And so, you believe your senses above and beyond any of your intuitions or innate skills. You only believe when you see.

Understanding your Brain Waves will help make more sense of this...

BUSY BETA BEE

In this sensory simulation, the human mind reverberates at Beta frequency. I call this "Busy Beta". This frequency is like a stressed-out bee buzzing around after losing her queen, frantically trying to find her...

"Queen?...Queeny??...QUEENY!?!??"

Busy Beta Bee, stressed off her tits!

I was THE freaking Busy Beta Bee!

In this Queen-separation-anxiety Busy Beta Bee space, you can't perceive, not truly. You can't make informed and intuitive decisions.

You're too busy *thinking* about how to put out the fire you've got burning inside your brain. You're super stressed trying to find your Queen. Most of the modern world spends their time in this space.

Whatever Primary Emotional "Resting State" [lol!] is most familiar to you (panic, anger, resentment, jealousy...), that Busy Beta Bee is running LOOPS trying to keep busy and figure it all out.

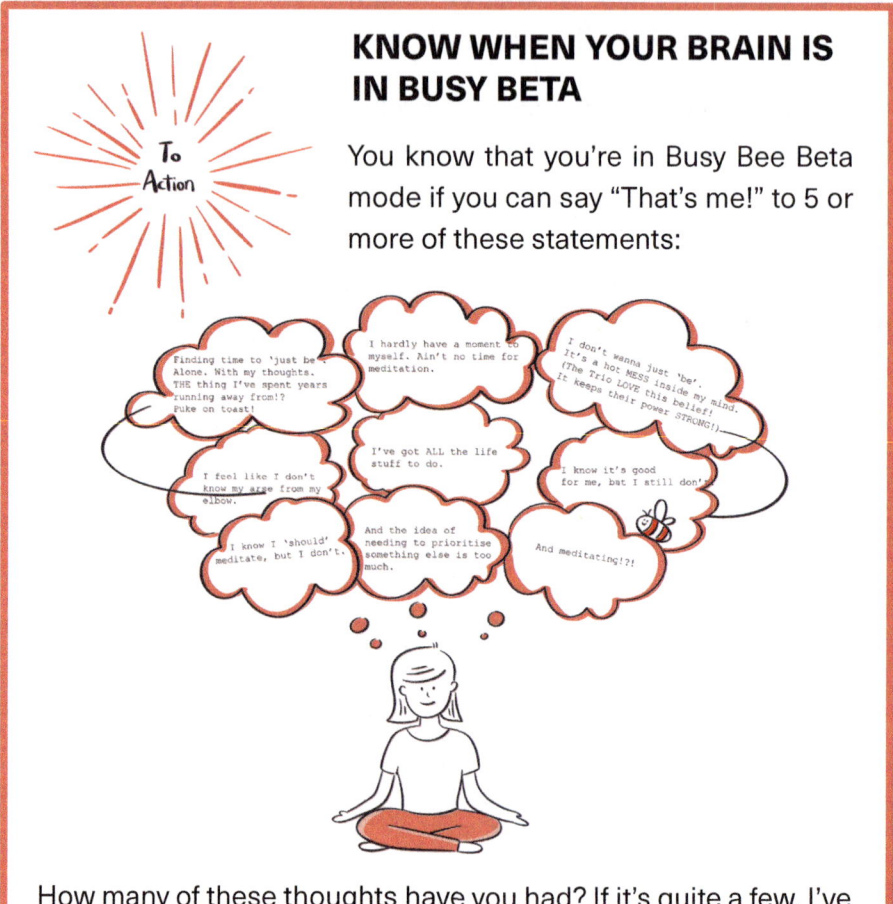

KNOW WHEN YOUR BRAIN IS IN BUSY BETA

To Action

You know that you're in Busy Bee Beta mode if you can say "That's me!" to 5 or more of these statements:

Finding time to 'just be'. Alone. With my thoughts. THE thing I've spent years running away from!? Puke on toast!

I hardly have a moment to myself. Ain't no time for meditation.

I don't wanna just 'be'. It's a hot MESS inside my mind. (The Trio LOVE this belief! It keeps their power STRONG!)

I feel like I don't know my arse from my elbow.

I've got ALL the life stuff to do.

I know it's good for me, but I still don'

I know I 'should' meditate, but I don't.

And the idea of needing to prioritise something else is too much.

And meditating!?!

How many of these thoughts have you had? If it's quite a few, I've got you! I know this space. I OWNED this space, like it was my biatch for around 30 years! And now I'm out, and I'm showing you **precisely** what I did to free myself of this mindset.

When your brain is working in Beta, all of your awareness is directed towards the stuff around you. Your Conscious Mind is always plotting and scheming around how you're going to navigate and manipulate everything out there to allow you to return to your brew and biscuit "best" life! You can't think straight when you've got a frenzied bee circling your head ready to sting you!

Remember: one of your primary jobs is to snap those familiar brain-pattern branches so often that Bob starts saying, *"Well this route is too much of an inconvenience to navigate. I'll just go another blooming way!"* THIS is what we want!! And **the** best Branch-Snapping Ally that you'll ever meet in your whole entire LIFE is your breath (An Alpaca breath, to be precise – more on that in a sec). Your breath takes your focus from the external Beta bee frenzy and brings it inside.

...and this is why Saturday Sitting is so BOMB!

Let's take a sec to learn what's actually happening to your brain when you're connecting to your breath.

ALPHA ALPACA BREATH

Theta and Alpha Brain Waves are dead different to Beta. They're some of the ones we want to be accessing on the regular. They help with processing, making memories and generally feeling more lovely about life.

When I think Alpha Brain Waves, I think Alpaca. Yes, you heard me right.

Think about those fluffy balls of glory for just a second. Have you ever seen one in a wide-open space? They're filled with JOY. Teeming with it from top to little fluffy tail. They're flitting[46] and frollicking, running and jumping without a care in the world. In these moments, they are the definition of living their best life in an Alpha state. So, when you're thinking Alpha Brain Waves, think of the totally free Alpaca and smile.

Don't panic. There may be some resistance to this. I hear The Trio:

"I don't want to bounce around cluelessly, Emma!".

This is ALL figurative (just so your brain "gets it" super easily [it's that Entry-Level Access Point we're looking for again here]).

This Alpha Alpaca state comes when you give time and energy to focus on your breath. Doing this creates space. You do this in two ways:

---

46   Dancing, skipping, playing.

Breath 1: A short and quick **Quickie**, or

Breath 2: Long and slow **Full Kit and Caboodle**

And I think that every woman knows that a good combination of both is the winning blend for bliss!

Tuning into your energies will tell you whether to choose a Breath 1 or Breath 2. To help, embody your rhubarb reds at **every** eventuality for maximum impact and ease (which is what we're going for here).

To become a Master Meditator, you must learn when and how to:

- Open up space to enter the Alpha Alpaca state as often as possible.
- Know when it's time for a quickie.
- Know when it's time to go full kit and caboodle.

BREATH 1: PAUSE THOUGHT™ – IN 2, OUT 6 EXERCISE

This is short and quick stuff right here. It can be as short or as quick as you want, so don't let The Trio go putting barriers in the way on Breath 1. Sometimes a planned quickie turns into the BEST long, slow, full kit and caboodle of your life. Stop letting The Trio make the rules! Noticing and touching that path (no matter how short and quick it is) is the name of our game here.

Let's use our Red Piggyback Sensory Hack™ stuff to help us.

To Action

A SHORT AND QUICK QUICKIE

Every time you see your Rhubarb Red sensory stimulant:

1. Ask yourself, *Where is my awareness in this, the only moment there is, right now?* (Remember, NOTHING exists outside of this moment)
2. Smile at you being a badass and noticing your awareness and wanting to OWN it. WHATEVER you are doing, bring heightened awareness to it by slowing down your inhale and exhale...
3. As the breath slows, focus on where it enters or exists in your body, or focus entirely on the completely mundane, super-regular, everyday stuff you're doing...
   - Folding clothes
   - Typing on your keyboard
   - Driving
   - Talking to your babes

If you become distracted, and you notice that your mind has wandered, allow your sensory hacks to bring you back to this moment of awareness.

But – and it's a big-ass **but** – please don't believe that it's possible to exist here permanently. No matter how profound your realisations are, you **will** get triggered out of this space (that's why I'm so passionate about teaching The 7 Steps). Your job is to re-align with yourself. Keep building that Rainbow Road so you can gradually spend more and more time in this space than out of it.

Breathwork done in Breath 1 ways has such profound impact whilst being super easy. It's super accessible, too, because it hardly takes a moment away from your everyday living. It's pretty hard not to fall totally and utterly in love with it.

Looking at meditation in *Breath 1* ways means that getting back onto that Rainbow Road, over and over again (using the rhubarb red sensory invitations), will come to feel like a solo Saturday night spent in your jammies with Netflix and your snack drawer filled with all of your best treats!

FRUSTRATION SOLUTIONS

If your Busy Beta Brain Waves are LIT, it might take a minute for you to start to think about breath in this snack-filled way. Being in Busy Beta means that any type of focused awareness through breathwork probably leaves you feeling frustrated. This is most likely because you've spent so much time in your head, which has caused a disconnect between the mind and body. That's okay (I was numb from the waist down for YEARS!). If that's you too, there's a little work to do on bringing a mind-body connection together.

DO A QUICKIE #1 BREATH

If you feel frustration when you get that rhubarb cue, follow this **#1 Quickie Breath** Exercise:

1. Drum your tummy with the palm of both hands, beating your belly like a drum.

Don't seize this as an opportunity for The Trio to be unkind to you here. Be gentle but firm, just enough so you feel it and it draws your awareness. Flow with a beat of around one per second or so.[47]

2. Hold your left nostril[48] closed and breathe in through the right nostril for a count of 4. Then breathe out for 4...

3. Switch your finger holding your left nostril to the right and breathe through your left nostril for a breath in of 4, then out for 4 again.

4. Repeat for at least a couple of rounds or choose to fill up your **only** Right Now Moment with this for as long as you feel inspired.

Did you do it? GO YOU!! If not, ask yourself, "Right now, in the only moment of my existence, will I go to my breath?" Frustrated or not, it's a **perfect** opportunity to practise, so lets go...

Learning to say yes in these moments, if only for a second or two (to touch that Rainbow Road), **will change your entire existence**. It truly is THAT easy!

BREATH 2: SATURDAY SITTING – THE FINDER'S BREATH

This is **Breath 2, long and slow stuff** right here

As part of The 7 Steps, this Breath 2 is scheduled for every Saturday, although building this practice into your life on the daily will have deeply profoundly yummy Snack Drawer, Rockstar Results!

---

47 Skip this part if you're out and about, or with other people and it'd feel super weird to do this bit. Move onto the other steps. These can be done in the busiest of places, surrounded by people who will have no idea that you're doing anything other than being a "regular" (lol) human being.

48 If you have trouble breathing through your nose, switch to actively counting your breath through your mouth.

To Action

BREATHE THE FINDER'S BREATH

Have a big-ass snort of something rhu- barby or put on your best rosy lippy before you do this:

Connect with the ground – bare feet and (covered [lol!]) bottom is best). Outside earth = bonus points, but don't get hung up here. If you're in the middle of an office block[49], work with what you have. It'll still be powerful. Notice your feet connecting to the ground they're on. Push down into it, gently, and feel this connection to the earth. Close your eyes.

1. Breathe in with sharp inhalations (through the nose is most powerful, but again, don't let this deter you – breathe through your mouth if it feels best). As you breathe in, force your arms into the air, palms facing in the same direction as your eyes would be looking out if they were open.
2. Sharply exhale through the mouth as you quickly bring your elbows into your body. Palms should still be facing the direction your closed eyes are facing.[50]
3. Continue for as many rounds as feels comfortably chal- lenging. You will feel light-headed, but you do not need to go hard[51].
4. Lay the back of your hands on your lap and place your palms up to the ceiling. Return to your natural breath and watch it fall back into alignment.

---

49   *office building*

50   The move is a little like you're going up to catch a basketball heading towards you. Stretch as high as you possibly can and just as you max out, realise the ball wasn't intended for you and drop your arms, led by heavy elbows.

51   This kind of "Push" is what we're no longer here for. Build up to a deeper breath gradually by learning your limits.

You might feel a little light-headed as this happens. Notice how The Trio want to scramble and panic, "We're dying. We're going to pass out!" Remind yourself of just how in control of yourself you are and return to your natural breath. Be aware of this, without scrambling to "land". Indulge in the feeling of surrender here, and continue to realign back to your breath.

Remain with the breath for as long as it feels good to. The Trio will be close by, saying, "We don't have time. We have to do these things. Let's go get a snack. Let's just check 'this' for a second". Choose to stay with your breath in these moments.

Watch as your Conscious Brain is screaming, "WE DON'T DO THIS!!! WE PANIC AND 'DO'!" and will try **every** option available in the armoury to attempt to distract you from connecting to this moment. Here, sit for a moment or two more. You are in charge of your life now. Do this and you WILL transcend and establish a Rainbow Road which is UNSHAKEABLE!

It's impossible to be actively aware of all moments of everything that you ever do, although I'm sure The Trio is trying to tell you that this superhuman feat is precisely what I'm asking and expecting of you.

You are a human being having a sensory experience. Those senses that Bob, Toad, and Francis are ALWAYS on the hunt for will continue to exist. And they will continue to look for them. If you give them an inch (which we ALL do, thinking, "I'm too tired today. I'll just fall back into my familiar), they take a MILE...

To Action

BREATHE A KIND AND PATIENT BREATH

Don't beat yourself up. Be patient with yourself. Breathe. Then, decide where you would prefer to focus. When you become aware, just ask yourself: *Where is my awareness? Do I want it to be here?*

Breathwork can be played like the drinking games you played at Uni[52]. Take a shot. Make Pause Thought™ breathwork a less poisonous version of this. Whenever you're doing almost anything, see rhubarb and ask yourself, "Where is my breath?" A quickie or long and slow — who cares?

Just notice...over and over and OVER again.

You exist within this human experience, and you don't get to skip this part, no matter how good you become at getting on the Rainbow Snackway Express. This is why you must connect with the breath in order to bring yourself to your centre, a much easier place from which to operate than the one The Trio have you living in!

Your paradise is unique to you and everything you seek to substantiate. That's the beauty of this existence! The route to this space is universal; it is actualised through breath.

---

[52]   Short for *university*; college.

SATURDAY SITTING HIGHLIGHTS

1. Meditation enables you to stroll up to that Rainbow Road and walk it like you OWN it!!!!! It's the pathway to your paradise – **the** space where you get to walk into the high-vibe energies of ALL that you are.

2. There are two ways to meditate:
   - Breath 1 – Quick and often
   - Breath 2 – Long and slow

   You must create a habit of using both in your world to get some stable footing on that Rainbow Road.

3. **Breath 1 – Quickies:** Rhubarb Red reminds you to take Pause Thoughts™ throughout the day where you bring heightened aware- ness to whatever it is you're busying yourself with. For extra clout (or if you find yourself somewhat distracted), do the tummy taps and nose-hold breaths in for 4 then out for 4 on alternating nose holes.

4. **Breath 2 – Long and slow:** Schedule a regular time to indulge in your rhubarby reds (suck your rhubarb and custard, have your dif- fuser on, wear your best red lippy and put it on with INTENTION before you begin) to do Breathwork each Saturday. Bring joy to this practice and it **will** bleed into other days in the week too. The more often you make space to connect, the quicker you'll come to gliding on that Catwalk on the DAILY!

REMEMBER:

Mind-on-Mute Mondays:

Wear your Minty Greens and explore this mind-blowing fact:

There is a voice inside your head.

This voice is <u>not</u> You.

Seek to notice every time he's getting his knickers in a twist, and snap a branch from his most favourite, familiar neurological brain-loops so he starts to become less comfortable travelling these outdated routes. Get curious around the idea that if there is a voice speaking, then who is the one listening?

That voice is You!

You will not know it the first moment you contemplate it, but you will come to know it. And once you do, you won't care to "understand" and "know". You'll just let it be. Here you'll feel a freedom you had no idea could exist for you.

To access your Mind-on-Mute Monday supplementary supportive workbooks and videos, please CLICK HERE.

REMEMBER:

Trigger-Free Tuesday:

Wear your Orangy Tangerines.

Toad believes that everyone else is to blame and that it'd all be just fine and dandy if **they** all stopped being such arseholes! Your job here is to be like Teflon: create a Space to Choose Freedom between the stuff happening outside of you and how you are reacting or responding to it. Keep laying the tangerine part of your Rainbow Road. Notice every time you see you're on the hunt for your Toad/wanting to bathe in someone else's firework explosions and say, "I see you and it's **not** going down this way ANYmore!!"

To access your Trigger-Free Tuesday workbook and supporting video, please CLICK HERE.

REMEMBER:

Wake-up Wednesdays:

Wear your watermelon pink and learn how to be kind to your mind. You're only thinking this way because all of those harsh voices that told you that you weren't "good enough" for this world got so loud that they've become etched inside your mind. Now, on eternal replay as your Francis, you've listened to them/her for so long that you've got confused. You think she is you and that you are her. You aren't. And the way to see this is to notice where she is introducing poisonous, grudge-bearing and controlling toxicity into your life, telling you it's good for you/all you deserve. When you spot this, remember that she is the overbearingly over-protective friend, and **not** the fiend she's doing a REALLY good job of pretending to be. You aren't landing yourself in the Street, the Cell or in a Casket. You're moving into new spaces – a wide open sea. Once she realises that the water's fine, she'll come join you. But you must move first.

To access your Wake-Up Wednesday supplementary supportive workbooks and videos, please CLICK HERE.

REMEMBER:

Thankful Thursdays:

Embody your lavender purples as you quit the pursuit of finding ways to Quick-Fix yourself. Centre yourself in the knowledge that all the stuff that you want on the outside of you materialises through grounding yourself in being grateful AF for the present moment and all it contains: shit shows and all! Sometimes finding gratitude in these shit-show situations feels like a push too far, but without this, your hunt for Quick-Fix Plums will continue to **drain** the joy out of your life.

When you feel drained, you've simply forgotten that you get to eat ice cream for breakfast, lunch and dinner, and that the plum is merely the cherry on top. When you find yourself down the lane, driving yourself round the BEND, looking for that sweet-treat promise outside of you, call in Grace. Get willing to do it differently. Find something to get grateful for in this obscure ride around the sun that we're all on.

To access your Thankful Thursday supplementary supportive workbooks and videos, please CLICK HERE.

REMEMBER:

Feel-It Friday:

On Fridays, remember to sense your almonds and embody your blues so that feeling your feelings feels more inviting. Your Mama, Papa and any other adult who got the gift of being in close proximity to you didn't understand the glory of all that you are. Instead, they took it upon themselves to mould you into what **they** thought you "should" be. This involved a LOT of telling you to smush down any and every uncomfortable emotion, which made you into a Cow(ard). They were wrong! You're a freaking BUFFALO!

To access your Feel-It Friday supplementary supportive workbooks and videos, please CLICK HERE.

REMEMBER:

Saturday Sitting: Wear ALL of the rhubarb reds as you realise that breathwork is the bread and butter of an elevated existence lived on The Rainbow Road. Connecting to the moment of right now is actualised by slowing down your awareness, which is influenced directly by the speed of your breath. In this heighted Alpha Brain Wave space, you get to choose where your awareness lies:

Out there in everyone else's messed-up *umwelts*?

Or inside, in your internal snack drawer filled with feasts that your Conscious Mind can't currently think up (because they're too magical to believe, right now!)?

Use rhubarb reds as your reminder to come back to this space, over and over again. And don't "try", *do*!

To access your Saturday Sitting supplementary supportive workbooks and videos, please CLICK HERE.

Surrender Sunday
THE SUPERPOWER YOU DIDN'T KNOW YOU NEEDED

The moment of surrender is not when
life is over. It's when it begins.

—Marianne Williamson

Introducing The 'Ideal Self' Avatar upfront and personal

To Surrender is to let go of what you think something "should" be and allow what is actually meant to be to come forward. It's going to find you either way (and not in a creepy Freddie Krueger kind of way). Good things are meant to happen, so let them happen. It's okay to relax and lean into good things as they unfold.

*Surrender is an absolutely rock-solid skill which not ONE human being alive actively wants to do. **No one** is sitting around thinking, "Ahh, I really **don't** want to know the outcome of this before I do it". We **all** want to know! And we believe that our power lies in controlling it all. On Surrender Sunday, you will come to learn that your power lies in letting it ALL hang out, and go wherever the funk it's meant to...*

Learning to Surrender, when all you want to do is control, allows you to put that final colour into The Rainbow Road. It also allows the other colours to be restored along your Rainbow Road at super speed!

*Yellow citrus-y Surrender superchargers **everything** it touches! The more often you Surrender, the more "evidence" you'll bank that surrendering is actually a blooming brilliant thing, and it'll become more effortless. As you navigate yourself to this space, all kinds of glorious More gets to show up in your world.*

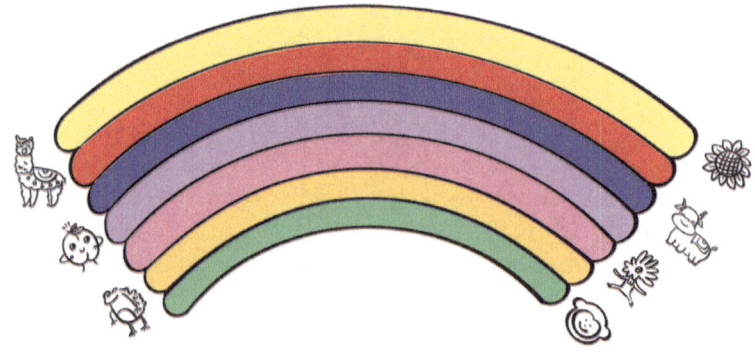

To do this, we're going to work on the yellow part of your Rainbow Road, which means you must:

1. Get bright – add citrus yellows to your life.
2. Read this Surrender Sunday chapter and do what it says, especially the sensory stuff. Your awareness of what's truly going on will continue to heighten here. Surrender is your newest Superpower.
3. Remember to say, "Fudge it", over and over again. Play pretend as you try on the freaking dress (and strip off that ill-fitting one you've been jamming yourself into for YEARS) as I share suggestions for how you can show your Trio that Surrender is actually Your best friend and not the foe they've painted it to be.

"You want me to go into situations without even looking for a clue as to what the outcome will be?! Emma, I'm pretty sure I can't do this..."

Say, "Fudge it," and try it on!

"You want me to 'go with the flow'? What if I stumble into something unsafe?"

Fudge this thought, up the bum! It'll all turn out better than you might ever think...

"What about other people? If I just let go and give freely, won't they just take, take, take?!"

Not if you take care of yourself FIRST (we'll get to that later!). Now go...

...as often as possible, using your Pause Thoughts™ and your Yellow Citrus Sensory Experience.

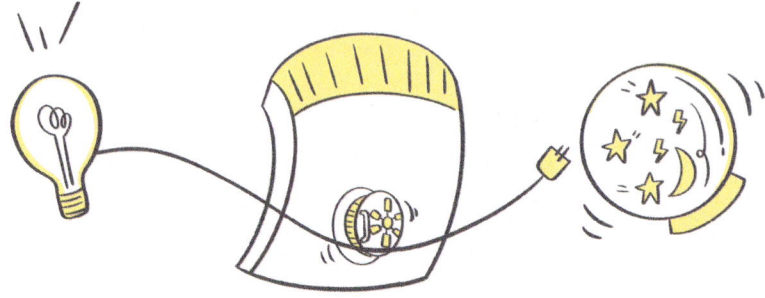

And one day, this silliness will slide on like a glove and you'll say:

"I had no idea that not needing to be so 'in control' was actually a good thing. WHUT?! Letting go means that the glorious things that are meant for me can open up in the most wonderful (unexpected!) ways. And the best bit is that they've been here the whole time, but I've just been hiding them from myself! Who would have thought that little old me was born for a higher purpose and that I'd spent so much time hiding away from it that I couldn't see the wood[53] for the trees?! Now I see ALL the trees. I know them by name, and we VIBE! A life of Surrender no longer feels like a resentful, 'I really *should*' It's more of a, "Well, who blooming-well KNEW!? Let's go!!"

---

[53]   Another word for *forest*.

Like everything else...It's bizarre but BRILLIANT!

HERE'S THE CHALLENGE...

Living life without learning the skill of Surrender often feels like you're riding a rollercoaster whilst trying to drink a scalding red-hot coffee with your best white outfit on. Surrender is actually the most powerful place of existence. You were born to navigate from a place of Surrender, but your brain and an anxious nervous system have a different plan. They're screaming at you, "Death and destruction lie in wait if I **don't** take charge".

The idea of Surrender sounds pretty appealing in theory – "Let go and let love" and all that – but in practice, it can feel like walking on a knife-edge. And all for what?! For it to just fall to shit anyway?!

But that's the point that we're **all** missing. When you continue to contort and control your world – white dress, coffee, rollercoaster, fall to your death or hold on tight – you miss **everything** that's meant for You. You're also making it impossible for anything new to get into **any** cracks, as almost everything new starts super small and comes into our lives in minute ways. Controlling it all means you keep doing and getting the same over and over, looping the loop again and again. And we want something **different**, right?

For it to get different, to invite a crack of something new into your world, you must learn to Surrender...

HERE'S WHAT YOU CAN CHOOSE TO SEEK...

On Sundays, use your Pause Thoughts™ to practise the elusive art of surrender. Surrendering is the scariest thing known to humankind. To Surrender is to go against our own survival skills, the thing that kept our ancestors alive. They acquired these skills by looking for patterns and predicting moon and season cycles to help them forage their path from birth to death less precariously. They forecasted events to avoid droughts, famine, high tide, low tide and other tribes' traps.

Throughout this chapter, you will come to know that Surrender is the art form your soul has been waiting for you to master. It's **the** missing piece of The Rainbow Road that means that everything else can come through. And you won't just come to know it in your mind. Conscious curiosity (alongside the Piggyback Sensory Hacks™) will allow it to penetrate through the belly of your Unconscious.

By the end of this chapter, you'll be able to:

- Do More than just survive

- Understand how to use the art of Surrender in your world, allowing it to take shape as it's meant to (and **not** how you think it "should")
- See how **easy** life and this process get to be
- Realise how letting go means you'll come ever closer to who You are
- Explore what More means for you and how it gets to be available for you too
- Stack your Evidence so you can see yourself constructing the yellow part of your Rainbow Road (awareness of this will spur you on to continue with vibes of snack-drawer excitement!)
- Go inside, and not wide, creating a heartfelt calling to lead a life dedicated to service (that doesn't feel like a tick list[54] of, "Well, doing this will make me a good person...")

Leaning into the lemony yellow art of Surrender will make your Rainbow Road complete. It will be ready for you to connect with it – for you to walk a million miles on it without **any** fatigue and truly make that Subconscious connection. Surrender Sunday is going to show you how you can get your life to feel like a high-vibe Anxiety-Free Dance Party.

To truly do this, and build that Rainbow Road, you've got to know that Surrendering and leaving an outcome open (to "fail" or "succeed") is You mastering the art of living. And the sooner you come to realise this, the more energy-filled your world is going to become. You'll begin to make time and space for what's meant for you (instead of exhausting yourself with what's absolutely not).

To truly do this, of course, you're going to utilise your Pause Thoughts™...

---

54   Another word for *checklist*.

PAUSE THOUGHTS™

On Sundays, use your Pause Thoughts™ to show your Trio that Surrender is a superpower and not a death threat. You've probably believed their deadly threats for a while, and that's okay, but continuing to believe them is **not**. You now know that you CANNOT change thoughts with thought; your job here is to accept this whilst simultaneously creating an Entry-Level Access Point by getting curious AF about making it different at a deeper level!

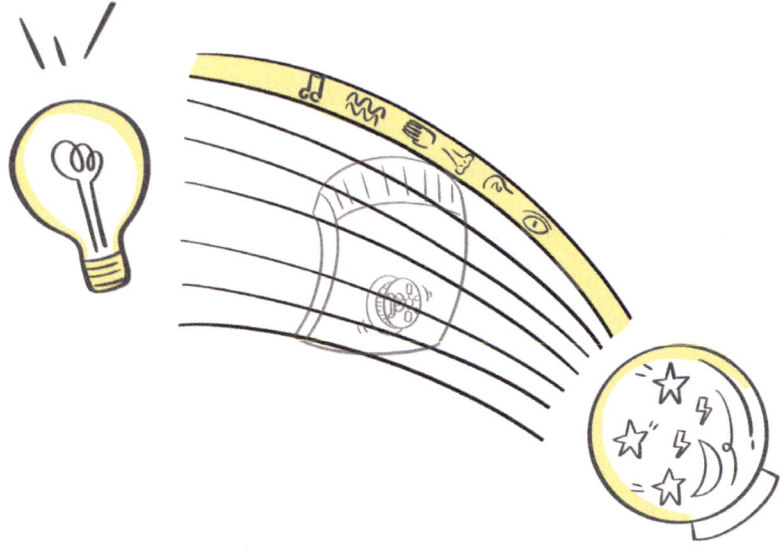

Your job is to create that lemon-y yellow part of your Rainbow Road, piggybacking the notions I share *from* your (doubting) Conscious Mind, *through* that Emotional change-making space of your Unconscious and *into* The Subconscious.

TO DO THIS EASILY, AS YOU READ THIS CHAPTER, YOU MUST EMBODY CITRUS YELLOWS.

Wear your citrusy top, your lemon socks. Suck on lemon sherbet drops as you sip on a limoncello shot. Plant your sunflower delights. Spritz your citrus perfumes and have a swig of your homemade lemonade. All the lemons, whilst reading about the power of Surrender, will allow the knowledge to marinate deep within and impress the Conscious Mind.

Then, once you've read this book, each Sunday, carry this citrusy sensory reminder with you. And each time you see, smell, taste or touch it, create a Pause Thought™ for yourself, making space within the Unconscious for more of what will bring your inner being into alignment.

When life gives you lemons, you Surrender the shit out of it and make lemonade. What else is there to do?!

The taste of Surrender isn't as bitter as The Trio are making it out to be.

It's bloody brilliant!! Ready?

SURRENDER MAKES IT EASY

One of the most profound moments of Surrender I experienced is so brilliantly mundane and utterly ordinary that it's *almost* impossible to see the power behind it. Almost...

The willingness to lean into Pause Thought™ moments is a lot more powerful than it seems. That's why I'm so blooming passionate about this work. I can't wait for you to discover this for yourself.

I'm totally here for the out-of-this-world, earth-shattering Snack-Drawer-Full-to-the-Brim moments, 100% (**so are The Trio**)! But I'm *more* here for the hidden gems, like the moment I'm going to describe below. I share this with you in the hope that it'll inspire you to be on the lookout for the magic that lies in the ordinariness of your life, where it's easy to miss.

MONSOON MAGIC

It was raining buckets and howling wind. I'd left the lid off my compost bin in an earlier attempt to not squish some of the wiggly friends who'd taken refuge at the top.

Upon realising they lay exposed to the elements, I ran to their aid (the love I've developed for nature is at a depth I didn't know existed within me before this work) and I couldn't find the lid.

"Perfect!" I thought. "Of course I can't find the bloody lid when it's blowing a gale[55]. I'm getting soaked and my soily BFFs are drowning!"

Frantically, I searched. No lid. Just wet. And cold. And drowning worms.

Then, my eyes caught the smiling face of a bright yellow sunflower, and it forced a moment of Surrender where my awareness came out of the panic of the moment. I stopped and could see myself scrambling to control the saga: *find the lid, save my worm friends, and just get back inside sharpish to warm up by the fire*. It was like when I was back in that Bone Doctor's office and my healing mission was to "*just get well enough to keep functioning*". But just like back then, The Universe, and her storm, had a different idea for me.

I looked up to the sky and imagined that big bright yellow ball burning down on me, instead of the super-thick, grey heavy rain clouds staring down. I remembered what yellow embodied.

"This is easy," I reminded myself. "I totally and utterly forgot how easy this gets to be. Silly me, scratching around desperately in my attempt to control in order to get the outcome I want! Here I am, completely and utterly missing the cool rain on my skin and the ridiculousness of what I must look like right now to any external eyes who happen to catch a glimpse".

---

[55] Stormy winds blowing.

I looked up at my imaginary ball of bright yellow and then at the sunflower. I gave the sunflower a little nod of, "Thanks, you absolute BEAUTY!" and then looked to the ground.

And there at my feet, **of course**, lay the compost lid. Literally sitting in front of me.

It was right there, in a yellow moment of awareness and Surrender.

Then, I squealed! Like I was 5 years old and had just opened the Christmas gift I'd been waiting all year for. I stood and danced in the rain, getting soaked wet through with tears and the drops pummelling my skin. I lifted the lid onto the compost bin like I was picking up The Nobel Prize and giving my acceptance speech to the worms (who had absolutely NO idea I even existed).

Becoming aware of these minute moments, which 99.99999% of the world miss, and celebrating them like you've just found the eternal cure for Covid will determine the level of success you'll create for yourself in this process.

Is it simple?

Not on your nelly![56]

Is it easy?

As easy as finding your misplaced compost bin lid!

I genuinely believe that being open to these cataclysmic moments of profound nothingness has a heck of a lot to do with why I'm here right now, doing what I'm doing today.

So don't roll your eyes (that's The Trio, not you!); instead, join me and think...

"Might this be happening to me too, and I'm missing it?!"

MIGHT THERE BE MORE?

You are made from stardust. Evolution has somehow compiled the remnants of a supernova explosion millions of years ago into a skeletal structure with muscle, skin, tendons and a multitude of other precise features to make You.

And you're bowling around like it all makes sense and (even more crazily!) like you know exactly how it's meant to go?! Sorry, whut?!?!

The art of Surrender is you being able to get a little more curious about the weirdness of the world. To open up a space where you can openly and curiously wonder...

Might there be More?

Might there be More? More than little old me who has allowed The Trio of Terror to become SO inflamed that I think that I am the actual

---

[56]   The opposite of easy – it's **never** going to happen!

*centre of The Universe? Might there be More than believing that every-thing that happens to me is like I'm on an episode of The Kardashians, with hidden cameras waiting to expose me in every room?! Like every move I make has such an obscene, earth-shattering impact on **every-one** that I have put all my energy into micromanaging everything I do?*

If this is what you're experiencing, it's because you have defined your-self as a role that was never meant for you. You've created an avatar, and you're always trying to hold up this avatar's mask. This mask is dull, super serious, and ill-fitting – and it's weighing Actual You DOWN!

Doing this means you've always got to think and remember your made-up rules for living and consult them **every** time you're going to do **anything**!

You can't live this way.

To Action

ASK YOURSELF, "WHAT IF?"

Ask yourself: *What makes me me?* Get curious around this, for more than a second.

THE WHAT IF LIST

Sit down with this one. Get out your pen and paper and answer these questions. Watch how HARD The Trio want to define you with absolute answers – get brave and challenge yourself on each question with, "Is this as true as I think it is?" The brave will get the most enlightening feedback from this...

Ask yourself: *Would I still be me if...*

1. I didn't have my name?
2. I didn't have a family?
3. I didn't have this role/job?
4. I didn't live where I lived?
5. I had a heart transplant?
6. I had brain damage?
7. My brain was put in another body?

Any frustration felt here is The Trio. This is meant to be mind-fuckingly fun. Be gentle to You!

If you're feeling super smug, or if you've contemplated matters like this before, maybe you understand that you're a spirit, that we're all one, that you're an awareness. But what in the world does it mean, actually?! Do you "know", truly?!

Na, me neither! Isn't it bloody BRILLIANT!?!

To make "sense" of all of this, that avatar version of you has been adopted and labelled as an "Ideal Self" version of you. If your arms are getting heavy from holding up the mask that's been created for her, it's time to get curious about this "Ideal Self" Avatar.

To Action

GET CURIOUS: YOU OR THE IDEAL SELF AVATAR?

Get clearer on what parameters you've constructed around yourself and the "ideal" version of you. Ask yourself:

1. *What do I think I should **not** be?*
2. *What do I think I **should** be?*
3. *How do I know when I'm doing a "good job" of being these things?*
4. *Is it fun navigating this?*
5. *(And this is your power question:) Am I open to doing this differently?*

When you feel yourself about to back out of something lovely that you wish you could be brave enough to do, or you're in the process of doing something you dislike because you feel like it's the "right" thing to do, take a moment to reflect on these questions. Do this a lot. Take a screenshot or picture of this page and put it as your phone's wallpaper. Consult it every time you feel yourself making a move to support the construct of your "Ideal Self". If you truly want to put an end to this pattern, say to The Universe, out loud, "I am open to doing this differently. Help me and I will do my part".

Remember: You (as in ACTUAL You and not the "Ideal Self" Avatar you) are limitless and FREE!! Bob, Toad and Francis HATE that you're starting to see this. They know you're onto them, and they are PISSED (and scared, all at the same time – the worst kind of pissed)!!! They deal in absolutes. And they're absolutely NOT on board with what you're doing here. Getting curious around your "Ideal Self" Avatar allows you to realise that the whole world isn't as interested in you as The Trio would like you to think they are. This opens up a vacuum of uncertainty.

Never forget: The Trio is mad keen on keeping You hidden behind the "Ideal Self" Avatar mask and holding you to the parameters of this construct because they think it's in your best interest. It's keeping you in the "known", in high-alert "Return to 'Safehouse'" mode. This "known" Avatar version of you is "safe" to them. To show them how it's *not* as safe as they're leading you to believe, to create an Entry-Level Access Point, you need to make a Surrender Evidence Stack. And you must start to stack counterevidence...

SURRENDER EVIDENCE STACK

Your Surrender Evidence Stack stacks when you Pause to say, "Fuck YES! I chose to let go..." Your brain gets the message of, "More of the chill, less of the control, please", and every time you do this, You add a percentage to your Surrender Evidence Stack and feel a teeny percentage safer in the unknown, and The Trio gets quieter.

Through this interruption, you begin to collect evidence for what a brilliant, badass human being you are at Surrendering (or doing any of The 7 Steps!) and you collect evidence of how Surrendering and getting yourself to think differently are actually really blooming good things!

The **ultimate** Surrender comes when you've stacked enough *believable* evidence that you start to recall this awareness more routinely. To get to this point, you must *remember* to stack evidence through the experience of using your lemons, sunflowers, and sunshine to interrupt you each time you spot yourself trying to control.

To Action

REFLECT ON YOUR 0% SURRENDER STARTING BLOCK

So, it's time to start surrendering in your real life. Answer this:

How many shitty situations have you navigated?

Lots, right?! If you'd have known what was coming before it came, could you imagine being able to handle it? Not in a million years, true?

Would you have asked for it?

"No!"

Were you glad it was happening?

"Emma...clearly not!"

But, despite not wanting it to happen, weren't you competent and able to get through it? You made it out alive, even if it was just by the skin of your teeth, correct? When you were **in it,** did you handle ALL of the uncertainty of it? The answer is yes! Maybe it wasn't the most eloquent moment of your life, but, in whatever guise, you did it. Acknowledging this doesn't mean you liked it, asked for it or want to go back to it. It's just a moment to recognise and celebrate how much more capable you are than you give yourself credit for. Taking you back there with different glasses on (and not Rose-coloured ones – we aren't sugarcoating SHIT!) allows your brain to process it all differently. To say, "Wow! We did pretty alright there. I wasn't in control, but I handled it".

I'm hoping that little exercise moved the dial at least 1%. So, why not join me in trying on those Non-Rose-Glasses in other areas of your world, too?

Like when:

- You let yourself have a pudding when Francis was saying not to – WIN +1%!
- You let your husband pack the baby bag even though you knew he'd forget something vital (and you left him to organise the solution when he realised) – WIN +1%!
- You let the kids decorate the Christmas tree and didn't go back and redo it when they were in bed – WIN +1%!

You are a source of power. And the thing standing in the way of your realising this is your willingness to Surrender.

Every time you notice a moment where you let go of what you *thought* should happen and allowed something different to unfold, you add to the Evidence Stack that The Emotional "Safehouse" isn't as safe as The Trio makes it seem and that Surrender is actually a really good thing!

To Action

GET CURIOUS AND ASK OTHERS

To keep adding percentages to your Surrender Evidence Stack, you must actively seek out and take opportunities to spot your automatic desire to control, and instead, actively **choose** to let go in those scenarios. THIS is The Art of Surrender.

Sometimes noticing these moments takes some trial and error. This is Conscious Mind stuff. This is where reading this with your lemons is going to help you notice at that deeper level and fast-track the process. Get curious by:

- Asking people who love and care about you for their thoughts by saying, "When do I take control when I don't always need to?"
- Noticing when you feel a deep desire to take responsibility for another and ask if they want or need what you're offering
- Being on the lookout for times when others offer assistance and you reject their help (because you "know" they won't do it the way you know it "should" be done)

Ask the people around you to help you see these moments and encourage you to release them (having a Coach in your life is POWERFUL for this). In Pause Thought™ moments of aware-ness, when noticing my own need to control, my favourite thing to do is to take a snort of citrus and scream the words:

"I'm choosing to freaking SURRENDER right now. I see this. And I am choosing. FUCK!!!" (I find a good fuck always helps, on all kinds of levels!)

You might not be able to Surrender in this moment – it might be the very first time you're seeing it and Surrendering completely might feel out of reach. But by saying it out loud, you are acknowledging and disturbing the thought, action or emotion currently rooted in your Unconscious patterns. Through drawing awareness to it, you're saying a big, fat "NA!!" to it. For extra power in these moments, call in Grace as a SUPER helpful ally – tell those other guys and gals, clearly, "no Terror Trio allowed!"

Doing this without force, in a loving and inviting way (just by noticing, celebrating and noticing some more) will lay yellow rainbow brick after yellow rainbow brick with ease, opening up space in The Unconscious where you've been STUCK for so long! Interrupting yourself in this way is you saying, "I can handle things that come outside of the known and I am brave enough to navigate whatever is sent my way".

And each time you do even 0.0000001% of a win, crack the lemonade out, and don't forget the lemon-rimmed crystal glasses. You've WON! Celebrate like you've just bought your first pair of Jimmy Choos. Francis, Toad and Bob won't know their arse from their elbow when you do this. They'll cry, "You don't deserve to celebrate this! It's tiny. Insignificant. It's a JOKE that you want to congratulate yourself on this!!"!

DO IT ANYWAY! Add it to your Evidence Stack. Double donkey dare you!! It'll feel weird at first. Weird is good. Weird is new. And we wanna go to **new** spaces, **right**!? Celebrating You in this way is to keep You on track, until your Evidence Stack gets so big that you just start trusting, leaping and celebrating on the regular.

To Action

YOUR SURRENDER EVIDENCE STACK RECORD

Write your Surrender Evidence Stack somewhere (a sheet on your fridge, in eyeliner on the mirror in the bathroom, a Notes page on your phone which is the first thing you see in the morning) to tangibly keep a record. If you have something tangible, outside of your thoughts, you'll be less inclined to believe The Trio the next time they're off on one about how rubbish[57] you are. Stack the evidence of the number of times you surrendered. Think back to times like:

- When you chose excitement in an unknown situation instead of fear
- When you looked for clues and cues in attempting to take control of situations, and you let go.
- When you noticed you were doing something so that Janet at the office would be pleased with how over-the-top competent you are, and you stopped
- When you asked the barista to choose your coffee instead of having your regular cappuccino

Any time that surrender doesn't feel like an option and you catch yourself in the grips of NEEDING that outcome, choose to see yellow (and not red!). Challenge yourself to see this discomfort as an opportunity for victory, irrelevant of the outcome. The victory is in how you chose to handle the discomfort. It will get easier and easier each time you do it, and it will inevitably produce *easier* outcomes to respond to. Tangibly mark this event down somewhere so you have **hard evidence** for the next time The Trio get a little loud.

---

[57] Garbage, crappy, a bit shitty. Not good enough.

Consciously witness how powerful you are! Observe how much discomfort you can actually tolerate, and realize it did not kill you to feel it. Be acutely aware of this. Celebrate it and collect tangible evidence of the new reality you're creating.

To help us establish this new reality *for good*, let's arm ourselves with the knowledge of all the cards that Francis, Toad and Bob are going to pull as you begin to practise the Art of Surrender Sunday. Their chatter will start the second you say, "Okay, what's happening here?":

What's happening?	Bob, Toad and Francis	The Art of Surrender Sunday
This is new...	**fight/run/hide:** I don't know how this is going to go, so I don't even wanna start!	**Explore:** What the funk does this mean?! Who knows!? Let's look...
I am being triggered...	**fight/run/hide:** This hurts. Hurt hurts. I want it to stop. I have to make this stop.	**Explore:** This hurts, and I know that hurt = unhealed = holding me back. Let's look...
It has to go perfectly...	**fight/run/hide:** There's a chance I won't get this right, so I'd rather not do it!	**Explore:** Getting things "wrong" is simply part of the process. Let's continue...
What will others think?	**fight/run/hide:** How embarrassing! Let's stop NOW!	**Explore:** I can't control the fact that others will have their opinions, and I'm okay with it.
This is hard...	**fight/run/hide:** If something is hard, I better not attempt it at all. Hard = failure!	**Explore:** How might this be easy? Am I missing the magic here?
(Add yours here:)		

Which voice in the centre *Bob, Toad, and Francis* column do you find yourself battling most regularly? You'll have the upper hand in this tug of war if you can anticipate The Trio's angle.

Have you got your own *What's happening?* to add to the left column as you read this? What Surrender thoughts might you try on in place of The Trio's objections to your noticing?

To add MORE to your Evidence Stack, I am going to show you how you can tune into the power of something higher...

HIGHER PURPOSE

The Art of Surrender allows you to go wide instead of inside.

No matter how frightening it feels (aka how much control Bob, Toad and Francis have over you – which, I imagine, will still be quite a lot if you're only just starting your Evidence Stack), you're here for Purpose. (Don't snigger or roll your eyes. Do I have to remind you again that the odds of you being here is 400 trillion to 1?!) You cannot get away from this truth. It's THE reason you're feeling so unfulfilled with what's happening with you right now.

Your heart and soul are squealing with delight at this fact. You are here for a Purpose bigger than yourself. Surrender to this and you'll come to realise that's it's actually a really lovely (yet **still** kind of overwhelming at times) thing. And all of this "control" that The Terror Trio are peddling, to keep up their illusion, is keeping you further removed from your reason for being here; from your Higher Purpose.

Without going too Woo, there are Universal Laws which, when left to their own natural devices, allow circumstances to unfold precisely as they're meant to. You are meant to fall into alignment with this flow. You and your life are designed to move towards and attract to you what is meant for you.

Relinquishing control will actually have the OPPOSITE effect to what Francis, Toad and Bob are telling you that it will. They're saying, "Oh gosh, if we take our eye off the ball, all hell will break loose. Coffee EVERYWHERE! White suit RUINED. And you jumped off the roller-coaster at peak height, so now you're actually dead. Dickhead!"

In actuality, the opposite is true. As you start trusting that it's impossible to control it all, you start Surrendering, which leaves you with a shit-tonne of extra energy to begin being intrigued by the idea of More. The path you're meant to be on will begin to materialise. This will not go unnoticed by The Universe; you'll be given a break. It's like The Universe sees you and says, "Okay, I see her making moves. She's showing up. Let's give her a minute to catch a breath". This **cannot** happen with all of your precision, planning, contorting and controlling. Your Conscious choices, influenced by The Unconscious Emotional "Safehouse", will just keep repeating if not addressed, no matter **what** you do.

As you build up your Surrender Evidence Stack, your Rainbow Road gets stronger. All of the evidence will reach your Conscious thoughts and you'll feel more **alive** with the knowledge that you're here for so much freaking MORE!!! You'll become so sure that you'll want to scream it from the rooftops!

THEN, the moves to take are easy. You Surrender knowing that with each step, the path will become More obvious. As you walk that Rainbow Road (which is getting sturdier by the day), each step will emanate from the depth of The Subconscious.

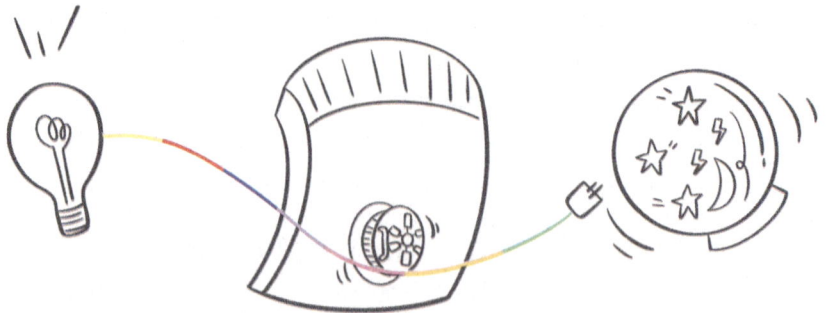

Experiencing this means that you see, in a way no other can or will (it's completely and utterly unique to you). And in this, you will perceive a new focus: creating a life with a different devotion.

A life devoted to others.

A life devoutly dedicated to making the collective *we* a priority is **guaranteed** to be a life filled with love, fulfilment, joy, abundance and any of the other good stuff you're in search of. This space is called Living a Life of Service. It's bomb! But there are some rules you must follow to make sure You feel empowered, not depleted, by serving others:

A LIFE OF SERVICE

> *The best way to find yourself is to lose*
> *yourself in the service of others.*
>
> —Mahatma Gandhi

When you align yourself to a life of service, a life of giving to others from a heartfelt drive, life will feel like the magical, unicorn dream you're hoping and wishing for.

Francis, Toad and Bob cannot exist within these spaces of giving. It's impossible. It's impossible because it's no longer about you.

But be warned: there are two ways in which you can give.

Way #1: You *want, hope and wish* for More. You *want* to serve, **but** only at a <u>Conscious level</u>. This way is often driven by lack and fear. This can look like:

- Wanting to be seen as a "good person"
- Wanting others to think highly of you
- Wanting to give to your community (donating to your favourite charities, sitting on the PTFA[58] at your kid's school, litter picking, baking cookies for the bake sale) to receive recognition
- Becoming a Coach and teaching other people how to clean up areas of their life that you haven't quite cleaned up yourself

Way #2: You have created a Rainbow Road so firmly rooted in The Subconscious space that you are able to embody your want for More totally and utterly, and therefore you can execute creating with **no** detriment to you and for the **full** benefit of others.

Most people don't know The Rainbow Road exists and therefore don't make it anywhere CLOSE to Way #2. That's why it always feels so "hard".

You've got to get real good at feeling when you're giving from Way #1 space or Way #2.

Bumbling around in the Way #1 space thinking you're in Way #2 is the WORST and it brings you into a place I call the Limbo Space.

---

[58]   *Parent, Teachers and Friends Association*

Limbo Space is when you want to serve but **only** through Conscious Mind thought. A big chunk of holistic therapists and online Coaches you see exist in this space. That's why so many of their businesses fail. This Limbo Space is as confusing for them as it is for the clients they are attempting to serve. These coaches would be much better off using the time they're trying to dedicate to others in self-service instead (bringing awareness to themselves [their Bob, Toad and Francis]) – AND getting grateful, feeling emotions, being rooted in their centre and their breath connection to the body AND SURRENDERING.

Wouldn't you rather be served by someone giving from a Way #2 space? On the receiving end, it feels much better and much more connected to receive from this space than from one that is (secretly!) lacking Way #1 ways. Way #1 is inauthentic, and this vibe often brings with it things we don't want[59].

To avoid this, give to others only when it's Way #2 –
where it takes nothing from you.

Going from Way #1 to Way #2 is a process that takes a bit of practice. The Narwhal Effect™ can help you here.

THE TALE OF THE NARWHAL HORN

---

[59]   If you find yourself lost trying to grapple, yet failing, with the Way #2 space, dive into The 7 Steps again. Continue laying down that Rainbow Road. Soon enough, you'll be able to skip along and #2 the shit out of your life.

Imagine your spine is a hose (weird start, I know. Stick with me). This hose is a vessel which has the potential to carry **ALL** the necessary energies you need. The base is your gooch. The hose then follows your spine to the crown of your head where the tip of the hose sneaks out. For fun, and a lovely visual for The Conscious Brain, I imagine this peaky hose-tip (when adequately connected) as a Rainbow-coloured Narwhal Horn.

You need a super strong and intact hose for carry-ing energy. Starting from the base of your being, this energy should peak to produce an overflow that pours out of your Narwhal-tip crown. When utilising a fully intact Energy Hose, you create The Narwhal Effect™: a process where energy is taken from your tail and through to the tip of your crown. It then bursts out, creating a Narwhal Horn of Rainbow Flow. The horn is the final outlet for this firehose of energy. With this struc-ture clear and in place, energy is then free to flow through and out of you in this way.

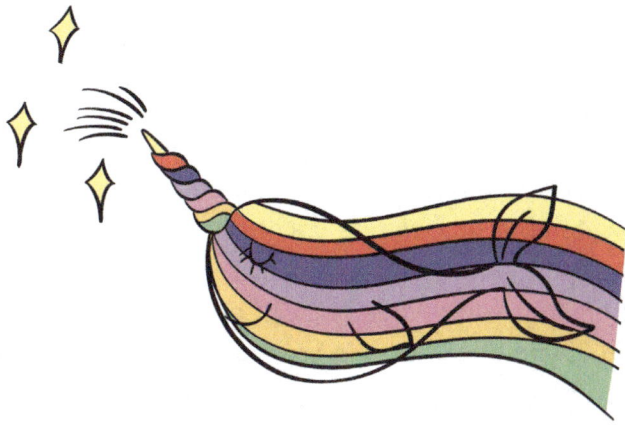

When you give energy to the world in this way, from your bootstraps up to the tip of your being with a Narwhal Effect™ overflow, it hardly ever feels like effort. It feels like an easy extension of you. In this space, You move your Horn to wherever it's needed, and blast! This is the epitome of the #2 Life of Service Way.

> *Living a life of service will feel like a Narwhal Horn Rainbow Explosion ONLY when your energy levels are full and overflowing in abundance.*

When you forget how to give in this manner and you are "giving" to others because you feel like it is something which you "should" do, it is the opposite of The Narwhal Effect™. Giving in this vein carries with it thoughts like:

- "If I don't do this, something I don't want to happen might."
- "They would like me to do this, so I 'should.'"
- "They might think badly of me if I don't."
- "A 'good person' would do this, so I should."

Giving from this space creates an effect just like everyone you help has a teeny little pin which they (usually unknowingly!) press into your Narwhal Spine-Hose with each action you do for them. Filled with holes, instead of energy moving up and through you, to climatic Narwhal sprinkle glory, the pin pricks instead allow remnants of your magical energy source to lightly dust them. They feel better, but you feel drained as funk!

The Energy supply that your gooch is tapped into is limitless. Energy continually attempts to make its way from the root of your being to your Narwhal Horn bonce. But it can't make that Narwhal climatic rainbow squirt finale if you're bleeding out all over anyone who wants a piece of you. If you have holes in your spine (aka lots of people have access to you and place demands upon you and your sprinkle system), you're sprinkling all over the place. And quite probably, if you're being completely honest, *you won't be having all that much of a positive impact on those beings. They're getting your last dregs instead of your full faucet.*

This way doesn't actually help other people in the long run, and it certainly isn't working for you. You cannot serve from this self-depriving space. That climatic #2 Narwhal Effect™ Rainbow Flow can only happen with a strong build-up of energy travelling from bottom to top. If you've learned to please other people for a good chunk of your life, this Rainbow Flow explosion has been stunted by sprinkles of your magic coming out of those tiny pinpricks before it reaches the top; this way, your energy never truly becomes full enough to climax!

To loosen the lock on a life connected to More (Rainbow Flow explosion and all!), you must learn the art of Surrender. Surrender is the magnet which draws everything that we have been learning together.

A lesson which you must learn is how to prioritise You and be able to say, "I deserve to take up space and do things for me until doing these things for others feels Narwhal-Horn easy.

SURRENDER SUNDAY HIGHLIGHTS:

1. Remind yourself, over and over again, that Surrender is easy, until one day...it'll just STICK!! Maintain an energy of, "Oh yeah, that's right. I FORGET how easy this gets to be. How silly of me!!"

2. Remain open to the question, "Might there be More?" Get curious about this mask you've been wearing for too long by asking yourself the questions from The What If List:
   What if:

   > *I didn't have my name?*
   > *I didn't have a family?*
   > *I didn't have this role/job?*
   > *I didn't live where I lived?*
   > *I had a heart transplant?*
   > *I had brain damage?*
   > *My brain was put in another body?*

   What makes me <u>me</u>?

3. Stack your evidence for when Surrender was actually a brilliantly helpful thing to do (despite it feeling SUPER uncomfortable!). Keep a tally next to your bed, in your diary, in your phone notes, or a piece of paper on the fridge. Stack the Evidence until it gets so big that you can see how letting go is helpful and you start to Surrender your way through life.

Go inside and not wide. Start to explore the idea that you are here for More, that you shying away from opportunities to do bigger things is The Trio and not You (with a Capital Y). Start showing up through acts of service to others and organisations bigger than you (but only with true Way #2 vibes to make sure it's not The Trio in disguise). Get curious around The Narwhal Effect™: notice when you're sprinkling others with your last dregs instead of blasting the world with your rainbow-coloured Narwhal Energy Horn! If you're on your last dregs, redirect yourself to The 7 Steps again for however long it takes to truly embody each Step.

REMEMBER:

Mind-on-Mute Mondays:

Wear your Minty Greens and explore this mind-blowing fact:

There is a voice inside your head.

This voice is <u>not</u> You.

Seek to notice every time he's getting his knickers in a twist, and snap a branch from his most favourite, familiar neurological brain-loops so he starts to become less comfortable travelling these outdated routes. Get curious around the idea that if there is a voice speaking, then who is the one listening?

That voice is You!

You will not know it the first moment you contemplate it, but you will come to know it. And once you do, you won't care to "understand" and "know". You'll just let it be. Here you'll feel a freedom you had no idea could exist for you.

To access your Mind-on-Mute Monday supplementary supportive workbooks and videos, please <u>CLICK HERE</u>.

REMEMBER:

Trigger-Free Tuesday:

Wear your Orangy Tangerines.

Toad believes that everyone else is to blame and that it'd all be just fine and dandy if **they** all stopped being such arseholes! Your job here is to be like Teflon: create a Space to Choose Freedom between the stuff happening outside of you and how you are reacting or responding to it. Keep laying the tangerine part of your Rainbow Road. Notice every time you see you're on the hunt for your Toad/wanting to bathe in someone else's firework explosions and say, "I see you and it's **not** going down this way ANYmore!!"

To access your Trigger-Free Tuesday workbook and supporting video, please CLICK HERE.

REMEMBER:

Wake-up Wednesdays:

Wear your watermelon pink and learn how to be kind to your mind. You're only thinking this way because all of those harsh voices that told you that you weren't "good enough" for this world got so loud that they've become etched inside your mind. Now, on eternal replay as your Francis, you've listened to them/her for so long that you've got confused. You think she is you and that you are her. You aren't. And the way to see this is to notice where she is introducing poisonous, grudge-bearing and controlling toxicity into your life, telling you it's good for you/all you deserve. When you spot this, remember that she is the overbearingly over-protective friend, and **not** the fiend she's doing a REALLY good job of pretending to be. You aren't landing yourself in the Street, the Cell or in a Casket. You're moving into new spaces – a wide open sea. Once she realises that the water's fine, she'll come join you. But you must move first.

To access your Wake-Up Wednesday supplementary supportive workbooks and videos, please CLICK HERE.

REMEMBER:

Thankful Thursdays:

Embody your lavender purples as you quit the pursuit of finding ways to Quick-Fix yourself. Centre yourself in the knowledge that all the stuff that you want on the outside of you materialises through grounding yourself in being grateful AF for the present moment and all it contains: shit shows and all! Sometimes finding gratitude in these shit-show situations feels like a push too far, but without this, your hunt for Quick-Fix Plums will continue to **drain** the joy out of your life.

When you feel drained, you've simply forgotten that you get to eat ice cream for breakfast, lunch and dinner, and that the plum is merely the cherry on top. When you find yourself down the lane, driving yourself round the BEND, looking for that sweet-treat promise outside of you, call in Grace. Get willing to do it differently. Find something to get grateful for in this obscure ride around the sun that we're all on.

To access your Thankful Thursday supplementary supportive workbooks and videos, please CLICK HERE.

REMEMBER:

Feel-It Friday:

On Fridays, remember to sense your almonds and embody your blues so that feeling your feelings feels more inviting. Your Mama, Papa and any other adult who got the gift of being in close proximity to you didn't understand the glory of all that you are. Instead, they took it upon themselves to mould you into what **they** thought you "should" be. This involved a LOT of telling you to smush down any and every uncomfortable emotion, which made you into a Cow(ard). They were wrong! You're a freaking BUFFALO!

To access your Feel-It Friday supplementary supportive workbooks and videos, please CLICK HERE.

REMEMBER:

Saturday Sitting: Wear ALL of the rhubarb reds as you realise that breathwork is the bread and butter of an elevated existence lived on The Rainbow Road. Connecting to the moment of right now is actualised by slowing down your awareness, which is influenced directly by the speed of your breath. In this heighted Alpha Brain Wave space, you get to choose where your awareness lies:

Out there in everyone else's messed-up *umwelts*?

Or inside, in your internal snack drawer filled with feasts that your Conscious Mind can't currently think up (because they're too magical to believe, right now!)?

Use rhubarb reds as your reminder to come back to this space, over and over again. And don't "try", ***do***!

To access your Saturday Sitting supplementary supportive workbooks and videos, please CLICK HERE.

REMEMBER:

Surrender Sunday: Use a yellow interruption to disturb anything that feels frustrating. Gently redirect your energy and say, "How silly...I forgot that life gets to be easy!" Be curious around the idea that There Might Be More. When you find yourself getting hung up on it all, ask yourself the questions on The What If List, which leads to the following 2 final questions:

What if you aren't all of those things you think you are?

What's underneath?

That's You! You're undefinable, in THE BEST ways! Serve others, **only** when you're connected with the true nothingness and EVERYTHINGNESS of who you are (the natural conclusion that The What If List brings you to).

Connecting with others is authentic when you are overflowing with the excitement of being alive, when you've grounded yourself so clearly in the fundamentals of The 7 Steps that giving feels like an abundant overflow to those who are receiving.

Every time you see yourself seeking to control and you surrender, stack the evidence for how powerful this choice is for you. Make a **physical** Surrender Evidence Stack note somewhere that you'll see on the regular as reminders of the magic of Surrendering. Observe all that it makes space for.

To access your Surrender Sunday supplementary supportive workbooks and videos, please CLICK HERE.

YOUR ANXIETY-FREE DANCE PARTY

Making time to explore these 7 areas, and embody them, on the daily **is** what's going to allow you to reach the climax of Maslow's hierarchy, making you an all-around bad-ass unicorn living out YOUR version of your Anxiety-Free Dance Party life. Before I begin to explain how life from this point on gets to feel like an Anxiety-Free Dance Party on the REGULAR, there are some Party Rules:

Party Rule #1: Be patient with yourself – it's meant to "go wrong".

Never forget that The Rainbow Road develops in pieces. This book came to be through trial (and a LOT of freaking) error. I made up this shit and I STILL had to go through the wringer (a number of times), so don't go thinking you get to skip this bit (AKA don't go listening to The Trio when actually you're just tired or just dealing with an extra big doozy dose of the #humanexperience).

Party Rule #2: Keep moving.

As long as you understand the essence of each Step and continue to use your Piggyback Sensory Hacks™, you'll be moving in a Rainbow Road building direction. Bring focus to your Piggyback

Sensory Hacks™ daily. This repetition will signal to your brain to always bring awareness to building your Rainbow Road as a bare minimum (The 1% Matrix is coming up and will concretely show you how to do this).

Party Rule #3: In moments of frustration, when it feels like what you're doing isn't enough, call in Grace.

Grace will remind you that it IS enough! Often, it's more than enough, no matter how small it is – I promise! She'll remind you that your best is good enough (even when you think it's somewhat questionable)! The most magical changes happen most often when you reach a point of, "I wanna give up" but you choose Grace and thus **choose** to keep going (with **no** *trying*!).

Party Rule #4: Choose.

Don't "try" and don't "hope". Keep sight of your dress. Keep choosing to try it on.

Now, I'm going to give you the HOW you get to keep going...

I knew that in order to create a new Anxiety-Free Dance Party *umwelt* (by letting The Subconscious, not The Conscious Mind, lead), you would need to feel Two Things about this work:

Thing 1: **That what I'm asking you to do holds IMMEDIATE TRANSFORMATIVE POWER** (mindset work needs to be *immediately and* **powerfully transformative** for your Conscious Brain to stay on board).

Thing 2: **That what I'm asking you to do promises EASE, FUN and CONVENIENCE (**transformative mindset work must also be unbelievably **easy, fun** and **convenient,** otherwise you'll be back at your "Safehouse" before you know it!)

For this to happen, I knew that this work **had** be different from anything else out there. This work HAS to be an **easy** and **immediately transformative** Mindset Strategy that **allows life to feel like an Anxiety-Free Dance Party**.

The Rainbow Road way means it gets to be **easy** and freaking **fun**! But parties take planning, and you have to **be** the party planner of your own life. In other words, you need to get your Conscious Brain over the hump to that Entry-Level Access Point so that you can begin to party plan.

When I first practised The 7 Steps, I actively made space to feel inspired to:

- Journal every day
- Read
- Listen to podcasts
- Wake up at 5 am
- Meditate for hours
- Fast
- Dedicate hours of my life to these 7 Steps, like...every day!!

When I learned the potency of practising these 7 areas, I got a taste of what my life might look like, and it was SWEET. I had **all** the evidence

I needed in absolute abundance that The 7 Steps worked! Squeak! I knew I'd nailed *Thing 1*: these Steps were divine; I was hitting **immediate, powerful transformation** with BELLS on. ***Powerfully transformative*** became the strapline[60] it carried! It felt like I'd struck GOLD!

Only...I *still* couldn't sustain it. Back then, I was only able to actualise all of these *Thing 1* things when I sacrificed my actual life by getting up at 5 am, neglecting my family and friends, and all of my other worldly duties that come with being a human being. I was missing ALL of The *Thing 2* Stuffs – the fun part! Back then, to get the *Thing 1* **powerfully transformative** results, "Push" was the only answer I had. I decided that if I wanted this enough (which I did), and if I worked hard enough (which I could), then it would come to fruition.

Just gotta push! Push harder. Be more. Do more.

But actualising this through "Push" alone was rough – I was all Pushed OUT! Back then, it was not fun. It was not easy. And it was NOT convenient! Keeping these 7 Steps alive left me burnt OUT (AGAIN!!!)

Just as I was about to add another chalk mark to my tally of "You're shite, Emma. Look at what you can create when you "Push" hard enough...but you're so rubbish, you can't keep going...then you burn out, you disgrace!!", my moment of *Thing 2* Inspiration happened...

ENLIGHTENING WOOD WALK

At the end of another "Push" cycle, where my grand finale was an extra impressive crash and burn that landed me in bed for an entire Sunday, I walked through the woods the following autumn morning.

I entered the woods and felt the too familiar sensations of a panic attack creeping into my body. The closing throat, the tightening chest,

---

[60]   Another word for *tagline*.

the tingling sensations crawling up from my toes and hands into my torso.

In my exhausted state, I didn't resist. I didn't panic. I didn't respond. I slumped to the forest floor and sobbed, uncontrollably – think the ugliest kinda cry you've ever seen, then 10x it! Mouth open/dribble hanging out kinda sobs. Snot EVERYWHERE! I was burned OUT! And as I sat on the ground, unable to fight any longer, those words came back to me...

There is more than this.

And I started to see it. I started to sense what this actually meant for me. I started to hear whispers of ideas and shades of colours that I hadn't seen before. A moment of:

"EMMA!! What you need hasn't been birthed yet. That's why none of it is 'working'...You ready to FINALLY do this?!"

I picked myself up, out of the heap on the forest floor, and got down to business...

THE 1% IMPROVED MATRIX

It was in this moment, whilst not crushing strategy or listening to a podcast or meditating for 5 hours, that it happened. At a very reasonable time when the rest of the world was also awake, when I was out doing something lovely that didn't include ancient Pali or journaling until my hands bled, I had this enlightening moment that allowed me to realise that the first step of *Thing 2* was to listen and work with my own energies. From this moment, The 1% Improved Matrix was born.

It looks like this:

HIGH ENERGY Little Resistance			LOW ENERGY High Resistance
You feel inspired to actively sit with The 7 Step Formula. Your energy is high. You feel little resistance.	The idea of doing a bite-sized element of the work is appealing to you. Your energies are middle-of-the-road and so is your resistance.	The idea of doing a bite-sized amount of work is feasible. Your energies are fleeting, but so is your resistance.	The idea of doing any formal, tangible work is overwhelming. You have high resistance to doing any formal work.
ACTION: Indulge in the active, tangible work. Read the book, use as many of the Piggyback Sensory Hack™ elements as you can at as many opportunities as possible. Check in EVERY time you become aware of a Piggyback Sense and check in with its Step.	ACTION: Do some of the active, tangible work. Read the book, use some of the Piggyback Sensory Hack™ elements. Check in as often as possible as you become aware of a Piggyback Sense and check in with its Step.	ACTION: Recognise an opportunity to do a small element of the work. Use one of the Piggyback Sensory Hack™ elements and check in with them when you feel inspired to.	ACTION: Make peace with your decision to choose out of the work today. As you embody that day's Piggyback Sensory Hack™, make *calling in Grace* when you get your sensory cue your #1 focus for today.

Learning to listen to your energies means you can apply yourself dili-gently when your energies are high and your resistance is low. Actively doing the work in a space of High Energy means you are in a state where you have extra energy in your brain to compute new information. Here, you're ready to step outside the parameter of your Emotional "Safehouse" and move a little further outside of your "known".

If and when it doesn't feel like this, rest. And not "Pretend Rest" where you aren't doing the thing but are still very much thinking about the thing (and giving yourself a pretty horrible time about not doing the thing). Rest. Actual rest. Know that truly resting your energies will give you extra potency when you *are* in that High Energy flow space to actively and intentionally create. Your resistance levels will naturally drop as you stop "Pushing" and being so hard on yourself, and **then** you'll feel more inspired to do the work. A new cycle that's naturally inspired – with not a hint of "Push" in sight!

When I reflected on how to put this work together, I wanted to make overcoming anxiety one of the best goddamn experiences ever. When someone who was done with anxiety wanted to create More and got curious around an opportunity to do this work, I wanted it to feel like a hard YES to them.

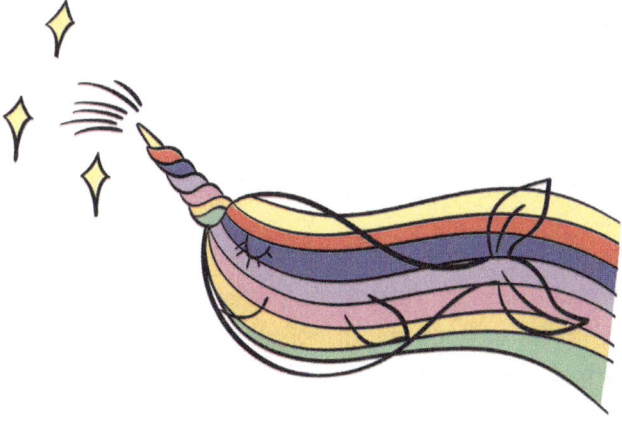

I wanted them to feel like a Narwhal in rainbow-coloured water, swimming all the strokes, having THE time of its freaking life whilst easily overcoming anxiety.

And now, I've taught you the strokes. All 7 of them. So now it's time to make that Anxiety-Free Dance Party come to life!

YOU'RE AN ANXIETY-FREE DANCE PARTY GODDESS!

You freaking **did it**! You made it all the way to the end (or you're an end-page peeker and you're EXCITED to make it to this magical point in real time) and out of your overthinking thoughts. You've made it into a world of magic, make-believe, and **more truth than what most psychology books possess**. The Trio might still be there, loudly protesting. Let them. We know what to do with them now.

Make this book your Bible. Put it next to your bed and place the day's Piggyback Sensory Hack™ on top of it. Every night before you go to bed, give thanks for that day's Piggyback Sensory Hack™, as you switch it out for tomorrow's. Let it be the first thing you see in the morning before you dive into your newly Rainbow-sprinkled world, and let it be the last thing you see before you close your eyes and drift off to your Rainbow slumber party.

Cement that Rainbow Road in your Unconscious **eternally**. Being out there, using your Rainbow Skills in real time, is the best way to firmly set your Rainbow Road. Use The Trove of Techniques at the back of this book when you spot:

◊ One of The Trio at work
◊ A space in which you're feeling less than your thankful self
◊ An overwhelm of emotions you don't know how to process
◊ A space where you want to connect to your Snack-Drawer Breathwork highway
◊ Your desire to Surrender the bejesus out of something

Reference the relevant part of The Rainbow Road you need, get your Piggyback Sensory Hack™ out for it, and get into your actual life to practise the magic.

If you're struggling to get your Piggyback Sensory Hack™ stuffs together (or you want to get your hands on some genuine Feel-It Friday Buffalo blue crystals or Mind-on-Mute Monkey Mints or ANYthing for any of the other 5 days of the week), we have ready-to-go Piggyback Sensory Hack™ Packs that we can post out to you ANYWHERE in the world. They're made with love and tenderness, each personalised to fit your unique needs to help with what you may be particularly navigating right now. You can buy them at www.thereismorethanthis.com.

Our *Free from Anxiety Flashcards Deck* is filled with moments of inspiration you can summon in moments when you're calling for inspiration – a new angle for an Entry-Level Access point to open up for you. Tune in further to the power of your intuition and draw the perfect card for what you need that moment. You can buy them at www.thereismorethanthis.com

If you feel inspired to explore any of this work at a deeper, personal, even more magical level:

- Join our FREE Live Masterclass held by Emma by CLICKING HERE
- Find me on Instagram: @morethanthisbyEmmaUpton
- Email me and my team at morethanthisbyEmmaUpton@gmail.com
- Visit our website at https://www.thereismorethanthis.com

YOU CHOOSE

This work happened when I made a choice...

I chose to not die so that I could write this for you. I chose. You must choose too...

Choose to do; **don't** try. Choose to anticipate; **don't** hope. Choose to use your Piggyback Sensory Hacks™. Choose to build your Rainbow Road. Choose to use The 1% Improved Matrix.

Choose to smile when it's The Trio of Terror. Choose Grace when it's too much.

Mind on Mute. Be Trigger Free. Wake up to everything that's **not** you. Get Thankful. Feel your Feelings. Sit with your breath, and Surrender the shit out of this wild ride around the sun we all find ourselves on.

Choose – over and over again. One day, you won't need to choose; You (with a Capital Y) will lead you to your More. And you are free!

You aren't here to exist. You're here for More Than This. Your Rainbow Road is the route which will take you there…

It's been a wild and trippy ride! Trying on that dress, over and over again. Exploring the depths of your being that you forgot existed…

Now it's time to land whilst still maintaining the heights you've actualised in reading this book.

The techniques presented in this book are the keys to your reawakening. To keep this work easily accessible, I present to you The Trove of Techniques, complete with the Remember sections and the Terminology you came across whilst on this trip. The Trove of Techniques which follows was created for your daily reference in order for you to embody the purest essence of this work.

To access the downloadable Trove of Techniques and supporting video, please click on the image below.

THE REMEMBERS

You've collected Remembers throughout the book at the end of each chapter. Now they've been compiled into one central space altogether for your convenience and accessibility. Use them alongside each chapter's downloadable workbook to keep this work alive and easy each and every day.

REMEMBER:

Mind-on-Mute Mondays:

Wear your Minty Greens and explore this mind-blowing fact:

There is a voice inside your head.

This voice is <u>not</u> You.

Seek to notice every time he's getting his knickers in a twist, and snap a branch from his most favourite, familiar neurological brain-loops so he starts to become less comfortable travelling these outdated routes. Get curious around the idea that if there is a voice speaking, then who is the one listening?

That voice is You!

You will not know it the first moment you contemplate it, but you will come to know it. And once you do, you won't care to "understand" and "know". You'll just let it be. Here you'll feel a freedom you had no idea could exist for you.

To access your Mind-on-Mute Monday supplementary supportive workbooks and videos, please <u>CLICK HERE</u>.

REMEMBER:

Trigger-Free Tuesday:

Wear your Orangy Tangerines.

Toad believes that everyone else is to blame and that it'd all be just fine and dandy if **they** all stopped being such arseholes! Your job here is to be like Teflon: create a Space to Choose Freedom between the stuff happening outside of you and how you are reacting or responding to it. Keep laying the tangerine part of your Rainbow Road. Notice every time you see you're on the hunt for your Toad/wanting to bathe in someone else's fire-work explosions and say, "I see you and it's **not** going down this way ANYmore!!"

To access your Trigger-Free Tuesday workbook and supporting video, please CLICK HERE.

REMEMBER:

Wake-up Wednesdays:

Wear your watermelon pink and learn how to be kind to your mind. You're only thinking this way because all of those harsh voices that told you that you weren't "good enough" for this world got so loud that they've become etched inside your mind. Now, on eternal replay as your Francis, you've listened to them/her for so long that you've got confused. You think she is you and that you are her. You aren't. And the way to see this is to notice where she is introducing poisonous, grudge-bearing and controlling toxicity into your life, telling you it's good for you/all you deserve. When you spot this, remember that she is the overbearingly over-protective friend, and **not** the fiend she's doing a REALLY good job of pretending to be. You aren't landing yourself in the Street, the Cell or in a Casket. You're moving into new spaces – a wide open sea. Once she realises that the water's fine, she'll come join you. But you must move first.

To access your Wake-Up Wednesday supplementary supportive workbooks and videos, please CLICK HERE.

REMEMBER:

Thankful Thursdays:

Embody your lavender purples as you quit the pursuit of finding ways to Quick-Fix yourself. Centre yourself in the knowledge that all the stuff that you want on the outside of you materialises through grounding yourself in being grateful AF for the present moment and all it contains: shit shows and all! Sometimes finding gratitude in these shit-show situations feels like a push too far, but without this, your hunt for Quick-Fix Plums will continue to **drain** the joy out of your life.

When you feel drained, you've simply forgotten that you get to eat ice cream for breakfast, lunch and dinner, and that the plum is merely the cherry on top. When you find yourself down the lane, driving yourself round the BEND, looking for that sweet-treat promise outside of you, call in Grace. Get willing to do it differently. Find something to get grateful for in this obscure ride around the sun that we're all on.

To access your Thankful Thursday supplementary supportive workbooks and videos, please CLICK HERE.

REMEMBER:

Feel-It Friday:

On Fridays, remember to sense your almonds and embody your blues so that feeling your feelings feels more inviting. Your Mama, Papa and any other adult who got the gift of being in close proximity to you didn't understand the glory of all that you are. Instead, they took it upon themselves to mould you into what **they** thought you "should" be. This involved a LOT of telling you to smush down any and every uncomfortable emotion, which made you into a Cow(ard). They were wrong! You're a freaking BUFFALO!

To access your Feel-It Friday supplementary supportive workbooks and videos, please CLICK HERE.

REMEMBER:

Saturday Sitting: Wear ALL of the rhubarb reds as you realise that breathwork is the bread and butter of an elevated existence lived on The Rainbow Road. Connecting to the moment of right now is actualised by slowing down your awareness, which is influenced directly by the speed of your breath. In this heighted Alpha Brain Wave space, you get to choose where your awareness lies:

Out there in everyone else's messed-up *umwelts*?

Or inside, in your internal snack drawer filled with feasts that your Conscious Mind can't currently think up (because they're too magical to believe, right now!)?

Use rhubarb reds as your reminder to come back to this space, over and over again. And don't "try", **do**!

To access your Saturday Sitting supplementary supportive workbooks and videos, please CLICK HERE.

REMEMBER:

Surrender Sunday: Use a yellow interruption to disturb anything that feels frustrating. Gently redirect your energy and say, "How silly...I forgot that life gets to be easy!" Be curious around the idea that There Might Be More. When you find yourself getting hung up on it all, ask yourself the questions on The What If List, which leads to the following 2 final questions:

What if you aren't all of those things you think you are?

What's underneath?

That's You! You're undefinable, in THE BEST ways! Serve others, **only** when you're connected with the true nothingness and EVERYTHINGNESS of who you are (the natural conclusion that The What If List brings you to).

Connecting with others is authentic when you are overflowing with the excitement of being alive, when you've grounded yourself so clearly in the fundamentals of The 7 Steps that giving feels like an abundant overflow to those who are receiving.

Every time you see yourself seeking to control and you surrender, stack the evidence for how powerful this choice is for you. Make a **physical** Surrender Evidence Stack note somewhere that you'll see on the regular as reminders of the magic of Surrendering. Observe all that it makes space for.

To access your Surrender Sunday supplementary supportive workbooks and videos, please CLICK HERE.

TERMINOLOGY

In 7 **Easy** Steps, you can overcome overthinking and live free from anxiety, **but** you must be willing to come on a mindset adventure with me.

This book is Mindset work meets Alice in Wonderland. For those of you daring enough to believe that a life free from anxiety **forever** can exist for you too, I've created a defining guide of terms from the book to make remembering how to walk this road together a little easier to "understand".

Overarching essential concepts that must be applied to EVERYTHING we do together from here on out...	
Trying on the Dress	**In moments where your brain is screaming, "This is ridiculous. This will never work for me", and you remain curious around the concept being considered, you're *trying on the dress*. The dress is figurative; it's a repeated moment which must be tried on over and over again, with kindness, ease and alignment, until, all in one moment, it fits – of COURSE it fits!** The dress in question is You living an Anxiety-Free Life **Forever.** It fits and becomes Yours, not by dieting, or budgeting, or borrowing, or any other temporary means; Your Anxiety-Free life becomes yours **forever** when you've tried it on *your* number of times. One day, you simply realise it **is** Yours after all, and it fits phenomenally. **In these moments, choose to seek...**

"Shoulding"	The word "should" gives the impression that there is a "correct" way to do something, instantly implying that there is an equally weighted incorrect way also. There are **SO** many ways to approach life. When the verb "should" comes up, ask yourself, *"What would my world look like if there were no 'shoulds'?"*
	In these moments, choose to seek...

FOUNDATIONAL CONCEPTS

The "Ideal Self" Avatar	**The version of a person that they think the world wants.**
Actual You (with a Capital Y)	**The ACTUAL person behind the facade of The "Ideal Self" Avatar.**
Entry-Level Access Point	**A foundational thought or idea which is inviting enough to get The Conscious Mind intrigued whilst keeping it out of overwhelm.** The mind-blowing concepts I teach are beyond Conscious comprehension when explained in totality; the "logical" "thinking" brain might dismiss, belittle, or disregard many of the concepts I deliver. An Entry-Level Access Point is **the** foundation upon which **all** new, everlasting knowledge is built upon. It is appetising and digestible enough for The Conscious Mind to begin to explore something you want it to cooperate with.

The 7 Steps	**7 fundamental Mindset Principles which when embodied allow you to be Free from Anxiety *Forever*:**
	• **Putting your mind on mute**
	• **Living trigger free**
	• **Waking up to what's not You**
	• **Getting thankful**
	• **Feeling your feelings fully**
	• **Sitting and checking in with yourself**
	• **Surrendering to what is and Finding you are part of something bigger than yourself**
	All 7 Steps reconstruct The Rainbow Road.
The Rainbow Road	**The Rainbow Road runs through the Landscape of your being, starting from The Subconscious Mind, running through The Unconscious Mind, and ending up at The Conscious Mind.**
	Each of The 7 Mindset Steps (pieces of The Rainbow Road) has a colour, scent, time and taste ascribed to it. All together, they make up The Rainbow Road. Each individual Step allows the reader to perceive a different part of The Rainbow Road, a different aspect of overcoming anxiety.
Piggyback Sensory Hack™	**A means of linking each of The 7 Mindset Principles with a profound sensory experience.**
	The smell of your mum's perfume takes you back to bedtime as a babe; the taste of a Cherry Coke ice lolly takes you back to endless summers; deep oranges take you to Ibiza sunsets... The senses give us the power to transcend our current state. The 7 Steps practised alongside The 7 Piggyback Sensory Hacks™ makes the work a sensory submersion. This allows a transcendence beyond The Conscious Mind thoughts of "Push" and manipulation and into a flowing state of freedom.

Pause Thoughts™	**A brief moment in which you check in with your headspace and get curious around what's going down.** Every time you get a flash or hint of that Piggyback Sensory Hack™ when you're going to the loo (especially for a number two), when you're making a stew (or any kind of food), when you're standing in a queue, when you don't know what to do, take a Pause Thought™. Check in to see where your awareness is. What will you choose to do differently to step into Your Anxiety-Free Life?
The 1% Improved Matrix *(from The Anxiety-Free Dance Party)*	**A strategy for applying the work by tuning into your energies, wants, needs and desires in a given moment for MAXIMUM impact.** Eastern philosophies rely upon devout faith and patience. Western philosophies rely on obsessive thought intrusions and dissection. Both are "Pushing" through to "realisations". The 1% Improved Matrix is a system that abandons "Push" and nourishes the realisation that you are **not** a machine that needs dissecting and putting back together; you **are** a real-life human, living in the real world where you can't sit in the woods for 12 years to meditate and journal yourself into the anxious-free state you seek. Finding balance means that you get to lead as you increase your confidence.
The Narwhal Effect™	The effect of re-connecting The Rainbow Road from the tail of The Subconscious, through The Unconscious Emotional "Safehouse" space, and up to the tip of The Conscious. It is only through this effect (you pouring from a "full cup" as opposed to an empty one) that you can live your life in an overflow of energy with the freedom to serve others – or not. Either way, You are free.

Every human moves through three different terrains in their mental Landscape...

BRAIN WAVE STATES IN THREE DIFFERENT TERRAINS

The frequencies of your brain change as you move through The Three Different Terrains in your Mental Landscape. Actively learning how to move from one brain state to another is paramount to rebuilding your Rainbow Road and thus overcoming anxiety. This is how it's done...

TERRAIN ONE: **CONSCIOUS** CHARACTERS

BRAINWAVE STATE: Busy Beta Bee Brain Waves

Found in Saturday Sitting

A brain in Beta is heavily in The Conscious Mind. All awareness is directed towards the stuff "out there" – thinking, plotting and scheming around how to navigate and manipulate everything on the outside. Anxiety in Beta is best described as trying to calculate 3,754.5 x 73.56 with a frenzied bee circling ready to sting! It's pretty impossible to be clear here.

The Conscious:

The **only** part of your mind that you are actively aware of. In this part of your mind, you can think up, define and name things.

What resides there ⬇

Trio of Terror Member #1: Bob the Monkey	**Bob:** The voice in the head which never settles has been defined as a crazed monkey called Bob who spends his life *bobbing* from thought to thought, thing to thing, never able to settle.
Mind-on-Mute Monday	**Bob's communication is: Creating a Brain-Forest.** Bob is desperate to "make sense" of what should be a brief and passing thought as quickly as he can in search of a feeling of, *"Ah, well that feels better now. Phew!"* Each thought is like a branch on a tree – the more thoughts, the more branches occur, and the quicker Bob can monkey-dash and dart around inside the mind causing relentless chaos.

Trio of Terror Member #2: Toad *Trigger Free Tuesday*	**Toad:** A Poisonous Toad who's **desperate** to chase and track down an elusive, never-ending high to **finally** feel good. The only problem is: he's looking in all the wrong places and trying to beg, borrow and steal his way to a space of peace, joy, endless energy and happiness.
	Toad's communication is: Puke/poop and firework explosions when he's triggered. His poisonous ways evoke explosive results of harsh words and rash action which spill out covering everyone in a stinky, brown mess.
Trio of Terror Member #3 Francis *Wake-up Wednesday*	**Francis:** A fiend who takes on the voice of anyone who **ever** made out that they know best. It's easy to confuse Francis for Actual You (with a Capital Y) – she's a good liar, but her tricks are easy to spot with this third step.
	Francis' communication is: Red Rag Moments. These moments happen when Francis feels like she is being: • Overlooked • Underseen • Misheard • Taken advantage of • Ridiculed • Embarrassed • Made to feel guilty • Made to feel ashamed • Or made to feel any other intense emotion which is unpleasant to feel Red Rag Moments are those moments when Francis thinks you're being perceived by others as anything less than The "Ideal Self" Avatar (the strongest, best warrior in camp who no other tribe member, bear or snake would ever try to eat).
Cow(ard) *Feel-it Friday*	**Cow(ard):** The Cow(ard) runs, tries to hide, and condemns herself to endure more pain than is necessary as she runs along with and indulges in the storm, instead of into and straight through it like her Bovidae buddies, The Buffalo.

*These characters live inside your Conscious Mind and have free-flow access to The Unconscious. The Unconscious is where these characters interact with you and make sure you act according to their agenda. The Trio each use **all** kinds of tactics to peddle the illusion that The "Ideal Self" Avatar is you – they're so lost that they actually believe this and spend their WHOLE existence trying to convince their host of this too.*

TERRAIN TWO: **UNCONSCIOUS** CHARACTERS

Every anxiety that The Conscious Mind creates is projected into, and played out in, The Unconscious. With no free-flowing, beautifully intact Rainbow Road, every fear and anxious thought is stored here: it gets heightened <u>every</u> time you frequent this space.

The Unconscious:

An **unknown**, endless chasm filled with feelings, thoughts, memories and urges, stored up over time and housed in a central space which you have **no** considered control over. Until your Rainbow Road is up and running again, The Conscious Mind's characters treat this space like their playground at your expense.

What resides there ⬇

The "Ideal Self" Avatar	**The made-up version of the person that The Trio reside behind:**
	The Trio add fuel to The "Ideal Self" Avatar's fire. They breathe life into her and keep up the facade that this perfectly polished creation is **the** leading lady in life. She's actually a projection of all of the worst fears a person wants to hide from.

The Emotional "Safehouse" *Part 1:* *You Are Not the Problem: Learning Your Landscape*	**A familiar space which The Conscious Mind has decided is what you will ALWAYS be seeking to come back "home" to.** The brain's default setting is **always** "return to what's most familiar" (even if familiar is discomfort, fear, shame, guilt...). It will want to return here because it *naturally* defaults to "survival mode". What's most familiar and thus *seemingly* safe is what I've named as The Emotional "Safehouse", which can take many forms depending on the beliefs you adopted growing up. The Trio's life mission is to keep you locked inside The Emotional "Safehouse", thinking they are helping, but they're actually making matters worse. The Emotional "Safehouse" is familiar, but it is *not* safe.
The Poison Apple Storeroom *Wake-up Wednesday*	**A place where all of one's soul-destroying habits and tendencies are housed and locked in tight.** Energy is essential for survival. Food is required inside The Trio's Emotional "Safehouse". So, The Trio need to work out how to provide sustenance and where to store it so The "Safehouse" stays in full sight. Francis has made herself the sole provider of sourcing this sustenance. She does so through apples. And she stockpiles them in a "Storeroom" on the side of The "Safehouse". It's locked to keep all of those "bad people" out and keep all of The Poison Apple supplies tucked in TIGHT – no escape!

The way anxiety-inducing poison is inadvertently ingested – slowly killing a person from the inside out.

When consumed, ordinary apples provide energy. Energy is GOOD. So scranning down on apples, on the surface, is a pretty promising idea. Only...the kind of apples that Francis likes aren't your regular Farm Shop finds. There are three types and they're *different*: they each contain an undetectable deadly poison.

Toxic Poison Apples are mind-numbing people, places, things and activities that are held onto too tightly.

They might look like:

- Toxic gossip
- Toxic relationships
- Toxic workplace
- Toxic diets and body image

These things can feel like soul food in a moment of indulgence (they're familiar and often full of energy/excitement/drama to Francis, but it all slowly sucks the life out of Actual You [with a Capital Y])

Control Poison Apples are a thirst to control through <u>any</u> means available.

It's where Francis will manipulate, navigate, contort and control as much as she possibly can so she knows that she can **always** get access to what she thinks is needed – she sings the lie: *"If I'm in control, then it's safer, and we get all the apples we need. Apples are familiar, which means **these** apples keep us safe".*

Grudge Poison Apples are the poisonous need to hold onto pain caused by others because it all still hurts so much.

It's where Francis is desperate to keep contempt, hurtfulness and hatred towards others who have done "wrong" alive and as potent as possible.

The Quick-Fix Plum *Thankful Thursday*	**The Quick-Fix Plum is believed to be *the* answer to it *all*. That if "it" was actualised, then Bob's your Uncle, and Fanny's your Aunt...Life would feel great and there'd be an abundant overflow of gratitude.** It doesn't work this way, the way The Trio tell us it does – they'll keep you searching through the valley, over the mountain, down the track, round the freaking bend!! Just so you never find it!

> *The Emotional "Safehouse" is The Trio of Terror's favourite place to frequent – they feed you a diet of Quick-Fix Plums and Poison Apples there. They've made it so hostile and filled it with barricades, locks and bolts that The Rainbow Road, which once lay through here, has been shattered into smithereens.*

TERRAIN THREE: **SUBCONSCIOUS** CHARACTERS

BRAINWAVE STATE: Alpaca Alpha Brain Waves

Found in Saturday Sitting

Theta and Alpha Brain Waves are dead different to Beta. They're some of the ones we want to be accessing on the regular – they help with processing, making memories and generally feeling more lovely about life. I parallel them to Alpacas because they're filled with JOY. Teeming with it from top to little fluffy tail. The flitting and frolicking, running and jumping without a care in the world. In these moments, they are the definition of living their best life in an Alpha state. So, when you're thinking Alpha Brain Waves, think of the totally free alpaca and smile!

The Subconscious:

The all-knowing, omnipresent part of you which makes decisions based on your highest and greatest good; no words or active thinking/choosing exist here.

The Subconscious Mind cannot be accessed through any means of "thought". It's a Universal Energy Space which holds light, oneness and freedom. Every answer you might ever look for is stored within this Universal Energy Space. Access is granted here through making space in The Unconscious.

Grace *Thankful Thursday*	**Grace** is the archnemesis of The Trio – as they scramble and fret and bob and fight, she is an inner calm, peace, joy and love. She is balance and can be called upon to tackle any one of The Trio of Terror when they're up to their tricks.
Ice Cream Sundae Sanctuary *Thankful Thursday*	**Ice Cream Sundae Sanctuary:** The state of being grateful AF for the plate that's in front of you (your life as it is). This state allows you to be receptive to all of the blessings in life in a way that is healthy, sustainable *and* delicious. The Ice Cream Sundaes you get by being in this state as often as you possibly can, include everything you want in life *and* the sweet, juicy Plum on top (as opposed to the highly deceptive Quick-Fix Plums)!
The Plum (not the Quick-Fix kind) *Thankful Thursday*	**The (non-Quick-Fix) Plum:** A sweet and juicy plum on the top of the Sundae is the icing on the cake and the cherry on top. It's a *nice to have*, but it is **not essential** to be able to enjoy life – not when you've learned how to eat Ice Cream Sundaes for breakfast, lunch and dinner on the daily!
Emotional Bouncy Balls *Feel-It Friday*	**The Emotional Bouncy Balls:** Little friends which help process the inevitable emotions that life throws at all human beings. Moving with their nudges of encouragement, to feel (sometimes challenging) feelings allows these balls of emotion to leave each person who is willing to sit with the feeling.
The Buffalo *Feel-it Friday*	**The Buffalo:** The Buffalo is brave, courageous and faces all problems head-on. Channelling the braveness of The Buffalo speeds up reconstruction of your Rainbow Road, bringing you closer and closer to accessing the wisdom of The Subconscious.
Surrender Evidence Stack *Surrender Sunday*	**Surrender Evidence Stack:** Your collection of evidence that reminds you that everything turns out okay when you let go – which is the opposite of what has been previously accepted as The "Ideal Self" Avatar's way of being (the clamber to come back to the familiar of The Emotional "Safehouse").

This is the space where Actual You (with a Capital Y) resides.

THANK YOU!

Wade, your trust and faith in me and my skills to make a success of this work has been unwavering. You believed in me before I believed in myself. Thank you. I love you.

Rupert, your, "I'm so proud of you, Mummy!" makes my heart want to burst with happiness. I feel proud of myself, but hearing your words supercharges me to the moon and back. Thank you for being your Youest of You, Buddy – you inspire me every day. You're a gift, Roo!

Arthur, your enthusiasm and interest in what I'm doing makes me feel so seen. Your, "Yahoo, great job, Mummy!" with *big claps* and *whoops* **every** time I share a new milestone (no matter how small it is) lifts my heart to new levels I didn't even know existed. Thank you. You bring a lightness and joy to this world – keep choosing You, Art – you're a gift!

Mum, you are the definition of unconditional love. EVERYONE deserves to have a mum like you: you're love personified. I am so grateful for your wise words and council throughout my whole life, and especially now, in the bizarre world I've found myself in. I remember you being floored the first time I asked, "What is my purpose?" And now look at it all... I wouldn't be doing any of this without you and your love gifting me the foundation for it all (you old crone!). Love you a million blocks of flats. Thank you will never be enough.

To the people who have inspired me to create my More:

Thank you, Satya Narayana Goenka. You put me on the path which saved my life.

Thank you to The Venerable Dr Phramaha Laow Panyasiri for welcoming me to your temple to explore a new world of meditation at one of the darkest times. I have made some of the best friends I might ever wish for here.

Sandra Wissinger, you can make magic links with words in the same way that I make Rainbow Roads to The Subconscious. Together, our work on this book has been alignment personified. Your heart and soul are in the book, alongside mine. You go above and beyond and I'm so lucky to have you in this work with me.

Kayla Qu, the illustrations that you produced are a gift. They elevate everything to give that glorious visual which is a super important part of this work. I'm so glad to have found you. Thank you for making time for me in your incredibly busy work. Your dedication and illustrations are EVERYTHING!

Lewis Howes and your School of Greatness: we've been on too many walks together. Your story and the people you interview helped me to continue to trust deeper in the knowledge that More lies ahead for me too.

Wendy, Andrew, Imogen, Sydney the orphaned wallaby, and your alpacas at Acorn Glade: thank you for your love, kindness, and the last of your plums for the season. I didn't finish my book on my weekend with you – I got more than I EVER imagined I might.

My Library Crew – the people I met every Thursday at Lichfield Library, The Guild of St Mary's Centre, when working on this book: your kind words lifted my heart in more ways than you can imagine.

Beyonce's Renaissance Album – ESPECIALLY "Cuff it!" – it's been on repeat throughout this writing process.

And a special thank you to You and EVERY client who has ever trusted me enough to let this magic enter their world. I hope you feel inspired enough to believe that change is possible for you too, and practical enough to show you the tangible steps to implement it in your life...

ABOUT THE AUTHOR

Emma Upton went from having an anxiety breakdown to discovering a proven path for anyone looking to be free from anxiety and create More of the stuff they want in their world.

Emma enjoys taking incomprehensibly enlightening philosophies and placing them into a Wonderland which **any** willing participant can practically follow, implement and **choose** to use to transform their entire life.

During her 12 years of teaching, Emma developed a passion for transforming repugnantly difficult principles into delicacies. She's since learned that this process was preparation for her work as a Mindset and Expansion Coach now.

Emma's 7 tangible steps to overcome a busy brain are seeped in a magic which doesn't hold as much make-believe as your mind wants you to think. Her worldwide tribe of seekers of More has exploded as they've been overcoming anxiety and creating profound results since she left teaching in 2021. Seeking *More Than This* is now Emma's full-time passion.

IF YOU ENJOYED THE BOOK, THEN YOU'LL LOVE...

My 7 week Group workshop which creates a more interactive, personal approach to The 7 Steps

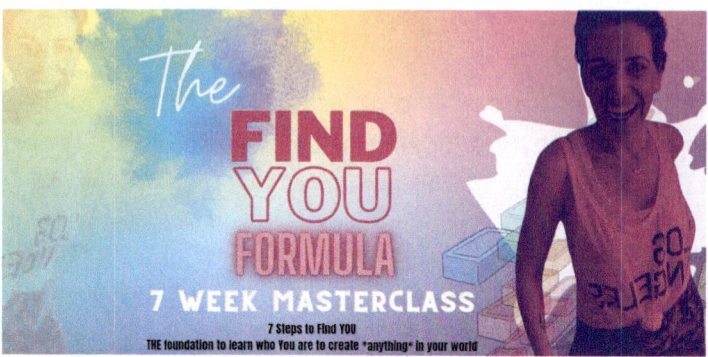

The Fearless Coach Academy where we work with The Narwhal energy flow to create your version of More

If you'd like more information about these, or any of my works, email morethanthisbyEmmaUpton@gmail.com or get in touch on Instagram @morethanthisbyEmmaUpton

REVIEW REQUEST

Thank you for reading this book,
You Anxiety-Free Dance Party Goddess!

I really appreciate all of your feedback and
LOVE hearing what you have to say.

Any input you're able to give will make the next version of this
book and future projects the best they can be. My mission is to
make as many people become Anxiety Free as humanly possible.

Will you help me with this mission, please?
https://thereismorethanthis.com/book/

Please go back to the Amazon page where you
purchased this book to kindly leave a review.

Super grateful for you. So much love.

Emma Upton

xoxo

Printed in Great Britain
by Amazon

24785427R00205